The American Grocery Store

Recent Titles in
Contributions in American History

The American Grocery Store

The Business Evolution of an Architectural Space

JAMES M. MAYO

Contributions in American History, Number 150

Greenwood Press
WESTPORT, CONNECTICUT · LONDON

Library of Congress Cataloging-in-Publication Data

Mayo, James M.
    The American grocery store : the business evolution of an
architectural space / James M. Mayo.
        p.   cm. — (Contributions in American history, ISSN 0084–9219
; no. 150)
    Includes bibliographical references and index.
    ISBN 0–313–26520–8 (alk. paper)
    1. Supermarkets—United States—History.   2. Grocery trade—United
States—History.   3. Architecture, Modern—20th century—United
States.   I. Title.   II. Series.
HF5469.23.U62M39   1993
381'.148'0973—dc20   92–45072

British Library Cataloguing in Publication Data is available.

Library of Congress Catalog Card Number: 92–45072
ISBN: 0–313–26520–8
ISSN: 0084–9219

First published in 1993

Greenwood Press, 88 Post Road West, Westport, CT 06881
An imprint of Greenwood Publishing Group, Inc.

Printed in the United States of America

The paper used in this book complies with the
Permanent Paper Standard issued by the National
Information Standards Organization (Z39.48–1984).

10 9 8 7 6 5 4 3 2 1

Every reasonable effort has been made to trace the owners of copyright materials in this
book, but in some instances this has proven impossible. The author and publisher will be glad
to receive information leading to more complete acknowledgments in subsequent printings of
the book and in the meantime extend their apologies for any omissions.

To Meredith and Mark

CONTENTS

ILLUSTRATIONS

CHAPTER 6

ACKNOWLEDGMENTS

Although there is a diverse literature on the design and history of the grocery store, almost nothing has been done to consolidate the American experience. A few writers, however, have made significant contributions. Historians Lewis Atherton, Gerald Carson, and Thomas Clark provided timeless works on the country store. Godfrey Lebhar and Max Zimmerman, journalists in the retail grocery industry, provided critical historic analyses of the supermarket in the twentieth century. Historian Chester Liebs has astutely analyzed the supermarket's architecture in relation to the commercial strip. Their contributions were essential to the development of this book.

This book would not have been completed without the help of colleagues and friends. Nicki Bromberg, Margaret Crawford, René Diaz, Charles Etheredge, Elizabeth Johns, Rita Napier, and John Reps were particularly helpful to me. Karen Kaiser, archivist for the Food Marketing Institute; Leslie McNulty, research analyst for the United Food and Commercial Workers Union; Shirley Palmer, librarian for the *Progressive Grocer*; and Carla Weiss, reference librarian for the Catherwood Library at Cornell University provided me essential historic materials for this book. I owe special thanks to Dennis Domer, University of Kansas, and Richard Longstreth, George Washington University, for their critical comments of my manuscript. Gera Elliott spent countless hours typing and retyping the book. Elizabeth Scalet proved to be a most understanding editor in sharpening my ideas. Finally, I owe a special debt to the University of Kansas for providing two summer grants and a sabbatical leave to complete this book.

PREFACE

When people think of a grocery store, they have a multitude of definitions and images in mind. Perhaps the most common one is a neighborhood shop on the corner, but it is just as likely they will think of the modern-day supermarket. Indeed, the term *grocery store* changes constantly as new forms of food retailing appear and become part of people's lives. For the purpose of this book, I use grocery store as an umbrella concept to describe the various food store formats that have been part of American history. This definition suggests a general boundary for the examination of food retailing in the built environment, but it is not sufficient to explain the political, economic, and historical circumstances that give the grocery store its full meaning.

The grocery store is a common ground for American society. By necessity, everyone shops for food to sustain themselves. The modern supermarket has become one of the few places where all classes of people can meet face to face. There is often a community atmosphere where shoppers meet friends and chat for a moment, a customer says hello to a familiar clerk, or one shopper helps another to find a food item. Sometimes bulletin boards are provided for community announcements, and promotional displays evoke images of a forthcoming carnival or public holiday. Shoppers do buy groceries, but they may do more. They can pick up a prescription at the pharmacy, get cash at a customer window or a bank machine, leave shoes to be repaired, leave clothes to be cleaned, or pick up flowers for a special occasion. All of these business transactions are reminiscent of people shopping in stores on Main Street or in stores surrounding the county courthouse square in a small American town.

With all these aspects of a community common ground, the local grocery store is still bound by the realities of economic competition. Although store

P.1 The Grocery Store as a Common Ground (Courtesy of the Photographic Archives, Eskstrom Library, University of Louisville)

management may help to create a community atmosphere and shoppers may socialize freely, the grocery store is first and foremost a business. Meat cutters, clerks, and cashiers are workers who are directed by store managers to help customers so that sales and profits are maximized. The hidden politics of the grocery store are the working relations between store employees and management. Although these are suppressed so that shoppers feel at ease in a community atmosphere, these politics periodically erupt. Union picketers parade in front of the store in the hope that potential customers will learn that employees lack adequate salaries and benefits. Although the local store is the place of protest, employees are often embattled with company management residing in a corporate headquarters far from the store. The grocery store offers a political duality, an image of community life versus the realities of economic conflicts.

The shopper's daily trips to the local grocery store touch only the surface of the political and economic conditions that underlie these visits. The modern-day store is not unlike other forms of business in the American economy. Like a factory, a supermarket is a plant designed for efficient economic production. Employees help to sustain the flow of goods so that profits are maximized, and they agree to a wage to compensate them for their labor. Store owners agree to those wage concessions, but they simultaneously ensure that their income exceeds their costs. Although profit margins in food retailing are not high, the volume of sales enables many owners to reap financial benefits greater than their costs. Through competition, both owners and employees adjust their economic expectations. To keep their employees satisfied with their current wages and to cover other overhead costs, store owners must maintain profits or expand their economic market. If they do not succeed, they face a variety of constraining alternatives. Store owners attempt to lower overhead costs by reducing employee positions, wages, and benefits and inevitably face potential conflicts with their employees. Even more devastating, store owners may be driven out of business by competitors. The grocery store is constantly under the economic pressures of competition.

Architectural design can play an important role in business competition. Grocery management can sustain and expand their markets even under severe competition when they gain a technical advantage that reduces costs. Architectural design has historically been one means for store owners to increase their profits. Through design, they can reduce the number of employees needed to operate the grocery store space and enhance the aesthetics of the store to attract shoppers. Introducing new designs can have consequences. Store employees and their unions may resist architectural improvements that increase their work loads or eliminate their jobs. Competitors can feel compelled to redecorate old stores or to build new stores to sustain their share of retail business. Architectural design shapes a grocery store, and the design remains in place as long as it is economically competitive.

Business competition helps to shape the grocery store, and as the historic conditions of the American economy have evolved so have the architectural designs of the grocery store. First there were public markets and general stores in cities, and country stores dominated retail trade in small towns and the hinterlands. The small all-purpose grocery store replaced its predecessors as mass distribution became prominent in the twentieth century. The supermarket replaced the small grocery store as automobile ownership increased. The supermarket grew in size, but eventually stores were designed to meet a variety of economic markets. Convenience stores, co-ops, warehouse markets, hypermarkets, and wholesale clubs appeared to meet the demands of a segmented marketplace. These architectural transitions reflected economic and technological changes that influenced the food retailing economy.

The purpose of this book is to provide a consolidated history of the American grocery store. Its economic and architectural character has a rich history that deserves to be understood more fully.

Chapter 1

THE PUBLIC MARKET

The history of the public market has been largely forgotten by the American public. Although people who live in eastern cities can still visit a marketplace, Americans in other regions have fewer opportunities for such an experience, because urban growth in the western United States came much after the heyday of the market. Although cities such as Los Angeles do have marketplaces, the market was more entrenched as a public institution in America's colonial cities, such as Boston and New York. Yet Americans know little about the history of the public market. Most market houses have been destroyed by city officials. Some buildings have been radically remodeled and converted into other uses. A few markets have been saved through historic preservation, but these widespread changes have made it difficult to understand the variety and magnitude of public markets that once existed.

The lack of recognition for public markets stems from an ironic combination of their importance and their expedient destruction. Public markets are a significant American phenomenon, because they were the main food emporiums for the nation much longer than any other building type for food retailing in U.S. history. For approximately three centuries, many eastern American cities and towns depended on the public market as their primary retail food source. Yet these buildings were rarely the grand architecture of their age. Market houses were taken for granted as "common" buildings. Most people were not upset by the destruction of a market house, just as few Americans today object when a supermarket is closed or torn down. People just assumed that another market building would be built. The historic value of public markets becomes apparent when Americans visit the few remaining ones that exist and when they realize that these institutions are often threatened by urban renewal plans.

The origins of public markets are not commonly understood. The first markets in the colonial era were transplanted from England and the Continent.

From colonial times through the nineteenth century, public markets were municipal financial ventures, but in the twentieth century, private investors began to plan, build, and maintain their own public markets. This private ownership trend was the direct result of the growing strength of the free enterprise system. The nation's cultural roots and evolving economic character helped to shape the historic identity of the public market.

THE OPEN MARKET

The first American public markets were open markets in streets without buildings, and these places were mainly considered to be a public facility in American colonial cities. A town had to be of sufficient size to have a marketplace, and its location had to meet the needs of both sellers and buyers. At the same time, public officials needed to control the time and location of the market to provide orderly control of transportation and goods, as well as levying taxes and maintaining sanitation.

For most colonial cities, the best location for a marketplace was near the town's business center and the town wharves. The first marketplace of record in the English colonies was established in Boston in 1634 by order of Governor John Winthrop. During the mid-seventeenth century in Boston, Great Street (now State Street) was widened to 113 feet to allow for an open market in its center. The market was at the town's center, but just as important, Great Street led directly and quickly to the town dock.[1] New York City's first marketplace was also established in the 1630s. Known as the market field, the area was located between the West India Company's storehouses. Although not immediately by the docks, the open market was near the fort and the town's main avenue, Broadway Street. In 1856, the city's first open public market was located near the shore in the area known today as Battery Park.[2] In the American West, St. Louis established its first market in 1768 at the town's center, immediately adjacent to the Mississippi River.[3] These early examples help illustrate the importance of water transportation to a successful public market. Country people and Native Americans brought their food products to market mainly by boats and canoes, and their goods were a major source of food supplies.[4]

Not all open markets were able to locate by a navigable water source. Spanish colonial settlements, such as San Antonio, were laid out in a grid plan according to the Laws of the Indies. Although plans are not specific, the marketplace in San Antonio was most likely held on the perimeter of the main plaza, and other Spanish settlements probably had the same arrangement.[5] When Mexican officials allowed Texas to be colonized by American citizens, they stipulated that their appointed colonial commissioner was to require one block to be designated as a market square.[6] In cities not dependent on water transportation, a location central to town activities was the main criterion because goods were usually brought to market by animal or cart.

Colonial open markets were scheduled events in the beginning. With produce and animals coming mainly from the countryside, people needed a time schedule. In New Amsterdam, Wednesdays and Saturdays were chosen in 1680 as market days. Mondays were never seriously considered by the community as a practical day for the market, because it meant that people would have to prepare for market on Sunday, a violation of their belief that no one should work on the Sabbath. Three years later, New Amsterdam enacted a law that allowed three market days per week while allowing dairy products, poultry, fish, fruit and some vegetables to be sold daily.[7] A daily market was too frequent for other goods, because farmers, who needed to tend to their farms, could not afford the time to make daily journeys to the market.

Open markets still persisted in the nineteenth century although market houses were clearly the preferred form. There were two reasons for this preference. First, city councils often converted vacant public property into an open market to generate tax revenues. Second, they were able to put markets in locations that had no other practical use. The size and shape of some Y street intersections often resulted in some of the street space not being used for traffic circulation, and cart vendors created temporary marketplaces in these areas. When a market committee decided to discontinue and to dismantle a market house because of a lack of trade, some vendors used the old site to take advantage of any remaining demand for trade. In addition, some villages preferred an open market instead of a market house. For example, as late as 1872, Ipswich, Massachusetts, used its town center commons as an open market.[8] Open markets in the nineteenth century represented either changes or stabilization of growth in cities.

FORMATION OF THE MARKET HOUSE

Market houses were eventually needed to replace the open market. Butchers, farmers, and customers wanted a permanent arrangement that enabled them to do business regularly, in good weather and in bad. City leaders and merchants also saw the opportunity to create a spatial-economic system to profit from the food trade. At these early marketplaces, business was both continuous and temporary. Butchers and vegetable retailers began to sell their goods daily, whereas the farmers still came to market on select days. Everybody wanted a profitable approach that provided a market in a fixed place on a flexible schedule. The eventual solution was that cities constructed and regulated the use of market houses. The local government paid for the market house and rented stalls to food merchants. By constructing market houses, the city fathers not only provided a facility demanded by the public but also collected considerable revenue once the market house loans had been paid.

The biggest health problem was butchered meat. During the seventeenth century, butchers slaughtered meat in private establishments in New York City, but the city fathers eventually required butchers to slaughter animals immediately outside of the city limits.[9] The separation of slaughter houses from public markets and the public control of both facilities solved many health problems, such as dysentery. Butchering practices in market stalls, however, needed controlling. Public ordinances prevented the selling of meat that was stale, spoiled, stuffed with fat, or tumorous.[10] The daily cleaning of meat stalls was eventually regulated. By building market houses, city officials provided not only improved health standards but also the means to profit from this public responsibility from the seventeenth century onward.

The creation of market houses and policies meant that local government had to manage them. Cities first hired a market master, initially called a market clerk. The market master was responsible for seeing that public rules and regulations were obeyed, and he collected rent from the merchants who leased stalls. The market committee established rent rates and reviewed and decided on complaints made by market occupants. The committee assessed fines and reassigned empty stalls as they became available. Local governments could not afford to have the markets run poorly. They did not want to be responsible for health hazards, and most importantly, the city did not wish to suffer a decrease in market revenues.

With local governments providing the market houses at a fixed place, public markets were essentially organized as socialistic institutions. In the beginning, merchants did not see this public monopoly as a problem. Food retailing was typically a family enterprise, or was run by an owner who sustained a very small number of employees. These retailers were small entrepreneurs who could provide neither capital nor business management to the public market. The community thought of these markets as public facilities that did not compromise the principle of free enterprise.

THE STREET MARKET HOUSE

The street market house was the first major design type used to house public markets. Street market houses were built in the middle of the street, and it was a common practice in the layout of communities to have at least one wide street where the market would be located. Local city councils were mindful of economics. Streets were public property that could be neither bought nor sold. By locating a market building in a street, city officials were able to avoid buying building sites on a city block. Some limitations, however, did exist. The local market committee had to locate these buildings on streets wide enough to allow traffic to pass on both sides of the market structure. As a result, market houses were usually located on a major street that had been designated for public markets. Most of these structures were between twenty-five and thirty feet in width and as much as three hundred feet in length. City officials ultimately decided that the benefits of minimal site investment outweighed any traffic inconveniences that the public might be forced to endure.

The linear building shape allowed for some means of traffic control. A basic problem was how to disperse the horses and wagons that would bring goods to and from the market house while still allowing other traffic to pass. Wagons and carts could line up, parallel or vertical to the market building, and then load and unload goods. When side entrances existed, workmen could easily move goods to and from the market stalls. One side of the building was often occupied by carts or food stands facing the already overcrowded street. Street vendors along the market building's side wall exacerbated the situation by creating traffic problems that merchants, who were inside the market house, resented. Too much traffic meant customer inconvenience. Although the street market house layout and location were basically sound, not all of the traffic problems could be resolved. People managed the best that they could under the crowded conditions.

The building interiors were arranged into functional areas. Although some markets might be totally devoted to one food product, the typical street market house was divided by meats, fish, and vegetables and other produce. Exterior unloading areas were sometimes coordinated by particular food types, and these areas were adjacent to interior retail stalls that sold the same type of food. There was usually at least one customer corridor down the middle of the building. In a few market houses, cellars were built. Food stalls were leased in these basement areas, and in some instances the space was used for cold storage.[11] Not unlike the supermarkets of today, the market house was organized to maximize efficiency and customer convenience.

The structural design of street market houses was consistently simple. Most structures were built of brick or wood, and stone foundations were often used. All of these characteristics could be combined. In 1827, an ordinance to build a market house in St. Louis stipulated: "The foundations are to be of stone; the walls, piers, and pavements to be of brick; the timber of oak and walnut, and the shingles of cypress, pine, or oak. Separate proposals will be received for the masonry work, brick-work, carpentry-work, painting and glazing, plastering, and for the paving and making of stalls."[12] The most common method of building construction was a pitched roof, which was supported either by load bearing walls or a post and beam system. Because the street's width required the building's width to be narrow, builders used short truss spans in the building's framing system. As a result, they avoided structural problems associated with wide spans. Because the interior food stalls were typically the same size and laid out in a linear floor plan, the structural bay system overlaid a constant number of stalls with a repetitive grid, and this grid pattern was repeated until the desired building length had been reached.

Market facilities were often expanded. Some cities constructed a series of separate structures on the same street. For example, both Philadelphia and

Louisville had successive market houses on the same street, and both cities located these structures on Market streets, which were planned to contain them.[13] The market houses were not always on the same street. If sufficient space was available on side streets, a market structure would be put there.[14] These market expansions occurred because market trade was increasing for all types of food. Sometimes a particular food product would be added, such as a fish market. Old market houses were often dismantled, and the materials were used either to build a new market facility or to expand an existing public market.[15] Old street market house sites often became open markets in a street's neutral ground, and these areas sometimes were used once again as a site for a new market house.[16] When a city's market committee decided to make additions to its public markets, they tried to minimize public costs by continuing to build in the street, using the same plans and previously used materials.

Many street market houses also served as community buildings. A two- or three-story structure often abutted the end of the market house. The local police or fire station was sometimes housed in these buildings.[17] But the first floor was typically used for market purposes, whereas the second floor of larger market buildings was often used as a community meeting place. In New York City, sometimes the fire watch tower was added to the market house. Because there was no telephone system and there were many wooden buildings, city officials were constantly concerned about fire, and watchmen monitored the city as a fire prevention measure. Most market houses had a cupola and a bell to ring the beginning and the end of market hours, and watchmen used the same bell as a fire alarm.[18] Making these community functions a part of the market house was a practical matter. Street property did not cost the city anything to build upon, and including these community facilities with the market house meant that only one construction project had to be completed instead of two or more separate projects. By including other public facilities with the market house, city officials strengthened the common notion that the public market was the local community center.

There were variations in how street market houses were located and de-signed. Baton Rouge, Charleston, and Savannah had their market houses built on squares rather than in streets. In St. Louis, the first market was built on the square, whereas many of its other market houses were built in the street. In Sandusky, Ohio, the streets were broadened in two separate blocks on Market Street to provide more space for market buildings.[19] In New York City, a narrow triangular lot bordered by streets on both of its long sides was used for the Centre Market.[20] Yet no city provided a more unique public market than Boston. The city's most significant market house, Faneuil Hall, built in 1742, was two stories tall and made of brick. Even with the expansion of Faneuil Hall in 1805 and an added vegetable market house, Boston's Market Square was overcrowded. Other market houses had been built in response to Boston's growth, but Market Square was the city's main public

1.1 Community Hall for Public Market Sheds, Philadelphia, 1900 (Courtesy of the Print & Picture Department, Free Library of Philadelphia)

market.[21] In 1826, Mayor Josiah Quincy declared a major project "by filling the Town Dock and building over the wharves between it and the Long Wharf, thus creating space for a new two-story granite market house, 555 feet long and 50 feet wide, that was flanked by harmonious granite warehouses, fronting on the newly created North and South Market Streets."[22] No single public market project in the nineteenth century matched the magnitude and design quality of Boston's Quincy Market. These variations in design and location were uncommon. If a city had a square, it was usually a park, and the market house was usually made of wood or brick, not granite. The Quincy Market was built with a dome and classical colonnades at its ends, whereas Faneuil Hall was constructed with a finely designed cupola. These architectural fineries were rare, because most cities treated the market house as a necessity rather than as a public building that deserved architectural articulation.

Substantial public markets of the early nineteenth century were often more ambitious than those of the early eighteenth century. In 1707, Philadelphia officials built their Town Hall and market sheds in the middle of High Street. The Town Hall was brick, with gables and a cupola on its roof. The first floor was used for the public market, and the second floor was devoted to local government activities. The market sheds behind the Town Hall went through numerous transitions. The first sheds were made of wood with a post and triangular truss structural frame. By 1793 or earlier, brick piers replaced the wood posts. In 1836, city officials replaced the brick piers with cast iron supports and extended the market sheds. The Town Hall was demolished in 1837.[23] Similarly, other growing American cities undoubtedly improved and remodeled their public market structures as they continued to be profitable and as new building technologies, such as cast iron, became available.

The street market house proved to be the most popular alternative among American cities. The design type was not an American innovation; it was used in Europe before the first market house was built in the United States.[24] But by the early nineteenth century, Baltimore, Boston, Chicago, Cincinnati, Detroit, Lexington (Kentucky), Louisville, New Orleans, New York City, Philadelphia, and other American cities had adopted the street approach. Western cities often imitated American cities in the East. Robert Peterson and John Filson played an essential role in the founding and physical planning of Cincinnati, Louisville, and Lexington, Kentucky. To prepare their plans, they borrowed not only the original plats from Philadelphia's gridiron street plans but also the linear shape and location of its street market houses.[25] The street market building type expanded to other cities as local officials realized that this design approach provided the greatest flexibility for locating a market at the least cost.

Street markets continued to flourish through the mid-nineteenth century, but change was eminent. The street market house was still operative at the end of the nineteenth century, and today a few such market houses still exist,

1.2 Quincy Market and Faneuil Hall, Boston, 1826 (Courtesy of the Library of Congress)

1.3 Market Terminus, Market Street, Philadelphia, 1859 (Courtesy of the Print & Picture Department, Free Library of Philadelphia)

such as Lexington Market in Baltimore. The initial limitation of the street market house, creating traffic congestion, led to other market design schemes. With cities growing larger, it became more difficult to devote more or existing space to the public market. A few cities found it necessary to make adjustments.

THE MARKET ON THE BLOCK

Beginning with the mid-nineteenth century, city officials began to build new market houses on city blocks and to eliminate many street market houses. American cities were becoming larger and more industrialized, and public streets were increasingly needed to carry commercial trucking and public transportation. Market houses were taken off the streets due to business interests motivated by economic gain and to technological problems within the system of street market houses.

The dynamics of land speculation, which initially put markets into the street, now created the economic conditions for their removal. The primacy of property rights was much stronger than any notions of the public interest. Moreover, most municipal governments were dominated by vested business interests of all kinds. Maury Klein and Harvey Kantor, urban historians, note the consequences of this purely free enterprise approach: "The outcome for most cities was a common pattern of land use that favored economic development at the expense of almost everything else . . . it was the market mechanism that organized the process. Where land was available to the highest bidder, it went to those economic interests best equipped to exploit it."[26] The public interest assumptions of public markets took second place in fast-growing cities that were thriving under the land use assumptions of free enterprise.

Urban growth in the nineteenth century influenced the shape of the public market. There were huge population increases in American cities due both to immigration and to population movement from rural areas. To embrace this growth, cities grew laterally, and as a result, cities introduced new modes of transportation to handle increased traffic, both business and public. Business interests saw street market houses as expendable, because these markets occupied valuable space that could be used for more profitable purposes. Streets were increasingly congested with people, but at the same time, the streets were increasingly being filled by wagons and carts for business trade other than the public market. At the same time, people increasingly used public omnibuses—horse cars—and later streetcars to go to work. Street traffic became congested as commercial and residential areas became more densely populated. With the invention of streetcars and the increasing public demand for them, city officials ordered that market buildings be removed so that streetcar tracks could be installed.[27] To make the city's economy more efficient and profitable, people and materials had to be moved more quickly. In growing cities, market houses were seen as unnecessary dams in an economic river, the street.

American business attitudes toward government itself led to the lack of care for street market houses. Business interests made sure that city taxes were low, but local governments made up for these tax losses by making profitable revenues from their street market houses. The major problem was that market house revenues were often pilfered or redirected to other city expenditures, and market buildings inevitably deteriorated. These problems were infamous in New York City during the 1840s, as noted by historian Edward Spann: "The City Corporation had the responsibility for doing many things. The trouble was that it seemed to do all of them badly. In striking contrast to the progressive tendencies of the city's commerce, its domain reeked of decay: Decrepit, dirty, cluttered public docks and markets; dusty, muddy, garbage-laden, stinking, disorderly public streets."[28] The lack of city management systems and sanitary engineering led to some of these dilemmas, but more critically the domination of business interests over government led not only to greater profit margins as a result of low taxes but also to the deterioration of public facilities. The street market house system was a victim of political neglect.

The nation's economic development influenced the street market house. The system of wholesaling food became increasingly important in the nineteenth century. The public market had become more than just farmers and livestock growers selling their products to market business people. Food wholesalers were middlemen who enabled food retailers in the markets to focus on their trade. A few public markets had facilities for food wholesalers, but most wholesale markets were separated from the retail public markets. Food wholesalers wanted some larger public markets in order to handle the volume of their city trade. A mixture of wholesale and retail business meant that a big public market could be more economically stable than a small one, but the existing street market houses were usually too small for wholesale trade.

There were technical problems impeding the growth of the street market system. As cities grew larger, bigger market houses could offer a wider variety of food goods under one roof—if sufficiently good market space were available. For merchants, the good space criterion meant short travel distances within the physical confines of the market. When small market expansions were made, new buildings were sometimes located on side streets.[29] Large expansions, however, were usually on the same street as the existing market houses. The typical market street was wider than local streets, and sizeable building extensions could be built on a market street and it could still manage local traffic. Big expansions meant that the public market was physically longer, and customers had to walk longer distances to shop. If market houses were to become bigger and have shorter walking distances, the buildings needed to be more square in shape. The street market house was no longer the most efficient building system to meet the business needs of food retailing.

The placement of the market house on the block resulted in two basic approaches. The first approach was to keep the same basic plan as the street market house but with some modifications. Second, some market houses were radically different in plan and structure, because the linear design plan was abandoned. In both cases, the political-economic aims for expanded growth were attained.

The market house on the block was often a modified street market house, because many functional arrangements were essentially the same for both types. A two- or three-story structure was often built at the front of the market as before. The first floor included market offices and food stalls, whereas the upper levels were used for military regiments and community meetings.[30] The majority of the ground-floor space was devoted to the market, and food groups were still organized in separate areas. Wagon docks were sometimes on one side street, as they were for the street market houses.[31] Although the new markets had a different location, public officials saw no reason to change the physical arrangements previously used for business and public functions.

The major difference in modified markets on the block was that these structures were significantly wider than the old street market houses. For example, the largest street structure in Baltimore's Lexington Market is 50 feet wide and 290 feet long. In comparison, Washington, D.C.'s Northern Liberty Market, now destroyed, was 126 feet wide and 324 feet long.[32] The market houses on the block usually at least doubled the floor space that existed in the street market buildings.

Structural systems that provided wide, open spaces were needed to achieve this added floor space. By the late nineteenth century, the development of iron- and steel-framed structures made possible lengthy spans and open spaces that previously could not have been built. The biggest spans used arched, latticed trusses that were supported by steel columns and brick buttresses, and this structural frame was reinforced from below with tension rods that tied one end of a truss to its other end, much like an archery bow and string.[33] This framing system allowed significant economic benefits. Floor plans could be made and then rearranged as needed. Most importantly, the skeleton structure occupied little floor space. Brick, load-bearing walls and columns not only fragmented floor space but also occupied valuable square footage that could not be rented for food stalls. The architectural technology of the age made possible an efficient spatial alternative to the street market house.

Not all of the market houses used the arched truss as a structural system. The traditional triangular truss was adopted for narrower building lots. The Center Market in Washington, D.C., was built in 1871. Over seventy feet wide, it was wider than any street market, but not as wide as the city's Northern Liberty Market, which was 126 feet wide. The Center Market's size was achieved by making it two blocks long.[34] Although building on the block allowed some market buildings to have wide spans, old techniques of triangular trusses and long buildings were also used to make market buildings larger than those in the street.

The second design approach for putting the market house on the block was to build an almost square structure with a covered quadrangular court in the center. In the modified designs, floor plans remained much as they had been, for example, with butchers having an aisle along one side of the market building's wall, but in the square-shaped markets innovations were made. In the Union Market in St. Louis: "The great inner quadrangle, devoted to the sale of meats, had a vaulted roof supported by iron arches."[35] Pittsburgh's Allegheny Market included a quadrangle, and the building's outer ring of space was used to organize market activities. A square pavilion was fitted into each of the building's four corners. These corner pavilions were linked together by long market halls, which were built with low pitched roofs supported by columns and arched trusses, and these combined structures formed a square ring. The center space of this square ring was a quadrangle that was roofed with a clear story.[36] The quadrangle building type was unlike any approach taken before in designing American public markets.

The main advantages of these buildings were economic benefits and flexibility in the design of floor plans. The traditional aisle system could be used, but the square plan could have a perimeter aisle for circulation or could be divided into square segmental units as in Pittsburgh. Just as with the modified markets on the block, iron and steel technology provided the truss system that allowed these wide spans to be built, but more importantly, floor space was conserved and flexible. The square building had one distinct economic advantage: it required less linear feet of wall space than the long market buildings used in the past. For example, a 20′ × 80′ building has 1,600 square feet with 200 linear feet of wall space. In comparison, a 40′ × 40′ building also has 1,600 square feet of space, but only 160 feet of wall space must be constructed. Although the iron and steel trusses increased building costs, reducing the exterior wall costs resulted in significant savings, because a building's exterior walls were usually a major cost item in construction.

These square dimensions also meant that goods and customers traversed shorter distances when they made trips across the market's interior space. Architectural experimentation was the connection between these building variations. Where markets were once formed by the shape of streets, floor plans and structural systems were emphasized in the quadrangle markets.

Whether the modified or quadrangle plan was used in these new public markets on the block, buildings tended to be different stylistically from the street market houses. Some market houses included ornamental towers on their corners, and architects added gables and clear stories to allow for natural light through the roof.[37] The cupola and bell were used less often, because fire stations were increasingly built separately from the market. Window and

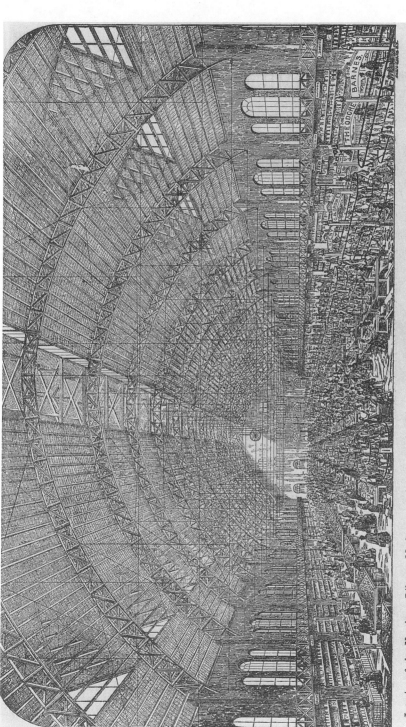

Interior of the Northern Liberty Market, covering the entire West End of the Square bounded by K, Fifth and L Streets, Washington, D. C. Size of room, 130 feet wide by 320 feet long, and 75 feet high. Erected 1875. JAMES H. McGILL, Architect.

1.4 Northern Liberty Market, Washington, D.C., 1875 (Courtesy of the Historical Society of Washington, D.C.)

1.5 Allegheny Market House, Pittsburgh, 1900s (Courtesy of the Carnegie Library of Pittsburgh)

door arches as well as patterned cornices became common sights. Compared to the engineered simplicity of street market houses, James Van Trump's aesthetic description of Pittsburgh's Allegheny Market is florid in praise:

the curving gables of the corner pavilions impart an almost Baroque feeling of movement to the rooflines . . . this curling roof gives an exotic, almost confectionery, effect to a utilitarian building, an effect which was further enhanced by the small ventilating turrets, which look vaguely Chinese . . . the solid, rugged, round-arched Romanesque vernacular . . . gave the building its particular character. . . . Over the arches of the main doors were carved representations of the fruits of the earth, all done in the heavy, slightly abstracted manner of the American mid-nineteenth century. . . . A mortuary of such municipal pleasantries would perhaps constitute an ironic riposte to many an urban statement today.[38]

In addition to following the prevailing architectural style, public markets on the block adopted these features for two important reasons. The public markets on the block cost considerably more than the simpler street market houses. Whereas street market houses were often conceived as being temporary, the new markets on the block were seen as more permanent, especially in light of the costs to use iron or steel trusses to build them. Thus, city officials were more willing to invest in these markets as public buildings which were to be politely accepted if not admired by the public. Second, many new markets were owned privately. Business people in the nineteenth century realized that a handsome building was good for business, and architectural style and ornament helped to further that aim.

SOCIAL LIFE OF THE MARKET

The squares are very full on market days; there are fruit and vegetables without number and garlic and onions to the heart's desire. Then again throughout the day there is a ceaseless screaming, bantering, singing, squalling, huzzaing, and laughing. The mildness of the air, and the cheapness of the food make subsistence easy.[39]

Wilhelm Goethe, *Italian Journeys*, September 17, 1787.

The social life of public markets has always been colorful, active, and a political reflection of America's economic life. Social and economic influences were interwoven in the creation of the public market as a meeting place in the city.

In the beginning, the temporary nature of open markets made the marketplace an event more like a fair than a part of everyday life. Many markets occurred only twice a week, and although some merchants inevitably took a given place on the market grounds as their own turf, the absence of buildings meant that rigid rules and boundaries for space were difficult to maintain. Butchers, hucksters, and farmers competed equally in the market space.

Social life in public markets became ritualized and stratified as market buildings were constructed and the market was open every day. The standardization of market space and its continuous use were the results of an expanding national economy and population growth in cities. Due to these changes, the roles of merchants became more defined as their differing demands for market space became apparent. Consistent, large volumes of food trade meant that merchants were potentially able to reap substantial profits from their business efforts. Determining which merchants could use which space influenced how market life was economically and politically reproduced.

The main players for space at public markets were butchers, hucksters, street vendors, and farmers. The butchers and hucksters (sellers of fruits and vegetables) depended on a daily trade in a fixed space for their profits. This pattern of business was in contrast to street vendors who moved about and to farmers who came periodically to market. In the nineteenth century and earlier, the butchers had the most profitable trade, and they were more able to afford the most desirable stall locations. Which stalls were best depended on the type of building design. For example, in the street market houses, merchants desired food stalls located at each end of the buildings, because these spaces were near the building's entrance and customers were most likely to visit these food stalls.[40] Food groups were normally separated by aisles, and the food stalls were clustered to form sectioned islands. Meats were in one area, vegetables in their own, and dairy goods in still another. Thus, there were comparative advantages within food groups as well as between them.

Street vendors were unable to maintain their food trade as well as merchants in the market houses. Compared to the butchers, street vendors were small entrepreneurs. They rented food stand space along the market house's outside walls, which faced the street. Street vendors, who usually sold fruits and vegetables, were unable to sell as much as their counterparts in market buildings, although the vendors' profit margin was essentially the same. Their overhead costs were less, but it was difficult for these vendors to save sufficient funds to become a market house merchant and to pay food stall rents. Market house merchants considered street vendors to be a nuisance, because the vendors made the streets more crowded and barked loudly to potential customers about the quality of their produce. The street hummed with human activity as a nineteenth-century observer, James McCabe, notes: "The amount of business conducted within them [the market houses] is enormous, however, but even this is surpassed by the aggregate transactions of the street stands and retail stores in the immediate vicinity, which to a stranger appear to form a continuation of the market itself."[41] But in the end, the market house merchants benefitted from the chaos of street vendors. Customers knew that the best goods were inside the market houses, and the quality of inside market space made shopping more enjoyable and susceptible to impulse buying. McCabe also thought: "Bad as the outward appearances of the markets is, the interior presents one of the most interesting sights of the city. The stalls are filled with the products of every portion of the Union, and with fruits and delicacies from foreign climes. The display of meats is extensive and enticing."[42] Street vendors could not compete with the products and interior atmosphere of the market houses.

Farmers in the nineteenth century were disadvantaged as much as street vendors in competing in the market houses. The farmers' inability to be in the market everyday made it difficult for them to protect their share of market space. Although exterior areas were made available for a farmers' market, the farmers continuously petitioned local market committees for space within the market houses.[43] Food stalls for the farmers were never plentiful in market houses. To make matters worse, market masters would often lease these food stalls to merchants who wanted a permanent lease arrangement or who would arrive at the market earlier than the farmers. Having to travel as much as thirty miles to market, they were often forced to sell their goods in the street, which was already crowded with street vendors and sidewalk displays of retail stores. Their lives were made even more miserable when the weather was bad.[44] Yet, customers thought that the farmers were an essential element of the public market, because these producers provided the freshest goods. Local market committees were eventually compelled to respond to petitions to resolve these problems, but more often than not, the cycle of merchants crowding out rural producers in the market houses was repeated.[45]

Country people and street vendors had more difficulty than market house merchants in presenting food goods for sale. The farmers had to be concerned about getting to market, protecting themselves from bad weather, and then returning home. Street vendors shared these problems to a lesser degree with the additional dilemma of moving about the streets when they used push carts. In contrast, the more permanent arrangements of food stalls in market houses enabled indoor merchants to be more meticulous about food arrangements than the street vendors and farmers who sold goods outdoors. The market house was a protective space that enabled merchants to decorate its interior on special occasions: "upon Christmas eve [in 1851]...No expense was spared by our butchers to give effect to this great pageant. The arches of the market house were illuminated by chandeliers and torches, and lights of various descriptions were spread along the stalls. Over the stalls were oil portraits—in gilt frames—of Washington, Jackson, Taylor, Clay, and other public characters, together with landscape scenes...The decorations and other items of special expense [that] these public-spirited men [provided]... reached in cost one thousand dollars."[46] Such expenditures for special occasions and daily stall upkeep demonstrated that market house merchants saw the need to have a decorative stage set to promote not only business but also their status. It was difficult for farmers and street vendors to match

1.6 Street Vendors, New York City, 1900 (Courtesy of the Library of Congress)

these gestures; they could not afford such expenses. Market house decorations and food stall design ultimately ritualized the competitive differences between indoor and outdoor merchants.

Spatial divisions separated work rituals among merchants, but consumer demand and shopping rituals separated the social classes by time within the city. In New York City and Baltimore, at four o'clock in the morning, the elites shopped first to take advantage of the best products. Many ladies would take the family carriage to market, and their servants followed them through the market houses with baskets for carrying purchased goods. Caterers for hotels, restaurants, and fashionable boarding houses also came at this time. Market prices were highest during this hour, but the elites could both choose and afford all the foods that they wished. At five o'clock, more shoppers came to market, but servants were not as prevalent as in the first hour. After six o'clock, the wives and daughters of workers, tenement dwellers, and boarding house keepers came to shop. By this time the best articles were gone, but shoppers could still purchase good products at lower, more reasonable rates. After nine o'clock, the poorer people came to market. The remaining meats and vegetables were coarse when compared to what was sold just an hour before, but the poorer people could afford the food at this hour. After ten or eleven o'clock, the poorest people, sometimes called the market vultures, were the blind, African-Americans, and the near destitute. Being the last to shop, these people bought the bony portions of the coarsest meat, such as neck bones, and they often came away with stale vegetables that merchants either gave away or sold for almost nothing.[47] This shopping pattern in New York City and Baltimore reflected the supply and demand of food goods relative to people's ability to pay. The market houses were open to the public, but food prices in these places often served to separate the social classes by time.

Although public market merchants unavoidably responded to differences among the American world of consumers, these business people also sustained and ritualized differences among themselves. The business life among merchants was more complicated than the daily social life in the market. How the public markets were governed affected the political and economic lives of all market merchants.

PUBLIC MARKET POLITICS

Public markets were primarily owned by municipalities. At first market masters were appointed by elected local officials to administer the markets. During the mid to late nineteenth century, market operations became bigger and more complicated. In New York City, for example, market committees were administered by paid officials, many of whom obtained their positions as the result of political patronage. These market committees sometimes included elected merchants from the markets who represented various trade interests, such as butchers, hucksters, and fish dealers.[48] Whether simple or complex, these committees were responsible for (1) where new markets should be built; (2) what existing markets needed to be repaired, expanded, or terminated; (3) financing market operations and improvements; and (4) the rules and regulations for market operations. These committees exercised powerful control over the fate of food retailing within the city.

The building of new public markets allowed for the economic expansion of food retailing and increased competition among market merchants. Neighborhoods petitioned for new markets to be built in their area to take advantage of shorter trips to market. But market expansion had a price. If a new facility were built, another market might need to be eliminated. As long as a city was growing in population, market committees found their decisions to build new market houses relatively easy. When population growth was stable or declining within certain locales, the committee had to decide not only whether a new market was needed but also if the existing market house should be repaired or eliminated.

Market committees were constantly concerned about market location and expansion. When a public market was stable and successful, market house merchants had few worries, but as the population shifted, market committees quickly saw that fewer market stalls were being rented, and some merchants began to default on their monthly rent payments for food stalls. These rent indicators told market committees that some action was needed. In some cases, a local market needed upgrading and repairs were made. The mix of goods was often out of balance. A fish market was frequently added to give a broader selection to customers. Market committees often created these imbalances. Some market stalls were normally reserved for farmers, but in the market masters' attempts to have food stalls rented every day of the week, farmers were often crowded outside of the market houses and sometimes away from the market altogether. Expanding market houses meant that the farmers could again be an essential part of a market house, a feature that many customers desired. Yet, the economic decline of most market houses was due to the success of other market houses that were newer and nearer growing population centers. Regardless of the reason for a particular market's economic decline, market committees were constantly on alert for any reductions in rent revenues. Public markets were located and expanded to produce profits, which then allowed the public market system to reproduce itself.

Merchants who worked in a public market threatened by closure actively petitioned the governing committee to retain the existing market. As small entrepreneurs, market house merchants depended on building a local clientele, and if the market was torn down, they could not easily rebuild the client relationships that they had cultivated over their years in trade. Yet, market committees often decided that building repairs and expansion were not sufficient to sustain rent revenues in a particular market. Some markets were practically vacant, and the committee's decision to eliminate them was inevitable. In some cases, a market house was still in operation but with more vacant stalls than the market committee was willing to allow. When such market houses were terminated, the butchers, hucksters, and other merchants who operated in these public markets were without a stall to sell their goods. Market house merchants and street vendors opposed the closing of any public market unless they were amply compensated.[49] As a result, the committee was usually pressured to provide the opportunity for these merchants to locate in a new market. Making the move from one market to another, however, was not an easy transition for merchants, and they were at the mercy of market committees that were responding to the growth dynamics of their cities.

Market committees financed public markets basically from their rent revenue accounts or property taxes. It was not unreasonable for public markets to net a 9 percent profit annually. A new public market was a good financial risk as long as market committees carefully tended to rent revenues. These profits were possible because market committees exercised a public monopoly over food retailing. Certain trades, such as butchers, hucksters, and fish dealers, required public licenses, and these trades were formally restricted to selling goods in public markets, although such controls were often ignored. By controlling where goods could be sold and by whom, market committees stabilized their control over market rents and the financing of new markets.

Although market committees exercised strong control over public markets, they faced many political conflicts. They had to police public markets for unfair business practices. At the same time market house merchants often questioned the fairness of regulations made by market committees. Political conflicts were mainly about who profited and at whose expense.

A continuous problem that merchants had with market committees was policing the illegal practice of forestalling. The offense of forestalling was traditionally "considered to be the private purchase of goods before they had reached the market, as well as any activity misleading a seller or dissuading him from bringing his goods to market."[50] This problem existed in New York City, Pittsburgh, and St. Louis as well as in other large cities. In the early nineteenth century, forestallers rode into the country to meet farmers who drove cattle to the public markets. They bought cattle for other butchers and themselves, and their price offers were less than if the cattle had come to the market. Cattlemen were willing to sell to forestallers, because the remaining cattle would be sold at a guaranteed but marginal profit. Butchers who minded their stalls paid higher prices, whereas the forestalling butchers left their stalls to be tended by unlicensed journeymen.[51] Farmers were especially hurt by forestalling. Forestallers, who had no goods of their own, pretended to be agents for farmers, and they rented stall space that had been allocated for the farmers' market. By being able to rent first the few stalls made available to the farmers' market, forestallers often prevented farmers from having a stall to sell their fresh goods. Farmers were forced either to sell their goods on the sidewalks or to accept a marked-down offer for their goods from forestallers. Soon afterward, the forestallers sold the same goods at a higher price.[52] Under these conditions, the farmers' profits were minimal at best when considering the time and effort spent raising their goods and bringing them to market. In contrast, the forestallers marked-down offer paid for the farmers' production cost, and their quick turn-around sales were pure profit with an adjustment for stall rent. The forestalling problem was made worse when stalls designated for the farmers' market were reassigned by market masters as stalls for the regular market. With fewer farmers' market stalls, forestallers were able to be more successful in monopolizing stall rentals before the farmers could arrive at public markets. When market committees attempted to fine these offenses, forestallers would become legitimate agents for selling farmers' goods, and with fewer farmers coming to market, there was a decrease in market fees.[53] Market committees continuously had to police their public markets in order to ensure that all merchants had an equal chance to sell their goods, but they often failed to prevent forestalling.

Perhaps no market committee policy in large cities, such as Baltimore and New York City, created more merchant unrest than the selling of market stalls at a premium. In every public market, some stall locations were better than others. Stalls near the corner of street market houses or near the entrance of market houses on the block were valued more than other stalls, because these locations had a high visibility to customers. To obtain one of these better stalls a merchant had to be a successful bidder at one of the market committee's public sales auctions. The merchant who offered the highest bid for a stall was paying a premium to have that stand, because a monthly stall rent still had to be paid. Moreover, the rent for a premium stall was higher than for other stalls. In the 1840s, stall premiums in New York City cost as much as $4,000, and the rental for such stalls could be over four times as much as other stalls in the market house.[54] Butchers were most affected by this problem, because their trade was the most profitable in public markets and they usually rented the most expensive stalls. They vehemently objected to the premium payment system as a form of extortion by the market committee. The butchers felt that the rental fee system was sufficient payment to determine who was able to occupy a stall. Matters became worse when non-merchants successfully bid for premiums and then subleased their stalls at a profit.[55] Due to loopholes in market regulations in New York City, some butchers were able to avoid temporarily paying a premium by obtaining a license from the mayor to occupy a stall for a given period of time.[56] Although merchant petitions against premium policies were considered, market committees were reluctant to eliminate premiums altogether. These funds were placed into the city's treasury, and when new markets needed to be built and old ones repaired, the premium fees helped to defray construction costs without an increase in local tax rates. Market committees considered stall premiums to be legitimate revenues for a public purpose, but market house merchants considered premiums to be an unjustified tax under a public monopoly.

The premium system was eventually eliminated. The misuses of market funds by public officials, as in New York City in 1858, did not help market committees who argued the necessity of premiums to finance public markets.[57] However, the elimination of premiums was due more to merchants' overhead costs and the inability of public markets to maintain a monopoly. Many merchants could not afford premiums, and when non-merchants bought premiums and subleased their stalls, the merchants who occupied these stalls were unable to sustain a safe profit margin. This problem was exacerbated by another dilemma. In New York City, licensed butchers were legally allowed to operate only in public markets, but the city was lax in administering this law. Butchers were willing to live with the cost of premiums as long as market committees controlled the market place. But as open competition increased, butchers in public markets were less able to compete with butcher shops, and premiums became a disincentive for butchers to remain in public markets. Market officials finally decided, as Baltimore did in 1870, that the short-run gain of selling stalls with the premium system was a long-range loss when compared to a competitive rent system, and stall premiums were eventually eliminated.[58]

The management of public markets during and before the nineteenth century was characterized by political struggles within the market system. Cities usually had a monopoly over these markets, and market committees were constantly mediating imbalances between merchant interests. Building new markets, expanding old ones, and destroying old structures represented a set of locational issues that market committees could reasonably administer. But over time, the market for food retailing coincided less with the public market. Grocery stores and butcher shops were becoming increasingly competitive with public markets. Market committees were able to monopolize public markets, but they were increasingly unable to dictate the larger world of food retailing. Technological and management changes in food retailing were on the horizon at the dawn of the twentieth century.

MARKET DESIGN IN THE EARLY TWENTIETH CENTURY

Many of the design approaches for public markets persisted into the twentieth century. Some market houses, such as Baltimore's Lexington Market, were so large and central to area food retailing that few changes were made. The linear plan of street market houses was still modified and built on the block, such as the Freemarket in Oakland, California, and the Pike Place Arcade in Seattle, Washington. The municipal markets of Birmingham, Alabama, and Winston-Salem, North Carolina, used the idea of squarer floor plans for economic reasons, although neither of these facilities adopted the quadrangle plan concept.[59] Architectural concepts from the nineteenth century and earlier were often continued in public markets because city officials still found these design approaches to be workable.

Technical advances in architectural engineering became apparent in public markets. In the eighteenth century and earlier, market buildings were built of wood or brick and sometimes with stone. Iron and steel truss frameworks, which were infilled with brick and glass, characterized advances in nineteenth-century market houses, and although they allowed for great flexibility in open space, these structures were expensive. Market owners needed a cheaper building system, and reinforced concrete provided the answer. In the twentieth century, market houses were often built with concrete framing systems and large areas of glass. Although many of these buildings had a traditionally oriented image, the architectural engineering was modern, and the modern shell for enclosing buildings was the next step in American architecture.

The most important advancement in building technology was refrigeration. Meat, fish, and dairy products needed to be chilled to prolong their freshness. New York City's Grand Street Market contained an ice house as early as 1820, and after 1825, fish were packed in ice from the New Jersey coast to supply Philadelphia's market houses.[60] Yet, refrigeration in public markets was rare and only the most progressive merchants used it before 1860.[61] Mechanical refrigeration was introduced in Boston's Quincy Market in the 1890s. Chilled brine or liquid ammonia was pumped from a central plant to food stalls through a pipeline system.[62] Refrigeration had finally made it possible for all merchants who rented food stalls to chill their products if needed.

Transportation dictated or modified the design of some public markets. Although an exceptional case, the Reading Terminal Market was built within Philadelphia's main railroad terminal.[63] But it was the automobile that influenced markets the most. As trucks replaced horse-drawn wagons bringing produce to market, people began driving to market instead of walking or riding some form of public transportation. Private market owners sometimes built parking facilities. The Crystal Palace Public Market in San Francisco had an L-shaped plan with a parking lot filling in the property to the street corner, and Kansas City's Stop and Shop Market had a similar plan.[64] The L-plan markets were basically two street market houses joined at one end to form an L. The grand age of the train was at its peak, but as a location for a market, it offered little to the public. The automobile was the future means of household travel, and if market managers provided parking, the car could easily haul the family's groceries.

No other public market was designed for changes in the twentieth century as much as Newark, New Jersey's new Centre Market. Constructed in 1924, the building was 115 feet wide and 650 feet long with a floor area of approximately four acres. The structural frame was made of reinforced concrete with a flat slab system for the floors and roof. The basement provided 60,000 square feet for wholesale storage, and a refrigeration system designed to serve individual market stalls. The market floor contained 250 food stalls that were arranged as square rings around structural columns upon which decorative light fixtures were mounted. The stalls were glazed with tile, and the market's floor had red tile with the walls being tiled ten feet high. The fish market was separated from the rest with glazed doors. At the rear of the market building, an open farmers' market was provided with loading docks for wagons. The top floor was a parking lot that could accommodate approximately five-hundred automobiles. There were two freight elevators for service from the basement to the market floor, and a passenger elevator was installed for service between the market and the parking lot above. The entrance facade was classical in design, with a colonnade and an ornamental clock centered on the building's cornice. Costing over $4 million, the Centre Market was an attempt by Newark's city officials to provide the most modern food emporium that money could buy; but within a few years of its opening, the Centre Market was unprofitable.[65]

The drive-in market was a new form of private development that was specifically designed to meet the needs of the automobile shopper. Built mainly on the West Coast, especially in the Los Angeles area, all of these markets were privately owned establishments, and they were smaller and in more suburban locations than public markets. A drive-in market typically had one concession stall for each food type. This type of market was usually located on a corner property, and a gas station was built on the corner lot. The building plan was normally a semicircular L shape so that the structure conformed to the automobile's turning radius and the lot's depth. Shoppers could park and then walk into the market to buy their groceries just as if they were shopping in other retail food establishments. The innovative design feature was that shoppers could remain in their cars, drive from one food stall to another, and make their purchases from each merchant. Salespeople would load their food purchases in the car.[66] The drive-in market was an attempt to continue the public market system while recognizing the need to address the changes in American life associated with the automobile and suburbia in the 1920s.

In contrast to creating an entirely new market place with the latest innovations, some private market owners built on past practices as well as adopting new ideas on a need basis. Seattle, Washington's Pike Place Market provides an example. The Main Market was built in 1907 as a four-story structure, and its innovations over most previous markets were concrete construction, mechanical refrigeration, electric lighting, and public toilets. In the 1920s, a public library and post office were located in the market, and these public uses are reminiscent of the community meeting places that were included in market houses during the nineteenth century and earlier. The Corner Market, Sanitary Market, and Economy Public Market were all privately owned establishments that had been added by 1916. At the north end of Pike Place

1.7 Centre Market, Newark, New Jersey, 1924 (Arthur Goodwin, *Markets*)

1.8 Plaza Drive-In Market, Los Angeles, 1928 (From the *Architectural Forum*, June, 1928)

Market a street arcade was built in 1911 to serve the farmers' market, and the structure is similar to the earlier age of street market houses. Like some large public markets of the nineteenth century, Seattle's Pike Place Market was comprised of multiple market buildings, which collectively form one marketplace.[67] Change in private public markets was often pragmatic. If some practice was outdated by a particular technological advancement, market owners made adjustments, but they kept old practices that still worked.

Private market owners often standardized internal design changes to impress customers that the public market was a fair, efficient way to do shopping. Many markets used the same type and style of weighing scales in every stall and in the shopping aisles to make the customer feel that every merchant was using the same standard of measurement, with the implication that merchant short-weighting was an impossibility. Owners selected the finish and color of market equipment to present an image of uniform sanitation. Scales were to have high-gloss white porcelain finishes. The favored finish on market stalls was high-gloss white tile. Meat, fish, and sometimes vegetable counters were enclosed with glass to make the customer feel that the presented food was fresh and appetizing.[68] The control of odors became a consideration. Inside the Stop and Shop Market of Kansas City, the fish department had its own walls and roof of glass with odors ventilated out of the building by fans. For poultry, both the killing rooms and the space for coops were glass-enclosed rooms.[69] Many public markets, especially old municipal ones on the East Coast, changed little, but newly constructed and renovated markets made changes toward standardized design schemes. These innovations minimized merchant fraud and reduced sanitation problems, but there was ever-increasing competition from grocery stores. Market management needed to demonstrate that public markets could be modernized to meet the needs of the contemporary consumer.

Market innovations had their benefits, but there were also expensive design mistakes. Mechanical, heating, and refrigeration systems were developments that market designers had not previously considered. For example, one public market was designed with the fish department located over the heating plant and the incinerator in the basement, and fish spoilage was inevitable. Another market had non-food retail stores along its street frontage, leaving the market essentially hidden from public view. Interior aisles were sometimes made too wide, and the visual impression was that there were few people shopping at stalls. Under-illumination gave a dull, gloomy atmosphere in some markets.[70] These mistakes were due both to designers and market managers who were unaware of or had not inquired about the consequences of these building technology and design choices.

In the early part of the twentieth century, the design of public markets was responding to new technologies that were significantly influencing American architecture. All of these technologies were aimed at reducing overhead costs. Concrete structures were becoming less expensive than other building frame-

1.9 Pike Place Market, Seattle, Washington, 1930s (Courtesy of the Seattle Times)

works. Heating systems made shopping more comfortable for shoppers, whereas refrigeration systems prevented food spoilage. Standardization of equipment was an attempt to eliminate inefficiency and to provide sanitation, both imagined and real. But public market management saw these new technologies more as refinements than as design innovations. In his management book on public markets, Arthur Goodwin comments: "Experimentation in the development of markets is past; the building and equipping of markets with the idea of permanency and durability holds sway. Competition amongst retailers has had a considerable effect because of the consumer's preference for institutions using modern equipment."[71] Although the rise of the automobile and the move to the suburbs would become important, technological developments in building technology and design were the initial influences in the twentieth century, and these changes were paralleled by new methods of public market management and their attendant problems.

NEW TRENDS IN MARKET MANAGEMENT

Management of public markets began to reflect general changes in operations that had been occurring elsewhere in the American food business. Increasingly, new public markets were privately owned rather than controlled by local governments. Moreover, grocery stores in suburban locations were beginning to provide serious market competition that had not existed previously. Running a market became an exercise in competing efficiently with other sectors of food retailing. Overhead costs needed to be kept low; volume turnover in all market stalls needed to be high; financing building improvements had to be well planned; effective sales promotions were needed; merchants' conflicts had to be mediated; and other brushfire problems had to be solved. Many of these problems were not new, but market managers had to adopt more effective business techniques if the public market was to survive. New planning and administrative approaches were called for.

Planning for public markets was an attempt to anticipate problems that could not be easily addressed after a market was opened for business. Location, design, financing, management systems, and ongoing administration were concerns that market management needed to anticipate.

Site location was a vital issue. During the era of street market houses, structures were easily located and built. The city owned the street, and building systems were simple. With property, immobile structures, and expensive mechanical equipment having to be bought, permanent locations for public markets became a necessity. A poor location meant a significant loss of capital whether or not the public market was privately or municipally owned. Although the locations of other grocery stores were considered, market experts recommended that the public market be located near department stores. The people who shopped at department stores were often the same shoppers that frequented public markets.[72] The rationale was that if customers could reduce their shopping trips, they would choose the one location that offered the best opportunity to save time. This argument recognized not only that department stores were located downtown but also that the central business district contained the essential transportation network for food coming into the public market. Locating a public market meant first deciding how to optimize private enterprise opportunities within a network of public city space.

For management, design concerns usually revolved around avoiding mistakes. Managers of public markets needed to know more than how to make architects aware of their needs. They needed to understand lighting, heating, refuse disposal, and refrigeration systems, because once these elements were in place, the costs of making changes could be prohibitive. Public market management had to be keenly aware of equipment design problems. Scales, cash registers, food counters, and other equipment were purchased in large amounts because most stalls were equipped with these items. Market management needed to know which hardware items were dependable and had low repair costs. At the same time, they needed to consider the equipment preferences of stall merchants as well as the public's impression of equipment presentation. Some market managers went so far as to control the design of business signs for stalls so that a favorable overall image inside the market could be attained. The more that these design issues were handled in advance of opening a market, the more market managers could then devote their time to other problems.

Financial planning was more complicated than in the nineteenth century, and the newly competitive environment meant that more preparation was needed to justify the expense of building a new public market. In the old system, a city's market committee could decide to build a new market and tear down an old one. Moreover, stall premiums helped to pay for a significant portion of building costs. Without a partial monopoly over food retailing and the premium system, public market committees were no longer financially self-sufficient. In municipally owned public markets, revenue bonds were increasingly used to finance building construction. Yet, such bonds required approval in public referendums, and cities had to offer a plan for retiring the debt on a proposed market. For financing private markets, owners could use mortgage bonds, common and preferred stock sales, or debenture bonds. These financial mechanisms became more prevalent as more markets became privately owned.[73] The growing alternative mechanisms for building loans in the United States meant that market managers had to become more aware of the potential costs and benefits of financing public markets.

Management systems for public markets became more complicated as market managers began to focus on lease agreements, accounting, product-merchant mix, and organizational structure. Although lease agreements had existed before the twentieth century, contract obligations had changed. New agreements identified responsibilities for furnishings or paying for items that had not been considered previously. For example, although gas bills had been negotiated before, electric bills and telephone installations were new areas of negotiation. Payment agreements were flexible. During the 1920s in Los Angeles, lease agreements called for market management to receive a percentage of the gross annual revenues earned by the stall merchant, a system much like tenant farming.[74] Accounting methods became more essential as public markets had to account for these new management complexities. City accounting departments usually handled these concerns for municipal public markets (as they had in the past), but the private markets were different. The advent of the federal income tax system further complicated private market accounting. Fixed assets such as buildings and equipment, as well as interest on notes and mortgages, were depreciable tax items that helped to reduce overhead costs. Advances in building technology and rental contracts placed more demands on management than in the past, especially in privately owned public markets.

Profit-conscious managers became concerned about the systematic mixture of products and merchants in their markets. Rather than allowing merchants to rent stalls strictly on a first-come, first-serve basis, managers saw the need to have an optimal mix of market goods that reflected customer demand. In a market where all stalls were rented, it made no sense to have twice as many butcher stalls as were actually needed. Close competition between meat stalls pushed down each butcher's profits and eliminated some other product, such as a specialized fruit stall, that might successfully meet customer demand.[75] In the farmers' market for country people's stalls, product mix was not controlled, but market managers had to develop a rotation system to prevent any one farmer from monopolizing the most desirable location.[76] Increasingly, the mixture of products and merchants required systematic management to sustain profit margins and to avoid merchant conflicts in an era when public markets faced growing competition from grocery stores.

Ongoing administration in privately owned public markets changed as market management spent more time helping stall merchants to be more profitable. Many public market managers divided their time between helping stall merchants who needed to increase profits and evaluating merchant performance and compliance with management's aims. For stall merchants to offer prices that were competitive with grocery stores, they needed volume sales; but they also needed volume buying power to reduce market costs. In privately owned public markets, managers helped merchants organize cooperative buying to purchase their food products.[77] Managers arranged for the temporary warehousing of goods in storage space within the public market. Although they paid rent for the space, merchants could then buy their goods on the basis of a best timely buy rather than restocking their stalls on a reactionary filling of available shelves. Managers coordinated advertising for all merchants, who were often required by contract to fund advertising costs. Still, merchants benefitted from this arrangement, because as a collective power, public market managers were able to buy good newspaper space and could also coordinate seasonal and special promotions. Market managers had to meet the special needs of merchants so that they maintained profits and were happy. Special privileges, such as allowing a coffee merchant to be the only stall to serve coffee, were demands that often needed to be met if a merchant was to be successful; but problems could arise if a lunch counter opened later and was allowed to serve coffee. Market managers often had to craft their lease agreements with tenants to meet such needs, but they were in constant jeopardy of creating havoc in granting merchant privileges.[78] Percentage agreements gave market management the incentive to retain merchants who were profitable and dependable, and these tactics were often successful in stabilizing management-tenant relations.

Managers in public markets intervened when they judged a stall merchant to be a problem. Whether in privately owned or municipal markets, rules and regulations had to be administered by management. To ascertain a merchant's performance, managers compiled complaint books from customers' comments. Management controls were often passive. By equalizing stall space, managers were more able to evaluate and control merchant productivity. For example, the new Municipal Market of Birmingham, Alabama, adopted the policy of equipping the stalls with scales, counters, meat blocks, and other merchandising equipment in order to secure tenants with small capital and to eject undesirable tenants on short notice.[79] Although they were individual business entrepreneurs, stall merchants were increasingly treated as employees by market managers who applied these administrative techniques.

In the early twentieth century, public markets were becoming modernized. New building technologies and business management techniques were being applied to make these markets more profitable, meet the needs of stall merchants, and satisfy customers. Management was changing both municipal and privately owned retail public markets to meet these competitive needs. Yet even with modernization, the public market was failing in most cities.

MODERN DILEMMAS

Public markets began to face economic problems in the early twentieth century. Some problems were due to the public market system itself, but changes in American business were external forces influencing the nation's methods in food retailing. In spite of advances in building technology and business techniques, management was unable to sustain the public market's dominant position in food retailing.

Public markets had competition problems within the food retailing business. Grocery stores were expanding into suburban locations where public markets could not easily follow. The markets had always depended on the principle of providing a large variety of fresh goods, and to implement that principle, market buildings needed to be large and located near warehouse markets. At the same time, grocery stores offered the service of home delivery, and with their decentralized locations nearer residential areas, they were able to provide home delivery more easily than stall merchants. Thus, home delivery overhead costs for stall merchants were often higher than grocery store owners due to transportation costs. The drive-in market experiment was an attempt to meet the demands of suburban growth, but the idea failed. A grocery store, especially a chain store, could be closed quickly if it was not profitable, but lease agreements with stall merchants did not allow public market managers to move so quickly. At the same time, public markets, even privately owned establishments, were usually local establishments that required a larger capital investment than a neighborhood grocery store, which was often in a leased building. Thus, public markets were not as flexible as grocery stores in service or in capital investment.

Public markets even had competition within the market system. Street vendors had always been problematic for markets, even during the nineteenth century. They added to the congestion surrounding public markets and offered limited competition by establishing curb markets. To control traffic problems around public markets, some cities required licenses for vendors and established curb market zones in some streets. This solution was advantageous to public markets when the market system was dominant, but eventually it became a drawback. Curb markets were very flexible. Having few overhead costs, vendors could establish a market quickly and offer good prices. As commercial and residential areas changed, curb markets could easily adjust to the local circumstances, as long as vendors could obtain approval for such revisions from city officials and were not harassed by local police.[80] Curb markets were never a threat to the large public markets, but when grocery store trade began to cut back on the dominance of public markets, trade at curb markets still persisted without any benefits to the public markets.

Municipal public markets also had internal problems. Although cities financially supported the market system as long as it was profitable, local officials centralized management in a city department without hiring good managers for each of their markets. As one market analyst complained: "In all cases we find the market master, the man who should be an executive head, a very underpaid individual; in almost all cases he is nothing more than a janitor, or the slightly elevated boss of a janitor or force of janitors."[81] This lack of investment in management indicated deeper problems. Although some public markets were built to include design innovations and new approaches to management, many markets did not introduce these changes. With increasing competition from grocery stores, cities were no longer assured that their public markets would be profitable or break even. Rather than attempting to compete or to out perform private enterprise, many cities took the position that retail public markets were a public service. If, however, private enterprise could provide a better system for food retailing, business people should not be deterred, because many local officials felt that government should not compete with private enterprise. This attitude often led to benign neglect in municipal public markets.

Conflicts occurred even in privately owned public markets. During the 1920s in Seattle, Washington, farmers who depended on food stalls in the farmers' market faced the same problem that East Coast producers faced in the nineteenth century. The Pike Place Market management was subleasing sidewalk stalls in the farmers' market to vendors who did not raise the produce. The motive was to have a steadier flow of rental income and to ease street congestion. The farmers were also to be put in stalls farther away from the market's center, and they were angry. The Pike Place Market had been created with the intention of eliminating middlemen who sold food products to retailers, and farmers argued that market management was now supporting vendors who were middlemen. Moreover, the City of Seattle contracted public property lease agreements with the private management corporation that operated the entire market, and the farmers' market was also on public property. Farmers felt that the city had an obligation to make sure that they were treated equitably. Farmers saw the set of circumstances as a contradiction to the public purpose of a market, and they organized themselves and sued Seattle's Board of Public Works. Court battles ensued, and the sidewalk stalls eventually were torn down and the farmers relocated in a new market building distant from the Pike Place Market's center of retail activity.[82] Although the Seattle incident represents only one case, it still illustrates the profit motives embraced by corporate managers of public markets. Rental space had to be maximized to ensure desired profit margins, and protecting these margins was becoming critical in the larger perspective of competing with the grocery store system. In such circumstances, it was difficult for management in privately owned markets to sustain the public interest of a "public" market while simultaneously maximizing profits in the increasingly competitive environment of food retailing.

Problems that were external to the retail market system loomed over the future of public markets. Land use issues, food processing, and corporate-labor arrangements were forces that led to the decline of public markets. Economics was the common thread that tied these forces together.

Land use issues were matters of public market location and transportation facilities. City officials traditionally placed public markets in or near business areas within the central city. Both producers who brought food to market and customers who bought these goods needed a convenient location. But as American cities grew in population and simultaneously spread to the suburbs, land use arrangements changed. The central city became more commercial with less land devoted to residential use. As a result, markets began to be located on the principle that they should be close to shopping areas and reasonably near to main traffic arteries. The idea was that the market needed to be conveniently located for shoppers and for transporting goods to the public market. But competition for urban land was increasing. Business interests used the principle of the highest and best use of land, but in practice this meant that the land use that could produce the highest profits was the best use. Although public markets were usually profitable, their profit margins were often less than for other businesses. Municipal officials were able to purchase good market sites without attempting to maximize profits, although they were unwilling to sustain public markets at a loss. The management of privately owned public markets, however, was less flexible about land costs because they needed to maintain profit margins in order to survive. In the end, neither municipalities nor private investors in public markets were willing to enter a fierce bidding war for urban land. Moreover, market management increasingly found it difficult to find property that was both affordable and sufficiently large for a good market site. As a result of these cost constraints, many potential sites for public markets that fulfilled shopping and transportation criteria were not economically viable locations.

Suburban growth was an insurmountable obstacle to public markets that were attempting to sustain their share of retail trade. For markets that were publicly owned, city officials had no incentive to build new facilities in suburban locations, especially when new suburban growth areas were incorporated as separate communities. The advantage of public markets was their huge size, and with a shifting landscape of suburban development that was low density, the elements of city compactness and slow expansion that had supported public markets were being gradually eroded. In the nineteenth century, city officials built some public markets on the fringe of dense development of their cities on a need basis, but they neither pursued aggressively the building of suburban public markets nor sustained sufficiently the maintenance of all their facilities.[83] Many municipal market houses were dirty and badly managed, and when the suburbanization movement accelerated, city officials were ill-prepared to respond to change. In the end, the public market was too large a public investment in rapidly growing suburban areas of American cities to respond to locational changes. It was one thing to locate in suburbia, but if the site did not generate sufficient revenue, the store had to be relocated. As an alternative, the public market was a poor choice because it depended on land use stability rather than change. Foreseeing these problems, many stall merchants left the public market to establish their own stores, often with a suburban location.

The nation's system of food retailing was transforming the public market. In the early part of the nineteenth century, retail public markets were sufficient to handle trade between food producers and stall merchants. But as American cities grew, retail public markets could not manage all of the incoming food to be distributed to stall merchants. A wholesaling system emerged as a means for channeling food imported into cities.[84] Whether transported by boat, rail, or wagon, depots were needed to handle bulk food deliveries that no one public market could functionally handle and continue its volume of retail trade. Wholesale terminal markets were built by a few cities to handle incoming food, but most cities began to combine wholesale with retail businesses in their municipal markets. By 1918, only 2 out of 118 cities with markets had markets that were used exclusively for wholesale trade.[85] With the growing competition from grocery stores, the wholesale trade business helped in filling market rental space that had been used previously by retail stall merchants. Public markets were increasingly becoming identified as including wholesale trade.

The introduction of the wholesaling system resulted in a more complex network for bringing food to market. In many cities, wholesale buyers bought incoming goods either directly from food producers or from their commission agents, and stall merchants could buy their food from this wholesale source. In metropolitan cities, there were also middlemen known as jobbers who bought goods from wholesalers and then delivered smaller units of goods to food retailers. In places like New York City, stall merchants could buy their food goods from wholesalers or jobbers, but the jobber network was more advantageous to grocery stores that were not near public markets.[86] Stall merchants could reduce their overhead costs by cooperative buying in the wholesale system, but grocery store merchants were equally able to organize themselves as a cooperative or to be part of a chain store, where corporate management made arrangements for volume buying. Both types of merchants were gaining equal price access to food goods, but public markets were not able to decentralize their locations as were grocery stores. With the increasing influence of the wholesale system, stall merchants in public markets began to lose their historic dominance over grocery store retailers.

The rise of national corporations in food marketing led to the decline of public markets. The decline was uneven, as Pyle notes: "The distribution of markets in 1880 may be summarized as regionally strong in the South and in the Northeast (except for New England, where markets had ceased to play an important role in food supply). In the Midwest, markets were being established in new cities and were declining in the old ones. In the Far West development was only just beginning, and markets were virtually nonexistent."[87] After the turn of the century, most public markets received regular shipments of food products from the immediate vicinity of their own communities.[88] After 1920, public markets declined throughout the United States. Public markets remained strong in cities, such as Baltimore, where governmental support was sustained. However, the regional persistence or decline of the public market had much to do with technical developments that enabled food corporations to first penetrate and then dominate cities served by the public market system.

The nation's railroad network and refrigeration technology facilitated the emergence of a corporate system of food distribution. The railroads connected American population centers to many sources of food that was harvested or raised by cheap labor in remote areas. Before the railroads came, the American system of shipping food to market was a very local affair. Farmers brought their crops and animals to market or sold their goods to commission agents who graded these food products and brought them to public markets. With an expanding rail network, corporations emerged that specialized in food processing, and they took advantage of the mass distribution possibilities provided by the railroads. Meat packers, canned food companies, and fruit companies were quickly able to process and distribute foods that had previously been available primarily at public markets. Moreover, advances in refrigeration technology neutralized the problem of transporting massive volumes of perishable goods. Public markets had sustained the historic advantage of a system that provided the freshest goods to the public, but national distribution of certain food goods became possible with the refrigerated rail car. For example, Armour and Company was not able to become a national meat packing enterprise until both the railroad system and refrigeration technology were in place. At the same time, Armour management bypassed the wholesale market by selling directly to food retailers, who were also increasingly becoming incorporated as chain stores.[89] The food processing companies did not provide food as fresh as that found in public markets, but these companies were able to manage mass distribution of perishable goods in large volume. As a result, a corporate system of food distribution increasingly replaced the more localized system of public markets. This transformation occurred unevenly across the nation, and where public markets were declining, there tended to be a growing influence from the corporate network of food processors and retailers.

The most radical transformation in the decline of public markets was the change in labor relations. Whatever shortcomings existed in the retail public market, it reproduced a system that enabled small merchants to operate as independent businesses. With local governments providing market facilities, the joint city-merchant relationship was at least a symbiotic agreement. Municipalities did monopolize the markets, but this public monopoly allowed many stall merchants to be their own entrepreneurs. This arrangement continued with privately owned markets, although leases based on gross annual profits began to treat stall merchants much like tenant farmers. As business corporations began to dominate both the food processing and food retailing industries, the small merchant system began to fail. Stall merchants often converted their trade, such as a butcher opening a butcher shop, whereas others went to work for grocery stores or retired. At first grocery store entrepreneurs were small business owners, but the rise of chain stores led to the corporate dominance of nearly all food merchants and the public market retailing system itself.

CONCLUSION

The public market system served the nation well. Cities were able to organize space, materials, and authority over food retailing that no single merchant could. Many of the location and design characteristics of public markets were brought from Europe by settlers. Public markets flourished in an age when the American economic structure was highly local or regional. But private enterprise expanded and became integrated not only geographically but also organizationally. Municipal controls over producers and food retailers were eventually overshadowed by a corporate enterprise system of food marketing.

The remaining public markets are much like they were in the 1920s and before, with few chances of once again becoming a dominant American institution. Historic preservation efforts by local citizens have done much to save public markets. Architectural changes are marginal enhancements to capture America's historic past as well as an attempt to keep these markets viable enterprises. For many people public markets represent not only a shopping choice but also a form of social life worth saving. Although most existing markets are financially viable, the public market was largely replaced first by chain grocery stores and then by the supermarket. This was a basic shift in food retailing, and the architecture to house this shift in retailing was changed as well. The rise and fall of public markets reflected the transition of the American economy from local mercantilism to national corporatism.

Chapter 2

FROM GENERAL STORE TO GROCERY STORE

The public market dominated retail food trade in cities from colonial times through the nineteenth century, but the grocery store was also an influential source of food. In cities, people used grocery stores for specialty products or for convenience, because there were far more of these stores distributed throughout the city than public markets. Small towns and rural areas, however, often did not have permanent public markets, and general stores and country stores were the primary source of food goods. Until the twentieth century, American retail food trade in the city was a dual system of the public market and the small grocery store. Whereas the public market dominated trade, especially in large cities, the grocery store's retail influence was dispersed throughout both urban and rural areas. As a result, the grocery store has its own unique history.

The evolution from the general store to the grocery store was dependent on changes in the American economy and human settlement patterns. From early in the nation's history, the general store dominated grocery trade in small towns and the hinterlands. In the early revolutionary days of American cities, general stores did exist, although retail food trade was dominated by the public market. Whether it was the country store, a store on Main Street in a small town, or a general store in the city, the rise of the grocery store depended on eliminating the economic barriers of space and introducing a money economy.

The era of the independent store was the era of the storekeeper. As small entrepreneurs in an emerging capitalist economy, storekeepers were largely responsible for managing all aspects of the business. Barter trade, wholesale buying, and serving customer needs all had to be mastered by the storekeeper. Store architecture was shaped to meet the different economic and spatial limitations that existed in the city, the small town, and the rural crossroad. The U.S. population growth and changing settlement patterns as well as technological developments, such as railroad transportation and the mass production of foodstuffs, changed retail food trade. Storekeepers were able to retail mass-produced food goods that were no longer dependent on local and regional supply sources, and with the growth of towns and cities, storekeepers were increasingly able to specialize in the grocery trade. During the time when the nation's economy was oriented largely to meeting the needs of small retail businesses, the storekeeper's independently owned store was the dominant force in the American grocery trade.

EARLY BEGINNINGS OF THE CITY GROCERY STORE

America's first grocery stores were the general stores that appeared in larger cities during the seventeenth century. Even America's largest cities, such as Boston, were too small for storekeepers to specialize in the retail food trade. General stores served not only the town but also the surrounding country. Some merchants who ran these stores conducted both wholesale and retail trade to sustain a high volume of trade. There were few storekeepers who bought from wholesalers and conducted strictly retail trade in the seventeenth century.[1] Retail stores, however, did begin to appear—Boston having the greatest number of storekeepers—and grocers were already identified as having a distinct trade. Yet, the number of retail stores was limited. In 1690, Philadelphia had just twenty-nine storekeepers, both large and small.[2] The expansion of retail shops was only as great as the rate of growth of the population to be served.

Grocery shops became more prevalent in the eighteenth century as America's few colonial cities grew larger. The population growth was sufficiently large that a few merchants could specialize in the grocery store trade. Large grocery stores offered specialty items such as sugar, chocolate, cheese in bulk, oatmeal, coffee, tea, fruits, olive oil, and wine. Many of these goods were non-perishable, and such items were largely imported. These stores served the needs of the upper classes who wanted specialty items, but most small stores served the hand-to-mouth trade of the lower classes who could neither afford to buy groceries in quantity nor pay for the best quality.[3] Yet, the continued population growth in the United States provided a growing number of retailers, and with increased competition, resulting eventually in lower retail prices.

In the eighteenth century, some grocery stores remained general stores rather than becoming specialized retail shops. Some merchants in major port cities served as factors for plantation owners. Plantation owners sold large volumes of farm produce and bought equally large volumes of grocery and hardware goods. As a result, they dealt with factor merchants who offered to accept crops for trade and to sell processed goods far below retail prices.

These merchants operated both as wholesalers and retailers, and they sustained a profitable high volume trade when compared to storekeepers with small grocery stores.[4] This type of practice resulted in regional differences in grocery trade. In eastern seaboard cities, such as New York and Boston, grocery trade was both retail and wholesale, but in the South the factorage system discouraged wholesale trade. In cities such as Charleston, South Carolina, retail storekeepers limited "their stocks to imported groceries, hardware, and dry goods, or to specialties such as millinery goods or wines."[5] Later wholesaling did develop in the South in port cities, such as New Orleans, but this dual role of wholesaling and retailing enabled northern merchants to be more than simple storekeepers in the grocery trade.

During the eighteenth century, some grocery store owners expanded into other business interests. Storekeepers attempted to diversify their capital by investing in other trades and financial ventures. By diversifying capital, storekeepers could expand their opportunities to prevent a total loss in any one business as well as being able to profit in one or more of their ventures. In some cases, the grocery store was a front. The earliest definition of a grocery store was a groggery, or saloon.[6] For conservative citizens, the selling of spirits was bad enough, but some grocery stores even used the retail liquor license for illegal activities. A Boston grocer allowed a madam to use the dwelling quarters of the store building as a brothel for years, and the madam was finally prosecuted in 1753.[7] Legitimate or not, the grocery store was a beginning point for many other business ventures.

Grocery stores began to offer an increasing variety of goods as well as diverse employment conditions. During the 1730s in Boston, grocery stores became more specialized as the market for retail goods expanded. Stores offered a variety of preserved fruits, jellies, syrups, and nuts, and Boston's largest grocery specialized in all kinds of sugar, fruits, sweet oil, and spices. During this same period, many women, usually related to the owner, worked as clerks and even shopkeepers, and they became attuned to the specialized nature of the grocery trade. In spite of this, storekeepers transplanted the English system of apprenticeship by using boys and girls as workers to learn the trade.[8] The professions continued to be dominated by men, and storekeeping was one of the few avenues of upward mobility for women in an age of urban expansion, although apprenticeships were also continued.

The architecture of the grocery store during colonial times was essentially similar to other retail stores. In the seventeenth century, buildings in colonial cities were small, and for most of this century, commercial structures included living quarters for the storekeeper's family.[9] In the eighteenth century, cities gave more attention to building more permanent structures. Although wood was used initially in colonial cities in the North, structures with brick walls and internal wood framing became more prevalent, because owners considered totally wood buildings to be a high risk due to the ever-present danger of fire. But wood structures remained the predominant method of building construction. Many commercial buildings, like residential structures, had common walls that significantly reduced a single owner's construction costs.[10] The great leveler in design was the lot and building tradition. All lots, whether commercial or residential, tended to be narrow and deep, allowing the maximum number of frontage lots on a block, and the typical lot was often no larger than 20×100 feet. These lots were small due to economic conditions. Urban land was densely developed, packed, and somewhat costly, but building costs were quite high because both labor and materials were expensive. Builders constructed mainly narrow building spans, and traditions of designing narrow facades fitted well with lots delineated by narrow street frontages. Samuel Bass Warner, Jr., an American historian, noted about eighteenth-century Philadelphia:

The high cost of building kept houses small, cramped, and in short supply. The common... storekeeper's house was a narrow structure about seventeen feet wide and twenty-five feet deep. A story-and-a-half high, it offered about eight hundred square feet of floor space on its ground floor and attic. Most often the owner plied his trade in the largest front room.... If the... shopkeeper prospered he would likely add a kitchen ell or more likely move to a house of similar proportion with a kitchen ell at the rear. The house of an ordinary merchant... who had grown rich, would be like the... [storekeeper's] house with the ell, but would be two and one-half stories instead of one and one-half.[11]

Facades emulated the vernacular architecture of the time, but storekeepers were becoming aware of the need to present an image to potential customers. Glass windows were introduced so that food products could be displayed. Awnings of painted cloth and duck were installed over store windows and doors, and reached over the sidewalk to the street's curb to protect customers from the summer heat.[12] As cities grew in the eighteenth century, dense development forced city officials to be more aware of coordinating the configuration of streets and blocks. These same constraints of growth combined with increasing business competition shaped the architectural spaces that enabled grocery storekeepers to sustain a profitable business.

The high costs of land and building construction resulted in more than the high density of buildings and the clustering of retail activities. As cities grew, increased density and clustering meant that townspeople made shorter trips to buy their goods. Without quick means of transportation, the shopping trip to the market and nearby grocery stores had to be short. The spatial barriers of city size were minimized by townspeople using land use density as an economic means to reduce travel time within the city. A high-density city was spatially an economical city that served consumer needs.

Grocery retailing in cities during the eighteenth and nineteenth centuries eventually became dominated by the public market. The public market offered a small merchant distinct advantages over a grocery store. A grocery storekeeper had to have more financial assets than a merchant renting a

2.1 City Grocery Store, Philadelphia, 1868 (Courtesy of the Print & Picture Department, Free Library of Philadelphia)

market stall. Grocery stores were bigger, had a larger inventory, and had higher rents with a larger floor area than market stalls. Storekeepers who owned their own buildings still had to pay insurance and to make building repairs. Owning a grocery store required more capital and management abilities than were needed by hucksters who sold their produce in the public market. Yet, the earnings of an ordinary storekeeper who was frugal could adequately support a spouse and family.[13] Although their retail trade was complementary, grocery storekeepers had the opportunity to be petty landlords, whereas stall merchants remained part of the tenant class.

Grocery stores and public markets often complemented one another. Public markets were often held only two or three times a week in the seventeenth and early eighteenth centuries, but grocery stores were open every day. Some storekeepers located their grocery shops immediately adjacent to public markets. The street markets offered fresh meat, vegetables, and fruit, whereas the nearby grocery stores on the block sold non-perishable goods, such as tea and sugar. Within the same block there were sometimes porters who sold ale and confectioners who sold sweets.[14] Grocery storekeepers undoubtedly purchased some perishable goods from stall merchants and sold such produce at higher prices than in the market. This enabled storekeepers to sell quality produce late in the morning after the best produce in the market had been sold, and to sell such goods on days that the market was closed. The clustering of these retail activities meant that customers could do all of their shopping within the same area with multiple choices between market stall merchants and storekeepers.

There were eventually political conflicts surrounding grocery stores, and these problems were most intense in larger cities. By the 1830s, the public markets were being challenged by retail food shops. The old market houses were overcrowded and unsanitary. Butchers, grocers, and fruiterers were establishing stores away from the public markets in the better residential parts of town.[15] Public market officials responded to stall merchants by enacting laws limiting peddler sales and restricting meat sales to butchers who leased market stalls. Such laws were selectively enforced, because many people felt that the free enterprise system should prevail. During the 1840s in New York City, the Whigs and Democrats challenged the public market policies that were attempting to monopolize food trade. They complained that public markets led to longer walking distances for shoppers and to higher food prices which were caused by forestallers. These restrictive laws on food retailing, were rescinded in 1843. The elimination of such laws recognized the city's expansion, as a New York City observer noted in 1850; "it has become so fashionable to have a meat shop on almost every corner and fruits and vegetables in almost every grocery, and fish and oysters well nigh swimming through the streets that our large markets are to some extent forsaken."[16] Grocery storekeepers, however, were protectionists when such actions served their interests. They protested publicly when peddlers sold grocery products in front of their stores or nearby. Moreover, storekeepers were sometimes dishonest. Grocers had been traditionally defined as storekeepers who sold whiskey, and some cities, such as Rochester, New York, required these store-keepers to obtain a grocer's license for the sale of whiskey. Yet, many grocers sold whiskey without a license. When the Whigs replaced the Democrats in Rochester, they began charging very high fees for licenses. This significantly limited the sale of liquor in 1834.[17] In 1846, an investigation found that New York City storekeepers were charging an average of 100 percent above normal prices for small quantities of food. Such price gouging came at the expense of the poor who could afford neither high prices nor large quantities. Grocers also watered milk and doctored weights and measures when selling goods, and many corner groceries and butcher shops sold food that was unfit for human consumption.[18] Although grocery storekeepers saw themselves as the political victims of unfair trade, some grocers victimized peddlers and customers.

The distribution of grocery stores increasingly tended to be spatially de-centralized as cities expanded. During the nineteenth century, the urban land close to the city's center became the most valuable, because there was a limited amount of prime land.[19] Given such overhead costs, a grocery store-keeper had difficulty sustaining a profitable business downtown. It made more sense for a storekeeper to locate near a residential area where land costs were cheaper and potential customers were nearby. By 1860 in Philadelphia, grocery stores had appeared in every ward, and this pattern was repeated in other American cities.[20]

The growth pattern of grocery store trade in the East was repeated as national settlement moved westward to the frontier. Pittsburgh, Cincinnati, Lexington, Louisville, and St. Louis first established general stores and public markets between the late eighteenth century and the early nineteenth cen-tury.[21] As these cities and others farther west grew in population, storekeepers were able to specialize in the grocery store trade. At the same time, grocery store owners were often not only storekeepers but also became investors in other enterprises as they became financially more successful.[22] Labor con-ditions in the Midwest, however, were somewhat different from those in the East. There was a constant labor shortage in the Midwest during the first half of the nineteenth century. Commerce and industry were developing quickly, and there was a great need for workers to migrate westward. As a result, women and children increasingly had to work in shops to alleviate labor shortages.[23] Midwestern cities offered economic opportunities, and as these places became more urbanized, successful grocery trade became more pos-sible as the local public demanded more variety than general stores could offer.

The general store in the frontier city either became specialized or expanded into wholesaling. Conversion into wholesaling was often a profitable venture for merchants who left the general store business, because they knew the

2.2 Independent Corner Grocery Store, Philadelphia, 1901 (Courtesy of the City
Archives of Philadelphia)

wholesale trade. These wholesalers were able to supply another type of general store that existed on the western frontier and in the hinterland of settled areas—the country store.

THE COUNTRY STORE

The country store as a commercial vessel has all but disappeared. Many of the economic and technical transformations that led to the demise of the public market were also responsible for the decline of the country store. Yet, this rural form of enterprise had its own unique history that was shaped by political, economic, and spatial forces. Country stores were established by storekeepers to supply not only the settled hinterlands but also the western frontier. Such establishments were outposts, and when both travel time and unsettled space were reduced, the country store had served a major role in advancing commercialism throughout the nation.

When general stores began to emerge in American cities during the eighteenth century, the merchants who operated them were all-purpose businessmen. All types of products were bought and old, and such stores conducted both retail and wholesale trade.[24] The owners of these business establishments were merchants in the fullest sense. Although specialized trade within cities eventually limited the ability of urban general stores to compete within the city, their wholesale trade played a critical role in rural areas. City general stores were the primary wholesalers, known as jobbers, to country storekeepers. Coastal cities, such as Boston, New York, Philadelphia, and Baltimore, were the major locations for these general stores, because American commerce depended heavily on foreign trade at this time to provide retail goods. In the beginning, general stores represented both town and country trade.

Country storekeepers needed food supplies that their customers could not easily provide for themselves. Coffee, tea, rum, spices, molasses, sugar, tobacco, rice, and similar goods were items that settlers wanted or needed. Eggs, butter, and other locally produced goods were items that storekeepers sold, and local people traded these goods for other wares in the country store. Storekeepers were able to sustain a balanced supply of perishable and non-perishable foods by depending on this system of dual supply sources between settlers and wholesale jobbers.

The dual supply system was a critical link for storekeepers to sustain their accumulation of capital. Although they strongly preferred cash payments, storekeepers relied on locally produced goods as a form of wealth. Currency was a significant problem. Foreign currency and worthless currency from a variety of American locations compounded problems of efficient trade, and worthless bank notes and altered currency, such as clipped coins, were continuous nuisances for any merchant. At the same time, the United States was a developing country with a debtor status. Many people were poor, and in the country, the rural populace had little or no money.[25] Depending on food products, hand-made goods, and manual labor as forms of payment, storekeepers managed their business without complete dependency on currency. To supply their stores from jobbers in the cities, storekeepers used butter, goose feathers, and other locally produced goods that were accumulated through customer payments as capital. City wholesalers were willing to accept such goods as payment, because they could sell the butter at retail prices or sell feathers as a raw material to other wholesalers, exporters, or local manufacturers. The country storekeeper became a middleman between local residents and general store merchants, and these merchants became middlemen between the storekeepers and other entrepreneurs. Although storekeepers were able to profit from transportation costs to send their goods to wholesalers, they also faced the uncertainty of changing commodity prices in urban markets. Country storekeepers constantly had to balance the bartering prices that they made with customers with anticipated profits or losses that they could expect in commodity exchanges. Yet, they had no choice. Storekeepers became petty commodity traders in order to sustain their retail trade in the country store.

The economics of transportation was the primary influence over the location of country stores. Roads were few and physically modest, but such roads were the only market pathways that existed except for waterways. Country stores were located when possible at crossroads for practical reasons. A storekeeper could maximize any contact with potential passersby and be located at the one point where the greatest number of local settlers could take the fastest route to their supply source. At the time, settlers who were local producers could not profitably move heavy, bulky commodities for more than ten to twenty miles by land.[26] The maximum travel distance to country stores was normally determined by a settler's proximity to roads and road conditions.

Store architecture and site planning were a reflection of storage requirements as well as local building practices. In the eighteenth and early part of the nineteenth century, a general store was a wood, rectilinear building about twenty by thirty feet in dimensions. In settled areas, the structure was typically built of sawed lumber and unpainted, but some stores in new areas were log cabins.[27] Narrow doors were used, and windows had small panes. Windows were small because glass was expensive, and the idea of window displays was either unknown or unneeded. One-story structures were initially used, but two- and even three-story structures were commonly built in the early nineteenth century in settled areas. The upper floor space was either used by storekeepers as a home or leased as housing quarters or offices for professional men.[28] Country stores were often insufficient in size to contain bulky commodities acquired through bartering with local settlers. Such goods were often stored behind the store until a sufficient amount was accumulated for shipment to market. To protect these goods, some storekeepers built warehouses for safe storage of their bartered commodities, which were later sent to market.[29] The county store's site sometimes included a chicken shed and stables, much like a farmer's physical arrangements. Customer arrangements were relatively simple. In the beginning, a hitching post or rail was in front of the store. Porches were often built that served as a loading dock for customers to pack their supplies onto their wagons. The country store's building and site were designed as a processing center, albeit a relatively simple one.

As general stores became part of a settlement that eventually became a town, store architecture changed. Stores were increasingly being built from more permanent building materials. Brick structures became more prevalent due to better protection against fire, and for this reason insurance companies offered lower insurance rates to storekeepers with these buildings.[30] Buildings became larger to handle warehousing and larger retail space. Merchants advertised the physical size of their stores to promote the notion that a large quantity and assortment of goods could be found in their establishments. Window design became important as storekeepers used bay windows to emphasize product displays.[31] Building facades still remained plain with most signs limited to the name of the establishment. Store architecture in settled areas became more permanent because a settlement provided long-term stability for market activity.

Store interiors were practical but not always systematically maintained and arranged. Cleaning and dusting the shelves occurred during the slow business time of the year and perhaps only twice a year. Country stores always had a hodgepodge appearance. Lawrence Johnson notes:

There were soaps and spices, salt and salaratus, dishes, books and drygoods on the shelves. Hardware and leather goods shared floorspace with barrels of flour, sugar, and molasses. A cat in the cracker barrel was commonplace. Axes, log chains, kettles, pots, pans, kegs of nails were piled in corners or hung from the rafters on cords. Shoes were piled loose in a big "shoe box"; saddles and harnesses added to the variety . . . coffee, cheese, and tobacco crowded the counter along with piles of [cloth].[32]

Part of the problem in organizing goods was the storekeeper's need to offer many different items within a small area. Although a variety of products were needed to meet customer demand, there was no opportunity for variety or a large volume of any one product. At the same time, the retail packaging of goods by manufacturers was usually in bulk form or non-existent. Bulk storage was rather efficient because a desired volume of food goods, such as coffee, could always be spooned out for purchase, but the spillage on the floor was a constant nuisance. Other items were less organized, with only the storekeeper being able to find them. With little room to spare and objects of all sizes and shapes, the country store was a difficult candidate for modular storage systems.

Designated areas were provided within the country store for customer services and storekeeping. A special corner was sometimes set aside for the selling of patent medicines and other drugs. Of all the special functions provided in the country store, the post office was the best known. In its most sophisticated development, the post office was a caged space behind which the storekeeper performed the official business of mail postage or money certificates. Some storekeepers set aside a place to do their bookkeeping. At the turn of the nineteenth century, back storage rooms and cellars became more prevalent. Larger volumes of goods could be stored, such as cheese, butter, and molasses, either for warehousing purposes or replacement of goods on the main floor.[33] Although storekeepers were not able to store products in efficient modular units, they were reasonably able to plan the general layout of store operations.

Spatial efficiency in country store interiors was not absolutely essential because there was a lack of economic competition and low sales volume. Storekeepers typically had a monopoly over trade. Roads were too crudely built for fast travel, and country stores were the only retail center within reasonable distance of rural settlers. The cost of transporting goods from the wholesale jobbers to the hinterlands resulted in country storekeepers setting higher retail prices than general stores in towns. These higher retail rates were due not only to transport costs, but also to the lack of competition. Low product turnover meant that storekeepers did not need to be overly concerned about how and where to locate their goods. The combined influences of trade monopoly and the low volume of sales resulted in storekeepers not being particular about the interior design of their stores.

For storekeepers, the critical concern in merchandise control was the management of unit costs. An essential method of stock control was pricing codes. Storekeepers marked their goods with symbol, number, or letter codes known only to them in order to identify the wholesale price, and a markup quotient was used to give the customer a price. This technique enabled storekeepers to charge different prices based on whether a customer paid with cash, farm goods, or credit.[34] Although these codes were important for pricing imported goods, a storekeeper's scales were even more important, because scales were critical not only in controlling imported goods but also in measuring goods obtained through trade with settlers. For storekeepers, scales were the means to have exact controls over capital flow measured through goods. Country stores with a feed business had platform scales that enabled them to weigh stock and farm goods. But more important was the scale that measured both ounces and up to twenty-eight pounds. Made available in 1841, this scale enabled a storekeeper to measure ounces of tea or to sell flour or sugar in pound units.[35] Bookkeeping was important, but the number of sales per day was often so low that the scale was a more critical control over grocery trade than the storekeeper's ledger. Country stores were dominated by bartering

2.3 Country Store Interior, Thomas W. Wood's "The Village Post Office," 1873 (Courtesy of the New York Historical Association, Cooperstown)

and currency shortages, and pricing codes and scales enabled storekeepers to keep some systematic control over their inventories.

The distribution system for supplying country stores was not spatially efficient from the eighteenth to the mid-nineteenth century. Storekeepers normally made two buying trips per year in order to replenish their supplies. Buying trips took as long as six weeks, but shopkeepers tried to make these journeys during the down time of the year.[36] Although such trips were inconvenient, storekeepers enjoyed these trips as a form of entertainment and education. The salesmen for wholesale jobbers were called drummers, and as part of their ritual effort to obtain customers, drummers wined and dined storekeepers as well as taking them to the theater and less sophisticated haunts, such as the saloon. In time, storekeepers would visit a wholesale house to shop for the goods to be brought home. They were prepared and careful. Storekeepers knew what their customers bought, and even asked them what particular items that they would like to purchase before embarking on their buying trips. Yet, new products were constantly being made available, and drummers would attempt to convince them to invest in these new goods. It was during these buying trips that storekeepers became familiar with exotic foods from abroad. Varieties of tea, wine, brandy, rum, olive oil, spices, sugar, and other groceries were available from wholesale jobbers.[37] After storekeepers had made their purchases, they brought their goods back, and they were uneasy until all their boxes, bales, and packages were in the store. Although such trips were costly and time consuming, storekeepers were able to use these journeys as a means to gain status. They were able to experience the cosmopolitan life of the city. Storekeepers became aware of current events, technological advances, the arts, fashion, and other facets of urban life that were unknown in rural environs. The buying trip distribution system was an inefficient way to supply country stores, but it provided storekeepers a way to advance their knowledge and status in their communities.

Country storekeeping developed more quickly in the North than in the South. The North was developing into an industrial economy in which retail trade was becoming increasingly better organized. In comparison, the South was not advancing quickly, either industrially or commercially, because the feudalistic system of slavery for agricultural production impeded such improvements.

Country storekeeping in the North was characterized by a good wholesaling system and retail organization. Compared to the South, there were more and bigger wholesale centers in major ports. Boston, New York, Philadelphia, and Baltimore were the nation's major ports on the eastern seaboard, and the only equivalent southern ports were New Orleans and Charleston. The potential for volume and variety of goods was much greater in the North than in the South. Given the denser development of country stores and their proximity to wholesale jobbers, northern storekeepers were able to save time by making shorter buying trips.

This economic atmosphere in the North played a part in the advancement of country store trade with an innovation that later became important in the development of grocery stores. John Meeker was a Massachusetts businessman who developed the idea of a chain store system of country stores in the early part of the nineteenth century. Meeker organized everything: "He chose locations, set up stores, and with great good judgement selected young men as his partners to operate them. At one time he was reported to be operating fifteen stores."[38] Although he made a tremendous capital investment, Meeker's strategy meant that his company could purchase in volume to reduce wholesale costs as well as organizing shipping trips for multiple store destinations rather than making singular trips for each store. At the same time, Meeker was able to keep more attuned to the prices of agricultural commodities that he bartered from rural settlers for trade goods. The company was able to make more consistent and profitable price decisions because the volume of company trade kept Meeker more consistently informed than individual storekeepers could be. Meeker's chain of country stores was more workable in the Northeast because of multiple wholesalers and denser development than in other sections of the country.

The South operated much like a feudalistic state, preventing the advancement of capitalism through country store trade. The plantation system dominated rural life and wealth. The system was feudalistic not only because the slave system was the major labor supply for agricultural production but also because wealth was highly concentrated. It has been estimated that during the 1850s one thousand of the richest families in the South held approximately 44 percent of the region's wealth.[39] With planters controlling the wealth and not obligated to pay labor wages, they were able to establish their own means of retail trade, the factorage system.

The shortage of currency in the South and the potential volatility of agricultural commodity prices influenced by foreign markets meant that planters needed a stable means to sell their tobacco, cotton, and other products. The planter relied on people known as factors to be their economic agents. Planters brought their goods to market and sold them to factors, and in return, factors supplied the planters with slaves, machinery, and provisions. This business arrangement provided planters with a credit network and, in essence, a wholesale buying system. Much of the foodstuffs that rural southerners consumed were from the plantation and thus through the factorage system. The planters were indirectly retailers, because their bulk buying of goods prevented them from creating an expanding demand for retail trade or retailers.

Although the factorage system had significantly limited retail trade, the country store was the essential means that enabled retail capitalism to penetrate the spatial domain of planter feudalism. Planters did not monopolize the rural South, because many people settled the southern frontier to farm. For small farmers, the factorage system did not provide a feasible means to supply their needs, because factors were unwilling to trade with farmers who only produced a small volume of agricultural goods. It was more profitable for factors to handle fewer trade deals in larger volumes to maximize their profits and to operate as a merchant in foreign trade. As a result, lower- and middle-class farmers found it more convenient to operate in the barter trade system of the country store to obtain supplies. Just as in the North, the southern country storekeeper was an economic agent between rural settlers and wholesale jobbers.

The country store provided a capitalist presence that the factorage system could not stop from expansion. Country storekeepers were the pioneers of commerce in the South that followed the small farmers. In time, large plantations would follow, but the country store had often already created a market. Southern population growth created a demand for a more extensive retail system. In some areas, merchandise dealers from coastal cities initially used wagons to provide direct retail trade to settlers, but as interior towns and country stores beyond them began to develop, these dealers were forced to provide wholesale trade to these places.[40] Even the planters used the country store as a matter of convenience. Although the country store retail system could not eliminate the factorage wholesale system through competition, the geographic expansion of stores and the elimination of slavery after the Civil War led to the country store becoming a vital form of business.

Outside of the South, merchants in mid-America faced economic problems with their own country stores. With East Coast wholesalers being so far away from the geographic center of the nation, storekeepers had economic difficulties in transporting goods. Although Chicago and particularly St. Louis were the farthest wholesale centers in the West, merchants preferred not to buy in these cities due to high prices caused by transportation costs. It was less expensive for storekeepers to make the long trips back East for goods than to buy at nearby wholesale markets. The Erie and other canals opened up the Great Lakes and lowered shipping costs to Chicago, but St. Louis remained expensive. Yet, storekeepers used these most western cities to buy small amounts of goods when they needed certain items. Storekeepers in mid-America attempted to organize chain stores as was done in the North, but they were less successful. Three or four stores in partnership was the maximum possible number of stores that a merchant could sustain alone or in a limited partnership with local storekeepers. Distances between stores were sometimes far, and coordinating delivery could be difficult. Yet, the biggest problem was operating in bartered trade far away from wholesale markets. A chain store owner was unable to operate efficiently with a large volume of bartered produce and then sell wisely when goods were brought to market. Potential losses due to price drops in commodities multiplied for chain store owners. Cash payments were more secure but unlikely, because there was a shortage of cash. But storekeepers in mid-America did benefit in buying produce. Chicago and New Orleans began to specialize in wholesale groceries, and New Orleans offered better prices than the eastern markets.

Coffee, sugar, spices and some other items were obtained from Central and South America, whereas the Atlantic trade with European countries was primarily in manufactured goods.[41] The bartering system was used to trade for grocery goods, and storekeepers were more able to prevent economic losses on produce with shorter trips to frontier wholesale cities. Although the South was isolated from the East with its factorage system, the mid-American region was economically isolated from the eastern seaboard by the lack of an efficient transportation network.

The true American frontier was beyond the South and middle America because forts and trading posts in the West were the nation's outermost settlements, and although minimal, grocery trade did exist in these places. Many forts had trading posts that provided trade for Indians, soldiers, and settlers.[42] The early western posts were characterized by the fur trade era, which was in its heyday between 1807 and 1843. Hunters and trappers bartered their furs at trading posts to supply their trapping excursions, buying sugar, coffee, dried fruit, tobacco, and whiskey.[43] As time past, the fur trade subsided, and the military's presence became greater. Although the U.S. Army was responsible for feeding soldiers, the fort commissary did not provide all of the food. Military personnel were basically fed beans, salt pork, and bread, and many forts had vegetable gardens to add to the daily diet. But both the commissary and enlisted men got food outside of these channels. Cooks in the commissary would often trade surplus foods to the trading post or sutler, a civilian provisioner with a store on the post, for other groceries. Enlisted men would also buy specialty food items from the sutler whenever they could, because their army rations lacked variety. Food that was shipped was expensive, because freighters had to travel far and then face the danger of Indian hostilities.[44] Providing food through retailing was neither easy nor inexpensive, but the trading posts gained a commercial foothold in the wilderness.

In the settlement and frontier expansion of the United States, the country store was both a commercial outlet and the local community center as it was in more settled areas in the East. Receiving mail was a settler's contact with the outside world, and the trip to visit the post office and to go shopping was the community world. It was a time to hear local gossip and to sustain friendships. The community ritual had its shadier side, in the minds of some settlers. The country store was sometimes the local saloon. Liquor sales were a part of store trade from the very beginning, and with the country store being the only source unless settlers made their own, whiskey was a profitable item that provided the store a social function. Beyond its established commercial functions, the store was a communication center. When settlers needed to seek medical help for a family member, they went to the store. Politics of all sorts centered about the store, because it was where issues were discussed as well as where votes were cast. In addition to all of these functions, the storekeeper was the main player in all aspects of community activities. He was a banker, giving small loans with interest rates attached to payments, and he was the local tax collector. In the service trade, the storekeeper was a legal advisor, a pharmacist, and a part-time barber. The storekeeper played key roles in serious matters, such as choosing a school teacher and being a church elder. Finally, he was a funeral director, orchestrating the appropriate decor and selling the coffin.[45] All of these community elements came together at the store, and the storekeeper's name was eventually given to the cross-roads intersection or corners that the store abutted. Eventually, these place names were landmarks, directing travelers and defining surrounding neighborhoods.[46] The country store and storekeeper were the essential ingredients that helped to bind together the local community and its place identity.

The enduring community image of the country store is the sight of people sitting around a pot-bellied stove near the cracker barrel. The social space surrounding the stove was the community meeting place. Storekeepers enjoyed such company, but they were far more pragmatic in their views about local people in the store than the romantic views of modern times. As one Missouri storekeeper reported to a newspaper in 1825:

I am a storekeeper, and am excessively annoyed by a set of troublesome animals called loungers, who are in the daily habit of calling at my store, and there sitting hour after hour, poking into my books whenever they happen to lie exposed to their view, making impertinent inquiries about business which does not concern them, and ever and anon giving a polite hint that a little grog would be acceptable.[47]

Prior to the Civil War, the romantic images and the grumbling realities of country store life and trade held true, but more critically, the country store represented an essential commercial outpost in the nation's frontier and hinterland. Its spatial isolation and architectural presence in a landscape dominated by nature often meant that it was the only form of communal civilization that existed. But as much as it was a center of community life, the country store was also capitalism penetrating its spatial margins so that the economy of the nation could maximize markets through settlement trade. Without competition, prices were high, but unlike public markets that provided many choices and prices in the city, the country store offered an economic and political trade-off. The compromise was that settlers were able to become their own landlords and managers of production in the frontier, but they were forced to deal with the monopoly trade of country stores. Settlers provided as much food as they could for themselves to minimize purchases, but certain food staples, such as sugar, spices, and coffee, were impossible for them to produce. The storekeepers' dual system of barter trade between settlers and wholesale jobbers was a practical solution for retail transactions. Settlers had farm products but little currency, and storekeepers who were wise traders were able to survive successfully with farm commodities as currency.

Economic problems were made worse because cash was imported to the East or simply remained there. Farmers and storekeepers "frequently complained against the flow of cash and credit to the East."[48] Although prices were high in the frontier, profits were low, because premiums on bartered goods, interest on debt payments, and shipping costs were significant overhead costs to storekeepers. Country storekeepers went to great lengths to establish cash payments in the East. Silent partners in country stores often lived in eastern cities, and they provided cash and made purchases to take advantage of good prices with eastern wholesalers. Storekeepers used draft payments whenever they could. For example, quartermasters at U.S. Army forts often contracted for foodstuffs with traders who owned country stores. Because there was a shortage of cash in the West, a quartermaster instructed the Quartermaster General to credit the fort's expenditures on the trader's account with an eastern wholesaler. This meant that the storekeeper could avoid losing the cash in mail shipments back East as well as avoiding paying a premium for using bartered goods as a payment for past debts to the wholesale jobber.[49] The absence of currency in the West was always an economic liability to frontier storekeepers.

There was an ever present economic danger with country stores. Storekeepers typically accumulated debts with wholesalers in establishing their trade, and operating on credit, they had to pay not only higher prices for goods but also interest on their debts after a grace period. Bartered products did count as payment, but when economic depressions occurred, these bartered farm goods were worth less to a wholesaler than a storekeeper's cash payments. The indebted storekeeper was often caught. If the settlers' food products were worth less due to an economic panic, they could not buy as much at the store. Storekeepers were then unable to sell goods or sustain product turnover, because they had fewer bartered goods for trade. At the same time these bartered goods were worth less during economic depressions, and they had little currency to retire their debts. In good times, storekeepers had a running debt with wholesalers, but during bad times, such as the Panic of 1837, storekeepers went bankrupt and closed their doors for business.[50] The barter trade system enabled capitalist enterprise to expand, but this system was easily disrupted by commodity price fluctuations and larger economic currents within the nation.

Although the country store was a small business that depended greatly on barter trade, it was the only business of any consequence that provided retail goods in the frontier. In its early era, the country store was a compromise between advancing the nation's economic system to its civilized edge and using rudimentary trading techniques, like barter trade to compensate for the absence of currency. But this was a temporary trade-off. The nation's growth meant that country store crossroads often became towns with a stabilized capitalist economy. The country store was necessarily a generalized business to meet all needs only to be replaced later by a more profitable location with better architecture, and soon technological development brought about a new era for country stores.

THE MASS DISTRIBUTION ERA OF THE GENERAL STORE

The elimination of the nation's frontier as a spatial barrier was essential to the advancement of American capitalism. To expand economic markets, more people needed to be settled throughout the country, and a physical infrastructure had to be in place to accelerate economic activity. No technological advancements conquered the nation's frontier more than the railroad and telegraph. In 1800, a traveler needed six weeks to travel from New York to Chicago, and by 1857, the same trip took less than three days.[51] Because railroad depots included telegraph offices, business orders for goods were filled more quickly than before. Conquering the spatial frontier with reduced travel time and improved information meant that economic transactions increased significantly, and the railroad's physical freight capacity meant that larger volumes of retail trade became possible. The building of the nation's railroad and telegraph system enabled the American frontier to become an economic growth machine.

The railroad and telegraph became important to retail grocery trade in country stores, because these innovations finally made available commodity markets and currency to settlers in the frontier. Before the railroad came, settlers traded their crops at country stores, because storekeepers were often the only produce buyers and retailers within a reasonable distance of their farms. Both the railroad and the telegraph helped to eliminate the storekeeper as a middleman. These lines of communication accelerated economic activity between the hinterlands and cities, which operated commodity exchanges. Representing commodity dealers from these cities, buying agents traveled by rail to the hinterlands and dealt directly with settlers for their crops. The settlers who benefitted most were crop producers who were closest to commodity exchanges, because buying agents tried to control overhead cost by minimizing the cost of transporting goods. These buyers paid cash for farm goods, and this new purchasing method was a welcome change for settlers. The telegraph quickly enabled buying agents to inform their dealers about crop purchases, and this communication link allowed agents to make contract offers to settlers at the most current market rate. At the same time settlers were relieved of the responsibility of getting their crops to market or suffering any losses along the way. Once the crops were delivered to the railroad depot for sale, it was the buying agent's responsibility to get these goods to market. As new lines of communication, the railroad and telegraph enabled settlers to convert from a barter exchange to a money exchange economy.[52]

Country storekeepers were pleased with these changes in communication and economic exchange. First, they no longer needed to make time-consuming, costly trips to buy their goods. Previously, they had to haul their bartered goods to faraway cities and then return home with all their goods purchased hopefully intact. Wholesaler jobbers now sent salesmen into the hinterland to take orders and to furnish catalogues and samples for country storekeepers. The innovations in communication quickened wholesale dealings. Salesmen were able to make contacts with their wholesalers by telegraph or by post, and ordered goods were shipped by rail. Storekeepers no longer had to make two big purchases a year and sustain a large back inventory in their stores. Their wholesale purchases were smaller and more often, and this approach was more attuned to the store's cash flow.[53] Because the settlers were more able to pay cash for their goods, storekeepers were able to make cash payments for their wholesale orders. Credit was still extended to country stores, but for shorter time periods. The days of bartered trade between the storekeeper and the wholesaler were disappearing. Country stores still continued to barter with settlers, and storekeepers sold their accumulated, bartered farm goods to buying agents just as the settlers did. Some local barter trade continued at country stores, such as for butter, eggs, and some fresh vegetables, but the storekeeper's huge dependency on bartering no longer existed. The railroad and telegraph accelerated not only a money economy into the country store, but also changes in the management of the store's inventory.

As in the frontier era, the southern country store was an exception in the development of business trade. The railroad and telegraph helped to modernize the South, but it was the Civil War that economically transformed the region. With the elimination of slavery, the plantations were broken up into moderate farms, and factors were no longer needed to provide planters with large quantities of supplies. As a result, the country store, which had a small foothold before the war, became the dominant commercial force in the South.

Although most southerners did not have the cash to establish a business, the railroad companies and wholesale jobbers promoted the development of retail trade. Railroad companies were encouraging the construction of warehouses, stores, and railway stations in every section where railroads were being built. Drummers for wholesalers not only promoted such ventures but also played an active role in setting up business.[54] Thomas D. Clark, a historian of the South, describes a drummer's work: "In many instances he helped to establish stores in places where there were reasonably good trading prospects. He selected the locations, designed the buildings, bought stock, set up systems of bookkeeping and gave advice on general business procedures."[55]

Although the railroad and wholesale companies promoted business, poor roads and lack of railways also encouraged the demand for new stores. As on the western frontier, country stores were built at crossroads in the hinterland to reach every cabin. There were cash shortages in southern towns, but this circumstance was even more severe in the South's most rural areas. As a result, many storekeepers depended greatly on barter trade to sustain their businesses. Until the South began to recover economically from the Civil War, southern country stores had to operate mainly without cash trade as did western stores before the railroads came.

The railroad did not influence business trade the same in every region of the United States after the Civil War, but its freight system indirectly influenced the interior design of all country stores. More than anything else, the typical railroad freight car was a standardized packing unit. Although being able to contain freight of many shapes and sizes and not always filled, the freight car represented, in principle, a storage unit that could be arranged efficiently. Any retail destination, such as a country store, was ultimately affected by any systematic planning of efficient shipping, because mass distribution companies began to organize the crating of their food products for warehousing and shipping.

Although retail trade in various regions was affected differently by the railroad and cash trade, the processing and packaging of food products were beginning to influence every country store in America. In the 1860s, a few articles were being packaged. The need for transportable food during war led to the development of canned food, and stores began to carry canned meats, fruits, and vegetables, although such items were expensive.[56] Traditionally, many grocery items were delivered in bulk and often unprocessed. Sugar, flour, and coffee came in barrels, and coffee still had to be ground and then roasted in the family skillet. The Chase and Sanborn Company began to market coffee by totally processing it. Coffee was ground, roasted, and packaged before it was shipped. In time, the store's coffee grinder was discarded as an useless tool. Many food products were transformed into packaged units such as Quaker Oats and Eagle Brand Milk. The packaging of food into small units was preferred both by producers and storekeepers. Bulk goods were always subject to damage. Barrels often leaked, and bags of oats were sometimes torn in shipment. With barrels being constantly opened and closed during store hours, spillage was a common occurrence. Packaged goods were touched by the customer only after the product had been sold. Some customers were suspicious, because they were unable to see, touch, or smell the product. Customers blindly had to trust the food producer's guarantee that the package's contents were sufficient in quality.[57] Nevertheless, most people accepted the idea of packaged products, because they were able to afford small units of food that they could store in their homes without fear of spoilage. Packaged food goods became an increasingly accepted means of retailing food.

Food packaging began to influence the design of country store interiors. Whether it was canned food, wrapped soap, or boxed cereal, food packaging resulted in standardized units that could be systematically arranged on shelves. Before packaging, barrels were placed in different places in the store as a matter of convenience. Packaged goods allowed for orderly arrangements and displays. Although these items added visual order, the store was still dominated by a level of controlled chaos as Clark notes: "Keeping store was a game of guessing just where something might be found, and always involved hazy instructions of looking under something, or behind something else."[58] Much of a country store's visual chaos was due to the odd lots of hardware items that were piled at the back of the store or were hung from the ceiling. Yet, the systematic arrangement of packaged products began to permeate the country store's image. Packaged goods advertised company images, and as food goods began to be known by these images, the generic, practical images of store goods, such as the cracker barrel, became less apparent as a background setting of the country store. The manufacturer's paperboard cartons of packaged goods with names and pictures printed on them were quickly replacing the cracker barrel.[59] With multiple and often colorful labeling, food packaging, such as boxed cereal and canned goods, could visibly stand out as a single unit when these items were systematically arranged. The display of the manufacturer's packaged image continued to the checkout counter with the grocery bag. Manufacturers seized on the idea of the grocery bag as a way to promote their products and even supplied printed bags at minimal prices to storekeepers.[60] However modestly, mass distribution companies were beginning to influence the interior design of country stores.

Standardization of food packaging made uniform pricing an efficient means to manage cost control, and the cash register was being introduced in all retail stores in the United States to accomplish this end. The storekeeper's day book was the traditional way to account for store purchases, and it was a practical solution in an era when few sales were made. Barter trade had been so prevalent that prices varied depending on whether the customer paid cash, bartered, or bought on credit, but the introduction of a money economy into the locale changed traditional accounting methods. With systematic pricing, the cash register saved time, labor, and bookkeeping. The cash register gave a running account of recorded sales. At the same time, the storekeeper gave an image in the store of keeping up with the times.[61] The cash register provided the functional counterpart to food packaging in the country store. Food packaging provided a systematic input into the store's interior, and the cash register was both functional and symbolic of the store's output process.

The country store exterior was beginning to have a unified but multiple image in the last half of the nineteenth century. In many regions, and most certainly in the South, the store's facade was a square front, and this design became a badge of the trade much like a barber shop displaying a tri-colored pole of red, white, and blue. Some stores included a permanent awning made of tin over the porch. It was a new fashion to have a cast iron front for a building facade, and such storefronts often included false columns with decorative Corinthian details. The store's main sign often included not only the store's name but also company advertising. The store's doors were covered with advertising signs, auction notices, and announcements of local events. Some stores had Masonic lodges or other fraternal organizations as tenants

2.4 Nineteenth-Century Country Store, Bynum, North Carolina, 1939 (Courtesy of the Library of Congress)

on the second floor, and symbols, such as the Masonic square and compass with a G, were used as exterior signs. A post office sign was a common sight.[62] New and old symbolic functions were combined to give the country store its evolving identity as both a local institution and a vessel of mass distribution.

THE MASS DISTRIBUTION ERA ON MAIN STREET

The American small town and its businesses on Main Street became unavoidably intertwined with the growing economic forces of mass distribution. Some country stores on crossroads eventually expanded into towns, whereas others did not, as trade routes and trade centers became more important in settling the American frontier and hinterlands. Other towns were planned as speculative ventures to sell land for commerce and settlement. The railroads and mass-produced products both played a role in influencing town formation and character.

The railroad companies provided the growth foundation of new towns. When a railroad line was extended to or passed by an existing country store, business people and settlers realized the opportunity of minimizing the distance to receive or to ship goods from a given location. With the country store already the most feasible market location in a given area, a railroad line alongside the crossroad enabled business investors to build on a local trade area, however modest. But many towns were started from scratch. State agencies promoted town development as a way to populate their states.[63] But it was still the railroad companies that were the most effective economic boosters. Beginning in 1850, the railroad companies received federal land grants along the track rights of way as an incentive to extend rail transportation into the frontier, especially the West. To exploit these land grants, railroad companies actively promoted immigration and were involved in town-site speculation. The Illinois Central used a standardized plan to lay out towns. Standardized depots and buildings were built on company land.[64] Such land speculation enabled the railroads not only to recoup construction costs but also to profit immensely through land sales. At the same time, they monopolized profits from freight transport in new settlements. Most importantly, the railroads enabled towns to expand the volume of commercial trade and to handle business transactions more quickly. The combined economic result was increased profits based on the efficiency to import and to export trade goods.

Selling mass-produced goods in these town settlements was particularly advantageous to storekeepers on Main Street. They no longer needed to make long trips back to the East coast and to trade their bartered goods to wholesale jobbers. Moreover, grocery stores required only a small amount of capital to open for trade, and with reliable rail shipments of small quantities, storekeepers with little capital could continuously sustain their grocery stock with packaged goods without the large capital outlays required for two annual buying trips by wagon. Storekeepers now depended on drummers from wholesale houses to come to Main Street and to take orders for grocery goods that were increasingly packaged brand goods rather than generic bulk goods. Packaged food standardized quality, which put grocery store trade on a more even par with competing stores in the town.

The expansion and competition of grocery trade was related to the change from general trade to the specialized store. Initially, businesses were both wholesale and retail, and as cities came to capture the wholesale trade, storekeepers confined themselves to retail general trade. As towns grew and goods were increasingly mass-produced and distributed, store specialization began to occur incrementally. Rather than going immediately from general store to grocery store, combinations of specialized trade were done. Some stores combined provisions, such as hardware, with groceries, and many stores combined dry goods with grocery trade.[65] Storekeepers' particular combinations of specialized goods were undoubtedly the result of their trade knowledge of these goods and local market needs, but as the volume of trade grew and as there was a stable, continuous flow of specialized, imported goods by rail, retail specialization became more possible. National food companies increased their efficiency to mass-produce food, and railroads were systematically able to transport these goods in mass. As a result, specialized storekeepers depended less on piece-meal buying of many different items from wholesalers than general storekeepers were required to do in the past. Mass food production, the railroad network, and retail specialization were integral factors that made possible the grocery store on Main Street.

With town grocery store trade depending on a mass distribution system of supply, storekeepers increasingly had to rely on mass communication to foster retail consumption. Advertising in local newspapers became an important means to sustain a volume of grocery trade. Storekeepers sometimes advertised elsewhere when their own town had no newspaper, because they knew that the paper would be read locally, and thus the ads would promote their grocery store.[66] Food manufacturers helped shopkeepers by promoting their products in local newspapers and announcing that these products would be available at all grocery stores. Many of these campaigns were long and costly to manufacturers, but food brand advertising consistently promoted local grocery trade.[67] Both store and brand name advertising were used to go beyond serving face to face the known needs of individual townspeople or farmers in order to increase the number of potential customers.

The grocery store in the nineteenth-century American town was not visibly different from most businesses on Main Street. As in big cities, building lots were often narrow and deep to maximize the number of store fronts per block. Buildings were usually two or three stories high and were built of brick or wood. Roof cornices and window lintels or arches were often decorated in the Italianate motif between the 1840s and 1880s. Building signs were relatively simple, and names were straightforward, such as Smith Grocery. Canvas awnings over a planked sidewalk were typical entry markers for most Main Street buildings. The first-floor facade was fully glazed for window displays, and the door entrance was often recessed to create more linear feet of window display as well as a sense of entry to the store. Wooden floors and wood or galvanized iron ceilings were common, with walls lined with shelves that were filled from floor to ceiling with merchandise. Inside the store, a pot-bellied stove was in the center and toward the rear, and local men known as loafers sat around the stove during cold weather. When general stores became dual specialty stores, grocery items were placed on one side of the store, whereas the other specialty, such as dry goods, was arranged on the other side.[68] When canned foods and other packaged foods became more prevalent in grocery trade, window displays and wall shelves behind the grocery counter became increasingly seen as geometric displays that advertised company brands. As the grocery store replaced the general store, especially in the last half of the nineteenth century, the building's exterior facade remained essentially the same, but the presence of packaged food increasingly began to dominate the content and image of store interiors.

Although mass distribution enabled the grocery store to emerge in American small towns, it also created contradictions when mail-order houses took advantage of mass distribution opportunities. Sears, Roebuck, and Company established a grocery department in 1895, and groceries made their appearance in the company's catalogue in 1896 with ten pages of food goods.[69] Grocers as well as other small town merchants were threatened by mail-order grocery buying. A large company, such as Sears Roebuck, was able to buy products in huge lots, which significantly reduced per unit costs. Small town grocers bought their food goods from wholesalers who operated with much smaller volumes of trade than the mail-order houses, and they were unable to compete economically. To make matters worse, mail-order companies were supporting a congressional bill for rural free delivery of parcel post. Town merchants had to face free delivery not only of catalogs to farmers but also of boxed groceries, such as canned goods and flour, to the farmer's front door. In essence, the parcel post law that was passed effectively reduced transport costs and made mail-order house prices lower. Small town merchants and country storekeepers vehemently objected to the parcel post congressional bill and fought ten years to prevent its passage. The farmers were very resentful of merchants preventing them from being able to buy food at a lower price.[70] Small town grocery stores benefitted from mass distribution through wholesale services and efficient rail delivery, but they suffered when they had to compete as small businesses against a retail corporation that operated at a large-volume scale as manufacturers and wholesalers. The systematic advantages of mass distribution economically worked best for the retail mass distributors, which were the mail-order houses.

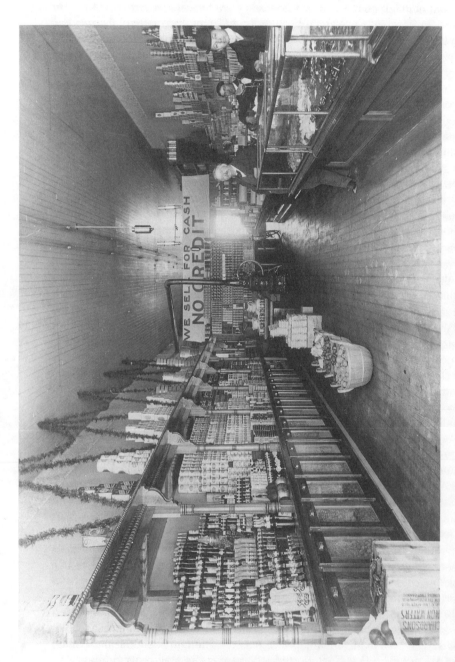

2.5 Main Street Grocery Store, Junction City, Kansas, 1901 (Courtesy of the J. J. Pennell Collection, University of Kansas Libraries)

THE MASS DISTRIBUTION ERA IN THE CITY

Urban industrial growth influenced the spatial organization and design of city grocery stores in the first half of the nineteenth century. American cities were growing quickly during this period, and some metropolises were five to ten times larger than a century earlier. The more cities grew in population the more complex became their spatial organization and economic activity. American cities were dominated by small businesses and industries rather than large enterprises.[71] Yet, there was a constant chaos in cities that were becoming industrialized, and this urban confusion was due in part to real estate speculation. The desire for profits shaped every spatial decision, not any sense of the public good. Building dimensions conformed to lot dimensions, and with many lot sizes being standardized, there was a uniformity of architecture. Grocery stores, like other small businesses, were in buildings that were built fully to the front and sides of their narrow lots, but the storekeeper sometimes used the rear portion of the lot for storage, garbage, and privies. Grocery stores were located in every area of the city. Small stores and residential quarters were either in one building or mixed as land uses on the same block. But as the nineteenth century progressed, streets became lined with continuous rows of offices, businesses, stores, and tenements. Grocery stores were frequently sprinkled among these businesses. American cities, however, continued to grow, and their downtown areas were converted into specialized business districts for factories, warehouses, mills, and retail business. At the same time, grocers with small stores were often unable to stay in business downtown when prime downtown land was surrendered to more profitable commercial business enterprises. As a result, grocers increasingly located their stores outside the city's central business district in nearby residential areas and beyond.[72] Ultimately, the size and wealth of a city dictated how many grocery stores were open for business and where they were located. With the haste that industrial cities were built, grocery stores were taken for granted by people as a part of nondescript architecture in the speculative buildings that came to dominate urban space.

In the latter half of the nineteenth century, a number of social and economic forces brought about new approaches and changes to the grocery trade. Immigration, department stores, and suburbanization were influences that emerged and redefined the role of the grocery store.

Industrial growth in cities was being matched by a growing work force of immigrants who supported specialty shops in their ethnic neighborhoods. Ethnic grocery stores reflected local culture. In the Jewish ghetto, kosher butcher shops abounded, with nearby grocery stores offering barrels of herring in brine and barrels of dill pickles in various stages of processing.[73] Push cart vendors lined the streets, and the sidewalk became a shopping aisle separating the push carts from first-floor shops, which were often grocery stores and butcher shops. As a temporary daily arrangement, the sidewalk became a public market without a roof. Whereas the factory labor force represented the beginning of immigrant involvement in the production side of the nation's economy, the shopkeepers' and street vendors' organized use of the street was often their initiation in the retail economy.

The city department store was involved in the grocery trade as department store owners sought out new markets for retailing. In stores such as New York City's Siegel-Cooper in 1896, manufacturers of branded food merchandise rented space in open booths to display their products and offer samples to customers. Shoppers could go from booth to booth and taste various goods while enjoying a small snack.[74] Given the customer composition of who could afford to shop at a department store, food manufacturers undoubtedly saw their displays as a practical means to spread the word among customers who would set a trend and pass a word of approval to their friends. Such displays enabled manufacturers to determine public reaction to their products. The decision among some department store owners to sell food merchandise on their valuable floor space was more than just a promotional scheme to increase customer traffic. Some stores had fully developed grocery stores. Unlike neighborhood stores and public markets, which were purely functional and sometimes unsanitary, department grocery stores in cities were elegant and large. In 1902, W. H. Simmonds, a British author of grocery trade, vividly described a New York City department grocery store:

It is one vast magnificent room 180 feet by 250 feet, the main feature of which is a large pavilion having a dome of opalescent glass lighted with 196 electric lamps. This dome is supported, or so appears, by four glass cylinders or posts.... These are hollow, and are filled with brilliant-coloured fruits, such as red and white cherries, cored pine-apple, Bartlett pears. This pavilion is surrounded by a glass display counter with round corners... filled with the finest foreign and domestic fruits and vegetables, and so arranged as to make effective colour groups.... Mirrors are at each end, and the cornice recessed in order to afford places for display. Opposite this, on the front side, is a large space, enclosed in handsome brass railing, elegantly carpeted, and filled with scores of tables and chairs. Five magnificent glass cases, containing samples of goods, are located at intervals within the enclosure. Here customers may be seated and give their orders to clerks, both men and women.

In the rear of the main pavilion are two round pavilions, with stained glass domes, supported by slender Corinthian columns. These pavilions are enclosed in circular glass display counters, 18 feet in diameter. The supporting columns are square, boxed in quartered oak, with mirrors on each side. They are surmounted with octagon shelves for the display of goods.

The different departments are all elaborately furnished. In the cereal counter, below the highly-polished counter top are... steel enamelled bins which... have half-round crystal glass tops, and are finished in silver and gold on a glossy black background. ... The coffee section is oblong, and consists of forty [such] bins [which] are set in an oak frame, and the entire section protected by a heavy brass rail with ornamental scroll pillars.

The delicatessen section "is a dream in mottled Italian marble," with verde-antique pilasters and base. The top of the counter is pure white marble, the counter being in reality a cold-storage glass case. These cases are lined with tiles, and are connected with a refrigerating plant... an elaborate dark quartered oak refrigerator, 56 feet long, 10 feet deep, 12 feet high [is] divided into three compartments—one for hams and bacon, a second for butter, a third for cheese. This cold-storage section has a plate-glass front, with extra-heavy plate-glass doors. It is lined with tiles, [and] fitted with electric lamps... the tea balances in this store de luxe are of silver, and of original design. Every detail is guarded.[75]

City department stores were able to capture an elegant presence in their food departments, but these stores were unable to monopolize or to gain merchandiser preference in the goods that were sold. Merchandisers were willing to limit the sale of high-priced brand items, such as perfume and cologne, to department stores, but mass food distributors depended on maximizing profits by volume sales rather than the highest price per unit. In contrast, department store owners had to balance profits by unit price with volume sales, because their stores had a limited amount of floor space on valuable downtown property. With profit margins for food goods being lower than most other store items, department stores eventually replaced food products with other goods that had a higher margin of profit per unit. At the same time, merchandized food items as well as high quality produce and meat were increasingly available at other grocery establishments.[76] Department stores were unable to sustain a profitable grocery trade with the profit constraints and competition which existed.

The early suburbanization of American cities in the nineteenth century began to affect the mass distribution of retail goods. Public markets, ghetto grocery stores, and department stores with grocery trade were confined to the realm of the central city, because most people required a commuter trip between home and work with a reasonable travel time. American cities were typified by tenements and row houses that were built without setbacks. With high property and building costs, most residents were forced to rent apartments or to buy modest homes. With the advent of the commuter trolley, space beyond the city was within reach of a reasonably priced, reasonably brief commuter trip. Developing the suburbs meant that real estate speculators could make great profits while more people were able to be property owners with ample living space instead of renters in a densely populated city.[77] Although work was separated from the home, not all retail shopping necessarily needed to be contained within the central city.

Grocery stores depended on volume trade, and shopkeepers who located their stores in suburban locations had several advantages in the late nineteenth century. Being a short distance from a store, a suburban consumer could walk to the grocer's shop for small purchases and carry them home. Home delivery of groceries from suburban stores was undoubtedly quicker than orders from stores in the central city. Although grocery stores dealt mainly

2.6 Siegel Cooper Department Store Food Demonstration, New York City, 1896 (Courtesy of the Museum of the City of New York)

with fruit, vegetables, and packaged goods, butchers also opened suburban shops to take advantage of the suburban trade. When located near to one another, grocery stores and butcher shops became a single marketplace and economically buttressed one another. It was undoubtedly in the suburbs where the notion of "corner" grocery store gained its full meaning. With suburban building being largely devoted to residential development, commercial enterprises naturally located at sites with the greatest traffic. Whether along a trolley line street or not, the corner lot was a visible location that was a more expensive property than the other lots on the block, and a commercial enterprise was more likely than residential use given these conditions.[78] Yet, suburban locations meant higher costs for grocers, because jobbers had to travel farther to deliver wholesale goods to stores. Moreover, locating in new commercial buildings meant that grocers often paid a higher rent than in older buildings within the city. Nonetheless, any increased costs were passed on to the consumer, and the grocer had the security of having suburban customers who could afford to buy a steady flow of goods and who could pay their bills on time. The suburban grocery store was a good investment strategy. Grocers were spatially able to follow affluent suburbanites who were a dependable clientele, to sustain a steady volume of trade with small profit margins.

THE STOREKEEPER'S AGE

From the nation's beginnings through most of the nineteenth century, storekeepers as individual entrepreneurs dominated retail trade. Storekeepers served to establish and expand trade in cities and towns, and they were business pioneers in America's frontier and hinterlands. The storekeeper system required a continuing balance between the constraints of space and the technical means and organization to conquer those spatial limits.

The constraints of space were initially an asset to the grocery storekeeper. Without efficient means of transportation, trade was very localized. Larger cities depended on fresh vegetables, meat, and some non-perishable goods to be provided by nearby producers. Many non-perishable goods, such as tea and sugar, were imported by sea, but once goods were on land, shipments moved slowly. Without efficient land transportation, mass distribution of food goods and companies to produce them were unfeasible. At the same time, the lack of time-saving means of transportation meant that customer buying trips had to be short, both in time and distance. These constraints of time and space enabled storekeepers to be the primary source of grocery goods for customers who lived nearby.

The constraints of space were also a liability to grocery trade. With a localized economy, a city grocery store could depend on a reasonable level of trade in the surrounding neighborhood. Public markets and grocery stores, however, were increasingly appearing in other city wards, and a grocer's ability to increase store trade was rather limited. In towns organized around Main Street, population density was much lower than in America's big cities, and as a result, small town storekeepers were less able to specialize in the grocery trade. Dependable, timely shipments of non-perishables were less assured in America's small towns, and with a smaller volume of trade, groceries were sold alongside other goods in the general store. The spatial constraints were greatest on country stores. Such stores monopolized retail trade on the frontier and the hinterlands, but country storekeepers were forced to run business in a barter trade economy in the country store's early era. The storekeepers' buying trips back East for goods were time-consuming and could result in damaged goods and economic instability. Dependence on trading in bartered goods for manufactured goods meant that country storekeepers were unable to plan for falling prices of commodity goods or to buy at the same wholesale price whether they paid with cash or barter. The constraints of space slowed down the volume of retail grocery trade.

The rise of technical means to conquer the constraints of space led to the successful development of the storekeeper system of grocery stores. The expansion of the railroad into all areas of the United States provided a network on which existing retail stores could flourish. More than anything else, the railroads along with the telegraph brought a money economy to all regions where these facilities were built. With country storekeepers, storekeepers on Main Street, and big city stores now operating on a cash economy, mass distribution of food goods produced by national companies became possible.

The technical means to conquer the constraints of space, however, were creating the conditions to dismantle the storekeeper system. American business realized that if mass distribution of food could be done for wholesale trade, then the same systematic advantages could be used for food retailing. The ability to use a large amount of floor space for grocery trade in department stores was an indication that a systematic organization of food retailing was possible, and that building space could be well designed to attract consumers. The ability to organize wholesaling, receiving, shipment, and retailing of food by Sears, Roebuck, and Company demonstrated that a corporate organization was potentially more able to manage mass food distribution in an advancing capitalist society than a local storekeeper. Although these particular ventures into food retailing failed, the use of large stores and corporate management eventually succeeded and dominated the grocery store system of storekeepers.

Chapter 3

THE CHAIN STORE AGE

The storekeeper's age began its decline in the early twentieth century as the economic logic of mass production extended to retail distribution. The nation's new transportation and communication structure in the nineteenth century made possible mass production. To manufacture goods in large quantity required rapid means not only to receive raw resources for production but also to transport finished products to market. Mass production depended on speed. Business people realized that there was a contradiction between methods of production and methods of distribution. Production was now based on large-scale economies, whereas retail and wholesale businesses were small distribution operations that were less economically efficient. Business people in the grocery trade realized that producers such as Quaker Oats and Armour and Company had adopted a corporate structure to centralize certain management functions and to focus on making every part of their operation profitable. The problem with retail distribution was space. Whereas most producers operated from a single factory, mass retail distribution required multiple locations where customers could shop, and these stores had to be efficiently designed for volume business, as did the manufacturer's factory. The solution was the chain store system.

THE BEGINNINGS OF MASS RETAIL DISTRIBUTION

The chain store concept emerged as an idea among storekeepers of all kinds who wanted a more systematic way of conducting business with lower overhead costs, and grocers were the first retailers to use the chain store system.[1] They knew that if they could buy in larger volume, their overhead costs would be reduced. They also realized that circumventing wholesale jobbers would allow them to accomplish that end. Bulk buying and dealing directly with food manufacturers were essential components of the chain store concept.

The first major grocery store chain emerged from stores that already used a system of bulk buying rather than from stores already specializing in the grocery trade. The Great Atlantic and Pacific Tea Company—A&P—was initially devoted to selling only tea. The company's strategy was to buy whole cargoes of tea and to sell it at cut-rate prices right on the docks in New York City.[2] The dockside location was replaced by stores, but the system of bulk buying and bypassing wholesalers was kept as the guiding principle. Some chain store owners were unable to initiate buying food goods without avoiding wholesalers. Bernard H. Kroger, who began his chain store operation in Cincinnati during the 1880s, was initially unable to avoid working with wholesalers because he began directly in the grocery trade instead of another trade, like tea. Even when he owned only one store, he made it a management practice to buy as much of a given product as was feasible. In dealing with peddlers who worked for wholesalers, he was often offered to buy a case of a product, but he inquired about the price of a carload.[3] The basic aim of bulk buying was to reduce unit food costs as much as possible.

Those storekeepers who expanded beyond a single store realized low unit food costs were only possible with volume trade, but to sustain volume sales, product turnover in the store was essential. Unlike the old country store principle of maximizing profits for every sale, the chain store grocer was motivated to offer the lowest retail price in order to sustain a volume trade. This principle gave such owners an economic advantage over their competitors who owned only a single store. By maximizing volume with lower prices, the net profit per sale was less than for the independent grocer, but this strategy was ultimately the most profitable. The chain store owners saw their stores as a means of maximizing dollar velocity within a given building space. To them, profits were better determined by estimating the net gain relative to the store's square footage. With bulk buying, advertising, and lower prices, chain store owners were able to yield a greater net profit per square foot of retail space than an independent grocer.

With a chain store owner being able to oversee many stores rather than one, organizational economies occurred other than bulk buying costs. Home delivery in the city was a necessary part of business. An independent store owner needed a horse, a delivery wagon, and a driver, but for a chain store owner, the requirements could be less. It was possible for a chain store owner to have less than one delivery wagon per store if another store was nearby. Just as important, if some problem existed for a delivery wagon at one store, a wagon from another store could help with deliveries until proper repairs or horse substitutions were made. If necessary, a food stock item in one store could be shifted to another in cases where temporary shortages of that good existed. In contrast, an independent store owner had to wait until a wholesaler could deliver a new order. In managing the flow of grocery trade, the chain store owner had more flexibility than the independent grocer.

The ability of chain store owners to control overhead costs and be flexible enabled them to channel their energies toward seeking profit-saving management devices. They were able to save on building insurance by having an umbrella policy over all of their stores instead of a separate policy for each store. This allowed them to get better rates. Advertising in the newspaper cost less for chain stores, because when there were multiple stores in the same city, one newspaper notice could serve all of the stores simultaneously. In contrast, an independent grocer's advertisements served only a single store.

The big advantage that chain store owners had over independents was the ability to plan efficiently. Unified systems of bookkeeping enabled management to compare store productivity. If one store had a lower volume of sales than the others, the chain store owner could analyze a number of conditions. Problems could be due to a poor store manager, insufficient collection on credit accounts, a bad location, insufficient store promotion, or other problems. Chain store management had the ability to make changes based on store comparisons, something that an independent was unable to do. By focusing their attention on more than one store, chain store owners were able to evaluate not only existing stores but also the possibility of building new ones. They learned to analyze which locations might be profitable and compared those sites in regard to building costs and rental rates. Independent store owners tended to be more locked in to a given location in order to develop a local clientele. At the same time, they often did not have sufficient funds to build another store or to rent at a different location. Chain store owners were also better equipped to manage overhead costs and to be more flexible about making decisions to invest in or to divest themselves of existing store properties. As a result, they were very competitive against independent grocery stores.

Chain store owners designed their company image to take advantage of their strengths: uniform management and advertising. Chain stores chose a lettering style to illustrate the company's name on building signs, and the same sign type was used repeatedly for every store to build a company image. The same care for design was extended to delivery wagons and horse tackle so that people would recognize the chain store company. Management was sometimes elaborate in attempting to create a company image. From its inception in the 1860s when the A&P Company sold tea, management consciously attempted to project a store image:

A great sign in the shape of a "T" extended above the street and blazing with dozens of small gas lights, beckoned passersby to enter a high-windowed building with bright red vermilion, imported from China and picked out with gold leaf. Around the windows—through which could be seen crystal chandeliers—curved arches of gas jets with glass cups glittering in red, white, and blue.

Inside, the pageantry continued. Walls decorated with gilt-edged Chinese panels; the ceilings a flowery canopy of fancy tinwork; the cash desk shaped like a pagoda; tea bins painted red and gold. In the center of the main floor a cockatoo on a stand welcomed the trade.[4]

The designs of most chain stores were visually more humble in their beginnings when compared to A&P's stores, but chain store owners did realize the necessity of creating an image for their stores. By developing a consistent image, they discovered that they could begin to gain the psychological advantage over the general public. If a family moved from one neighborhood to another, the household would either ask neighbors where to shop or depend on their past experience by shopping at a chain store that they had known or used previously. The consistent image was a sign of security to people who moved, and newspaper advertising using the company's logo helped to reinforce people's confidence. The independent grocers did not have such a psychological edge, and they had to attract people either by the store's location or by local reputation. Every store added to the chain helped to further the company image by increasing the probability that people would see more than one of the company's store. With systematic repetition of a chain store's image in its building designs, delivery wagons, and advertising, chain store owners began to capture the public's attention, which eventually resulted in their increased willingness to shop in the chain stores.

Grocer chain companies promoted the store's image with premiums. Customers were given vouchers for the amount of purchases that were made, and after saving a sufficient amount, they were able to trade in their vouchers for gifts, such as furniture, china, jewelry, and clothing. At other times, kitchen ware was offered at reduced prices when store purchases were made. In the 1900s, trading stamps came into existence, and S & H green stamps came into wide use.[5] In this, chain stores had the same advantages over independents as they did in other aspects of the grocery business. When chain store management bought premium gifts, they were able to buy in bulk, whereas the independents could not. In working with premium stamp companies, chain management was able to extract a better financial agreement than independents for issuing stamps, because the chain store management only had to administer one contract for many stores, whereas each independent had to arrange an individual contract. Moreover, if a customer went to another store or moved across town, the chain store's vouchers would still be valid, or in the case of stamps, the customer could continue to collect the same type of stamps, knowing that all stores in the chain used the same stamps and gave the same premiums. Chain stores were able to promote stamp premiums more economically and consistently than independents.

Although chain store owners did not own huge numbers of stores in the nineteenth century (as they would in the next century), they did experience the advantages of surviving physical hardships more easily than independent

3.1 Early A&P Chain Store, 1890s (Courtesy of the *Progressive Grocer*)

grocers. Major catastrophes often beset grocers. There was the ever-present danger of fire. Independent grocers were less likely to be as fully insured against fire as the chain stores because the chains were able to receive lower rates. Undoubtedly, some grocers had no fire insurance. When these independent grocers experienced a fire and a loss of capital, their businesses were closed permanently. Even the insured independent grocer who suffered fire loss could not equal a chain store. A new building had to be either built or leased, and afterward, the store had to be furnished and then stocked. During this period the independent grocer was unable to produce any income. The chain store owner had to make the same recovery arrangements as the independent, but during the reconstruction of such a store, the chain owner was still producing profits from the other stores in the chain. The same pattern followed when floods occurred. Although both chain and independent owners suffered, chain owners probably suffered fewer flood losses. Being able to afford higher rents or more expensive land, chain store owners were more able to locate stores on higher ground than independents. Yet, this advantage was marginal, because numerous towns were built almost entirely in flood plains.

Chain stores were more able to survive the economic depressions that occurred during the latter half of the nineteenth century than were independent grocers. A chain store owner could always close one store at a time until a level of financial stability was achieved. In contrast, independent grocers could either recover from losses or close their individual stores. During good economic times, the savings chain owners could realize on overhead costs often enabled the chains to stay in business. After depressions receded, many independent grocers had to acquire bank loans to finance their recoveries, whereas chain stores did not. In a recession, chain stores could use the savings they had accumulated during economic good times to cover financial losses without having to borrow money. As a result, an independent store had a greater probability of having a loan as part of overhead expenses than a chain store. The chain store system demonstrated not only that it knew how to compete but also that it knew how to survive.

With all these advantages, grocery chain stores did not dominate retail trade. The A&P Company, the largest grocery chain, had only 198 stores in 1900, and the Kroger Company had less than 30 stores.[6] Grocery chain stores were initially concentrated in cities, because company management had to sustain a velocity of trade while recognizing the constraints of space. Chain store owners were learning how to coordinate the flow of incoming goods and how to distribute these items to their stores. A store was more likely to be successful if goods could be sent to it quickly while sustaining a high volume of trade to maintain low prices. It was inefficient to ship goods to a single rural store in which the volume of trade was likely to be lower than in the city. As a compromise, some chains put the store on wheels. Peddlers drove horses and wagons to solicit orders door to door, giving the chain stores the opportunity to supplement trade at their store locations and to introduce new customers to the chain store. The A&P Company found this strategy to be quite successful.[7] Even with chain stores increasing their share of the retail sales, public markets, independent city grocers, and country stores dominated the nation's grocery trade.

Chain store owners learned to exploit the opportunities for expansion within the city as the spatial constraints of customer location and movement were gradually eliminated. Traditionally, the American city had been compact and densely populated, because there were inadequate systems of transportation to move people from one location to another. Although upper-class residents sequestered themselves into neighborhoods that were spatially separated from the lower classes, the well-to-do residents lived quite close to the central city in the nineteenth century. This density of buildings and population was well suited to public markets and small grocery stores. By being centrally located and largely oriented to the pedestrian, public markets dominated retail trade in large cities with grocery stores having a strong but secondary role. Both of these types of retailer expanded their spatial limits by making home deliveries. In these circumstances, chain store owners often limited themselves to selling manufactured food goods and select items of fresh produce which they often obtained from local wholesale jobbers. Economically, chain stores were competing directly with independent grocers in big cities, but they were unable initially to overcome the magnitude and variety of food goods offered by the public markets. No chain store could compete with the fresh vegetables, cuts of meat, and fish varieties that big public markets offered. These particular goods were still controlled by wholesale jobbers, and some foods were produced regionally rather than under the control of a mass food manufacturer. By focusing on goods that they could purchase directly from manufacturers, chain stores were able to expand into retail trade but in a limited way. Mass transportation in the city changed the opportunities for chain stores. As cities built trolley lines toward their city limits, suburbanization began to occur. City residents wanted more residential space, and they wanted to own their own homes. With land being expensive in the central city and its near environs, people often had to rent apartments, and they were unable to buy a home as a capital investment. The result of this expansion to the suburbs was that "many cities doubled, tripled, even quadrupled in area."[8] The suburbanization of the American city laid the foundation upon which the chain store built its future in the grocery trade.

Suburbanization of grocery stores was advantageous to chain stores at the turn of the century and through the 1920s, because these companies had greater economic and spatial flexibility than independent grocers. As suburban neighborhoods were built, residents wished to minimize their shopping trips and the length of those excursions. By the close of the nineteenth century, building speculators began to locate commercial buildings along streetcar routes, known as taxpayer strips, in suburban areas of American cities. Grocery stores were often located in these developments, and chain stores became the dominant presence in the 1920s as chain companies greatly expanded their number of stores. Chain companies grew steadily in the 1900s and 1910s, but the greatest growth was in the post World War I economic boom. In 1920, A&P, American, First National, Kroger, Safeway, and National Tea had 7,723 grocery stores, and by 1930, these chain companies had 30,453 stores. Although some of these chain stores replaced independents in the central city, many were new stores located in newly created suburbs.[9] Locating stores in suburbia was the obvious solution, but independent grocers and especially public markets were severely limited in their ability to exploit suburban opportunities. An independent grocer often lacked sufficient capital to open a store in a suburban location. If the existing, more centrally located store was only doing moderately well, the independent grocer was economically trapped in a downtown location. Many successful independent grocers were not able to afford an additional store, but seeing the opportunity for economic stability and growth, some independents chose to close their old store and open a new one in a suburban location.

With chain stores no longer having to compete with public markets, the owners turned their attention to competing with independent grocers in the suburbs. Chain companies had the collective advantages of bulk buying, being able to analyze and to select good store locations, and using their past profits as leverage for setting up stores with few or no loans. These conditions enabled chain store owners to work quickly in capturing suburban business trade. The suburbanization process helped to advance the chain store system, whereas public markets and independent grocers were less quick to respond.

The suburbanization process tended to include a general form of land development. Grocery chain store owners were not the only businesses that wanted to profit from suburban growth. As the trolleys extended into the countryside, commercial development followed the rail lines. The American experience with strip development had begun. The trolleys had stopping points along their route, and commercial development occurred first at these locations. Building development from the central city along the trolley route to the suburbs was being done by speculative builders. Property owners along the trolley strips had initially built commercial building space as a short-range solution to holding on to properties with the hope of larger profits in the long run. These real estate investors saw their speculative strip commercial buildings as an expedient way to net sufficient profits to pay for property taxes. They assumed that as the city grew in size, these properties would become more valuable and be developed for higher density development. These trolley line commercial properties became known as taxpayer strips.[10] Being attuned to the need to exploit new market opportunities, grocery chain store owners were better prepared than their competitors to select the best locations with the lowest rental rates along or near suburban trolley routes.

As the city physically grew in area, old site location practices still continued.

Many neighborhoods in the late nineteenth century and early twentieth century contained mixed land uses. Corner grocery stores, which were alone or with a few other stores, were still being located within neighborhoods. Not on major arterial streets, such as a taxpayer strip, these grocery stores maintained a very localized trade, and because such locations were less desirable than those sites on or adjacent to the strip, land costs and building rental rates were less expensive than strip locations. Undoubtedly, both chain stores and independent grocers located stores within suburban neighborhoods, but with the lower costs, independent grocers were better able to afford stores at neighborhood sites than on the strip. Chain store owners were not only able to move more quickly in locating a new store but also were financially able to make more site selection choices than independent grocers.

Just as they spread across the city, chain stores expanded across the nation in the 1920s. The strongest concentration of grocery chains was in the Northeast and Middle West. New York, Massachusetts, Connecticut, New Jersey, Pennsylvania, and Maryland had the highest density of chain stores in the 1920s. Ohio, Indiana, Michigan, Illinois, and Wisconsin had strong but lesser densities. The southern states then followed, and the Rocky Mountain states and the West Coast states had the least concentration of chain stores in the 1920s. Although the West Coast chains, such as Safeway, Albers, Alpha Beta, and Vons, were prominent, these companies were unable to match the number of stores and trade volume of Northeast and Middle West chains. In 1925, Safeway had 1,050 stores. In comparison, the colossal A&P had 14,034 stores with 1,792 stores for American Stores, 1,642 stores for First National Stores, 2,559 stores for Kroger, and 761 stores for National Tea.[11] The chain store movement was strong in the 1920s, but its geographical growth was unevenly spread across the United States.

THE STORE AS A FACTORY DESIGN

Before the twentieth century, chain stores were in the process of becoming physically organized much like independent stores. Corporate chains, such as A&P, Kroger, and Jewel Tea, were expanding from selling only tea to offering a variety of goods. All grocery stores, both chain and independent, were being influenced in design by packaging containers used by food manufacturers. Canned and boxed goods were building blocks that grocers used to design store interiors as bulk goods in barrels began to be used less and less. Chain store owners were more competitive than independents, because of their ability to avoid wholesalers and to plan for store economies was better. Yet, the physical designs of chain stores were not substantially different from the plans used in independent grocery stores.

Corporate chains began to modify store design as a means to reduce overhead costs and to become flexible in relocating stores. John Hartford, co-owner of the A&P Company, created a store system to maximize store profits through design and management standardization. His basic approach was to provide an economy store that offered the lowest possible retail prices. A&P's old-line stores maintained a staff of fifteen to twenty people, offered credit, made home deliveries, and gave stamp premiums. Such services added 20 percent to overhead costs. To capture retail food sales, the A&P policy had always been to offer the best product possible at the lowest cost, because the company founders always believed that customers responded to the bottom line of new household savings in shopping. To reduce costs, the economy stores eliminated credit, home deliveries, and stamp premiums in 1910. Besides eliminating delivery workers, the number of store clerks was reduced to a store manager and a part-time clerk. The A&P Company did not invent the cash-and-carry system to reduce costs, but it was the first corporation to put the idea into mass production.[12]

The economy store was designed as a factory assembly line for consumption. Each store was physically planned, stocked, equipped, and furnished with fixtures to be another economy store. A type of canned good in one store could be found on the same shelf at another store. Shelves, display cases, and check out stands were designed exactly the same, and by standardizing design, A&P was able to reduce construction costs by repeatedly building the same items rather than creating higher costs of designing and constructing fixtures for unique circumstances. With speculative commercial buildings being essentially the same width and depth on taxpayer strips and in other areas, A&P was quickly able to assemble a store in order to be aggressive in maximizing profitability, as Mueller notes:

Work schedules and specialist teams of carpenters were carefully organized. A lease signed on Monday meant the premises were open and ready for business the following Monday. Supervisors throughout A&P's system grabbed locations about any place the rent was right. Stores were closed, too, if they didn't make the grade. For that reason, leases were on a one-year basis, with renewals.[13]

The A&P economy store was designed to be located almost anywhere at any time to capture potential retail trade. Although company management sought out lower rental rates, it was not cost efficient to relocate unless desired profit margins were met. A&P management chose lower-rent side street locations over higher-rent locations on Main Street and required a minimum store size of $20' \times 30'$.[14] Grocery stores still depended on customers walking from and to home on their shopping trips, and with such short trips, multiple store locations existed. However, company management still had to consider the profitability of a location regardless of rental rates. Once a location was decided on, either new equipment or fixtures from a closed store were installed. Equipping a new additional store expanded a chain store's overall profits, whereas relocating a store reduced losses and offered the possibility of greater profits than before. The economy store was made to fit into any building and neighborhood, but it was not designed to remain. Stores were designed as fixed capital commodities with an expected rate of return. The economy store had no place attachment to the local community as the mom and pop stores did. The economy store was purely a mobile factory for profit production.

Store design standardization was followed by management standardization. The A&P Company prepared standard procedures in its manual for managers. Specific instructions were provided—for using thumb tacks and putting price tags on shelves, and for prohibiting both credit and delivery. Because the physical elements of the store were constant, company management could concentrate on the store manager and clerks and their ability to run a store profitably.

The economy store was a self-contained capsule designed to fit efficiently into a standard building and neighborhood. It was, in principle, a factory design that was similar to the Ford car factories. Internally, the principles of Taylorism were at work. Frederick Winslow Taylor was a research specialist in time and motion studies, known as scientific management. By designing where objects were placed and how laborers moved, work production could be increased.[15] By standardizing such practices, company profits could be multiplied as the design was repeated. In an automobile factory, workers became specialists with limited but very defined tasks. In the grocery store, clerks were unable to be as specialized as car workers on an assembly line, but store managers and clerks could move to another economy store and be able to understand and to work with the physical operations of the new store. Each A&P economy store was allocated a fixed amount of capital, $3,000. It was divided in equal $1,000 amounts for food inventory, fixtures and equipment, and supplies and operating expenses. Each store was issued a cash register and a small ice box. In stocking the store, three hundred standard grocery items were predetermined and placed on preplanned positions on shelves designed to carry the predesignated volumes. As a result, all managers and clerks learned the same procedures for stocking and processing inventory. Their work procedures were standardized as well as their input of time. Workers clocked in and maintained a constant number of hours of work. Each store manager had a company-issued manual to carry in a shirt pocket to help administer every store uniformly. Continuous work objectives were specified for ordering, receiving, and controlling inventory as well as how to price and to design commodity displays.[16] The economy store's physical design was shaped by management policies that standardized store operations in order to increase profits.

By being self-contained and operating on a cash-and-carry basis, economy stores separated the store as a commodity from its role as a community establishment. Independent grocers had allowed their stores to be community meeting places. Country stores had always been the community hall in rural America. The independent grocery store had some of the same atmosphere,

3.2 A Typical A&P Economy Store, 1910 (Courtesy of the Great Atlantic and Pacific Tea Company)

because the grocer attempted to anticipate individual needs of shoppers. Credit allowances were made, and through home delivery, the store kept close contact with the customer. The economy store appealed to the public's pocket book, and many people were largely unconcerned with the social services and local commitment that the local independent grocery provided. Although chain store managers and clerks came to know their customers, those acquaintances were strictly limited by company policies and the possible closing of a store in order to relocate it elsewhere.

Although design standardization had made the grocery store work more efficiently, the traditional floor plan was not designed to handle a high traffic volume of customers. The typical grocery store had been laid out on a counter-and-wall system. Packaged goods lined the walls and were stacked almost to the ceiling on long shelves. This display was put behind a counter where the clerk would remove an item off the shelf after a customer requested to purchase it. The middle of the store was a large vacant aisle where customers viewed wall displays and then made their selections. This traditional plan was labor intensive, with a clerk having to serve individual customers. In small stores, a clerk might help the same customer for every selection, and in larger stores, clerks were often assigned zones within the store to help customers with particular food items, especially if customer traffic was great. For managers, the problem with this traditional store layout was that it was labor intensive. A plan that reduced the number of clerks needed to operate the store while sustaining a high traffic volume of customers would significantly reduce overhead costs. The traditional store plan was economically inefficient for chain store owners who wanted to control costs and speed up the volume of trade.

A radical store plan revolutionized how stores were managed. In 1916, Clarence Saunders opened the first self-service market in Memphis, Tennessee. Owner and founder of the Piggly Wiggly chain stores, he decided to eliminate the counter and wall system. His grocery store was located in a typical building of the time with a deep lot and a narrow street frontage, which other grocery stores normally used. Customers entered his store, and after passing the window displays, they went through a turnstile and picked up a shopping basket. They began along a circuitous one-way route that enabled them to pass by every shelf in the store. Customers took what they wanted off the shelf and moved on to the next shelf display. Once they had completed the full shopping circuit, they entered a divided path that enabled them to choose between the shortest line to the cash register. After paying the clerk, customers went through a last turnstile and exited the store.[17] The purpose behind this plan procedure was to have the customers to substitute their own work for clerks in the store.

The Saunders plan was an assembly line system turned wrong side out. Instead of the products moving down the line, the worker, who was now the customer, moved. The shopper was given the psychological freedom of mak-

3.3 Counter-and-Wall Service System, Gem Grocery Store, Topeka, Kansas, 1928 (Courtesy of the Kansas State Historical Society)

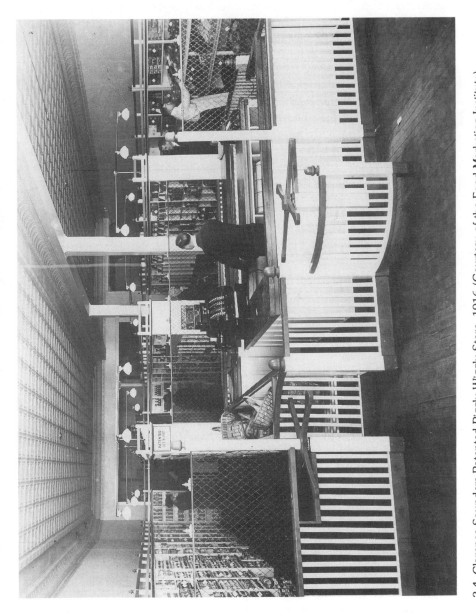

3.4 Clarence Saunders Patented Piggly Wiggly Store, 1916 (Courtesy of the Food Marketing Institute)

ing direct choices. In other stores where self-service was introduced, some customers felt as if they were stealing because only clerks had been allowed to handle merchandise before.[18] But chain store owners saw that the main advantage of self-shopping was reduced labor costs. Self-service shoppers were doing the work of handling goods, but most shoppers saw this additional effort as minimal. Self-service decentralized the work process into many hands rather than collecting it in the hands of a few clerks. The net effect, however, was that fewer clerks were needed to serve customers, and individual service was provided on a need basis. Some upper-class customers found self-service to be personally degrading, because they saw themselves being transformed into workers rather than being treated as an elite to be served. Some independent stores that introduced self-service maintained clerk shoppers and home delivery to serve this elite trade group.[19] Although a minority objected, the general public was willing to have self-service shopping aisles because they realized savings at these stores.

The Saunders plan of self-service allowed individual freedom, but it did not assume that the customer could be trusted. The turnstiles did direct traffic, but at the same time, shoppers passed through controlled check points that did not easily allow theft, the narrow waiting aisles by the cash register were like the cattle chutes that ranchers use to brand or immunize cattle. Where clerks behind counters had before policed customer theft, the cash register clerk by the turnstile now performed the task. The turnstiles did more than replace store counters, which were more expensive to build. These simple machines reduced the number of clerks required to police the store's inventory. As a result, the turnstile was both a security and labor-saving device.

Grocery chain store companies saw their stores as vessels that carried the flow of capital, and the best vessel was the one designed for maximum velocity. Bulk buying allowed chain stores to reduce unit costs, but this purchasing advantage was increased in one of two ways. First, more stores could be built to exploit new markets. Second, the store could be designed and managed to increase the velocity of trade. Chain store owners wanted building designs that increased volume sales, and the store plan that produced the highest net profit per square foot was the best design. By standardizing store layouts and introducing self-service, chain stores were able to reduce not only labor and equipment costs for setting up a store but also operating labor costs.

GROWTH AND EXPANSION

Grocery corporate chains were initially unwilling to expand into rural America, because many of the business economies that existed in cities were not present in small town America. Chain stores were unable to sustain a sufficient volume of trade in rural areas. The chain companies had the advantage over independent grocers of being able to buy in bulk, but this asset meant nothing if a sufficient stock turnover did not exist in their stores. With stock turnover being much lower in rural areas, chain stores were more willing initially to invest in expanding suburban areas in cities. The sales volume potential was significantly higher in the suburbs than in rural areas, and the result was that the suburban chain stores kept down unit food costs to supply store inventories. Some chain store owners began to venture out to smaller towns that were near their big city base of operations. In the 1900s, the Kroger Grocery and Baking Company began to expand outside of Cincinnati into nearby Hamilton, Ohio, where good rail connections for supply existed, and eventually the corporation located a warehouse in Hamilton. Yet chain expansion continued to go into large cities and towns.[20] Small towns were generally avoided, especially communities without a rail connection. The small town grocery store or general store still dominated local trade, although they were threatened by mail-order houses that supplied food on a cash basis through catalog sales. With profit margins for expansion being greatest in populated areas with good transportation networks for supply, chain stores chose to expand their business in urban rather than rural areas.

The critical barrier that prevented chain stores from expanding into small town America was the bad transportation system. Country stores at crossroads were still able to thrive in the late nineteenth and early twentieth centuries, because rural people had no fast way to travel to town. People traveled by horse and wagon over dirt roads that were poorly maintained. It was not unusual for country people to make an annual trip to the nearby town that was ten miles away.[21] People who lived nearer to town made more frequent trips, but wagons and bad roads resulted in fewer shopping trips. Rural Americans had to be more self-reliant by growing their own food or doing without certain goods from the store. Their impulse buying was held to a minimum. A poor transportation network in rural areas prevented chain companies from operating a store profitably while maintaining company operating policies of maximizing profits through volume trade.

The invention of the automobile had a significant influence on the retail economy of rural America. The first automobiles were curiosities, but cars such as the Model T were designed to drive on rugged roads. As the automobile was introduced, local citizens began to demand road improvements that would enable them to travel more quickly. With such mobility, rural people were able to make more frequent shopping trips. Volume retail trade was becoming increasingly possible in rural areas. The general store principle of maximizing profits per unit sale could not survive against an economic system based on maximizing profits through the lower prices made possible by bulk buying. The mail-order catalogue companies had already threatened the general store's economic principle by introducing mass distribution retailing into rural areas. But the chain store companies were prepared to challenge both of these retailers, as cultural geographer John Jakle notes:

The urban orientation of small-town consumers was nothing new. The mail catalogue had always been a popular device for avoiding higher local prices and limited stocks. It was once a mark of defiance against the town merchant for a farmer to say, "I'll order it!" By the 1920s catalogues lay on the counters of most stores for all to consult, with the merchant doing the ordering. But the automobile enabled customers to go frequently to the city, compare prices, and return with merchandise in hand.[22]

Although mail order catalogue companies did limited trade in the grocery field, the entrance of grocery chain stores into small town America eliminated their ability to be effective competitors. Mail-order houses such as Sears and Roebuck, which sold groceries from 1896 to 1929, were unable to provide nearby outlets for customers to buy their goods, although these companies were sufficiently competitive with chain store prices. Given the customer's ability to pay, chain grocery stores in small towns not only made lower prices more available to rural residents but also increased the potential volume of sales with readily available goods. Unless they planned extremely well, a family buying through a mail-order catalogue had to ration carefully from one order to the next because mail delivery periods were never exactly the same. With improved roads and an automobile, a household was able to restock its grocery goods quickly and with a greater variety of items than a mail-order house could offer. The chain grocery store offered more variety and quicker access than mail-order companies who sold food, and these mail-order houses eventually decided that they were unable to compete against chain grocery stores.[23]

As the chain grocery stores were expanding into rural America, a new form of chain grocery retailing was moving into suburbia: home delivery. Chain stores continued to locate more stores in suburban neighborhoods as new housing developments were built. Yet, A&P, American Stores, First National Stores, Kroger, Safeway, National Tea, and smaller chains were not able to reach the full potential sales volume of these neighborhoods. Suburban households typically had sufficient disposable incomes to make numerous purchases at grocery stores, but there was an insufficient means of transportation linking the suburban residence to the nearest store. In the beginning, household members traveled by horse and wagon, by streetcar, or on foot. Eventually, the automobile became a household possession. But even with these alternatives, the American family still maintained its traditional ways. The suburban housewife stayed at home and handled household matters because most wives did not have the employment opportunities of their husbands. Often, they were stranded. If the family had a means of transportation, the husband used it to commute to work, or the wife was not allowed or was unable to drive herself. Carrying groceries on public transportation or on foot was difficult, especially when many items were purchased at the store. In the beginning, chain stores offered home-delivery service, but as more chain companies converted to a cash-and-carry system of business, home deliveries were left to the independent grocers. But independents were unable to offer the cash savings that chain stores had gained through bulk buying. Families made travel arrangements to visit cash-and-carry stores, or used chain stores that continued home-delivery services. But there was a market gap. Suburban households were capable of supporting a higher volume of trade if the combination of chain store bulk buying to reduce overhead costs could be combined with home delivery.

Home-delivery companies exploited the last geographic gap of suburban retail grocery trade. Chain and independent grocery stores that provided home delivery did so as a reaction. They waited for the customer to call for an order and then delivered the groceries. The home-delivery companies went on the offensive by carrying food goods by wagon, and eventually by truck, to suburban neighborhoods. These companies became corporate peddlers for regular customers, and the best known chain was the Jewel Tea Company. In the early days, home-service routes were provided in rural communities before the chain stores began to capture those markets, but the front door delivery in suburbia was the frontier that chain stores were unable to capture fully.

Delivery wagons and trucks were designed to offer only a few select goods that salesmen could sell competitively against nearby grocery stores. Most home-delivery companies limited sales to fewer than two hundred items and some companies regularly sold less than one hundred types of goods. Any goods that required special handling or refrigeration could not be sold profitably, and common goods, such as canned fruits and vegetables, were considered by company management too heavy for shipment and handling.[24] Unlike chain stores that maximized volume in a stationary site with self-service, home-delivery companies had to sustain a volume trade with food products that would not slow down sales due to spoilage or difficult handling.

Home-delivery companies stressed good self-service with quality food goods that were not always offered at local stores. They attempted to sell new products to the housewife before they were available in the grocery store. Larger home-delivery companies offered their own food brands. Although the contents were the same as national brands, this tactic enabled the companies to create their own brand loyalty, which enticed customers to depend on home delivery. To have food goods brought to the home was a definite convenience for many housewives. Coffee, tea, baking supplies, packaged desserts, prepared baking mixes, macaroni varieties, cereals, cookies, crackers, and candy were all available. Soaps, cleansers, and toiletry goods were sold, and eventually kitchen ware goods were available. A home-delivery salesperson called about every two weeks on the same day of the week at approximately the same hour. Orders from the previous visit were delivered, and a new order was placed. Salespeople would show new products during these visits and answer questions about how to use them. By shopping in the kitchen, housewives could stay at home to take care of their children and could avoid bad weather.[25] Although home delivery and personal service resulted in higher food costs to suburban households, it was beneficial to

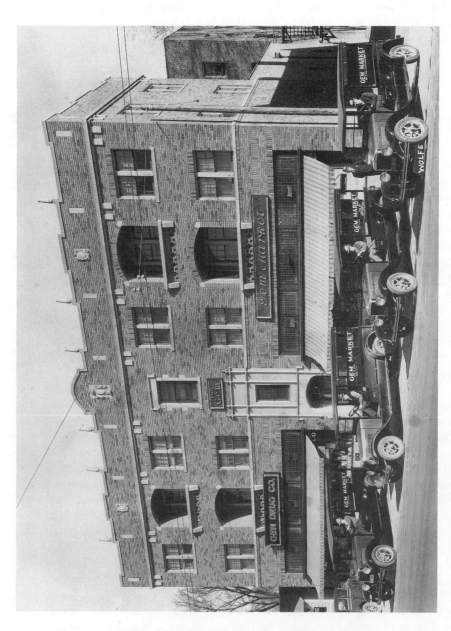

3.5 Home-Delivery Truck Fleet, Gem Grocery Store, Topeka, Kansas, 1928 (Courtesy of the Kansas State Historical Society)

housewives who were unable to be employed or had to remain at home due to weather, child care, or lack of transportation.

These circumstances provided the market conditions for home-delivery companies to succeed, but it was their promotional schemes using premiums that attracted households to home delivery. A basic strategy in offering premiums was to make the customer feel a psychological debt. In grocery stores that offered trading stamps, customers could redeem premiums for gifts. Many home-delivery services did the reverse. A customer was allowed to select and to receive an item before premiums had been acquired through food purchases. Working as a personal-service business, a salesperson contacted customers biweekly and was able to keep a running account of how many premiums the housewife needed to collect before she had paid off her premium merchandise. Premium goods were of high quality so that a salesperson did not have to face a disgruntled customer who had a premium product in need of repair. If a product proved to be faulty, the delivery salesperson replaced it with a new one. The premium system enabled the home-delivery companies not only to get through the front door but also to return again and again. The psychological debt of paying off premium merchandise as well as buying needed grocery goods made it possible for home-delivery services to sustain customers.

A less-used system of home delivery was the mototeria, a grocery store in a truck. It was a convenience store on wheels with an entrance door located in the middle of the vehicle's right side, which faced the curb. Invented by the W. K. Hutchenson Company in Massachusetts, the mobile store was called the Roly Poly. The company was selective in locating selling routes. The trucks traveled through only the better sections of family homes in suburbia. Because the truck was expensive to operate, it was necessary for the Roly Poly to travel through areas with a sufficient density of households who could afford the higher prices of convenience shopping. It was a cash-and-carry business that provided a variety of grocery goods. The truck stopped at every third house and rang a gong to call people to the curb. The driver was both manager and clerk. As customers entered, with shopping baskets, they were able to buy canned goods, relishes, baked goods, meat, soaps, and other items. As with the home-delivery companies, such as the Jewel Tea Company, the Roly Poly offered convenience to housewives who had to tend children, lacked means of transportation, or wanted to avoid bad weather.[26] But the Roly Poly was a self-service store on a small scale without the economies of an A&P economy store or the premium system of the home-delivery service offered by Jewel Tea. As a compromise, the mototeria was an expensive operation without sufficient customer advantages to be profitable, and it failed.

The chain company system of economy stores and home delivery was permeating all aspects of American life. Where small town grocery stores had been left unchallenged by public markets and independent city grocers for

3.6 Mototeria, W. K. Hutchenson Company, Arlington, Massachusetts, 1928 (From William J. Baxter, *Chain Store Distribution and Management*, copyright, New York: Harper and Row. Reprinted by permission of HarperCollins Publishers, Inc.)

decades, chain stores and even home-delivery companies began to compete effectively using the economic advantage of bulk buying. Suburban areas in American cities were eventually canvassed totally by corporate chains, either by nearby economy stores or home-delivery services, and as suburbia grew, these companies were quick to expand into new neighborhoods. The cycle was reproductive. The more the chains increased volume trade, the more they could lower retail prices. The chain store system was growing and expanding in the twentieth century, but so were the seeds of discontent and fear.

THE GROWING CRISIS

The chain grocery store system grew dramatically in the early part of the twentieth century. The A&P Company, which was the dominant chain, grew exponentially. Beginning with one store in 1859, A&P expanded to 200 stores in 1900, to 372 stores in 1910, to 4,621 stores in 1920, and to 15,737 stores in 1930. The combined growth of A&P, American, First National, Kroger, Safeway, and National Tea companies between 1920 and 1930 was 294 percent—from 7,723 stores to 30,453 stores. Among these five chains, A&P was the economic powerhouse, with 52 percent of all the stores operated by these five grocery companies in 1930.[27] In 1929, 17 percent of all American grocery shopping was done in chain grocery stores.[28] The chain store system was a serious threat to the independent system of grocery retailing and wholesaling.

The traditional wholesale system relied on a multi-tiered system of self-employed businesses. The primary market was comprised of brokers, producers, importers, manufacturers, packers, and commission agents. Buying raw food goods from the source, such as vegetables and grains from the farmer or livestock from ranchers, these businesses either shipped, processed, or manufactured food. The secondary market consisted of wholesalers who bought their goods from the primary market, such as wholesale grocers, broker and packer houses, produce and fruit merchants, and fish dealers. These wholesalers then distributed their goods to the tertiary market of retailers that operated as general stores, grocery stores, meat markets, fruit stores, street vendors, fish markets, and small mail-order businesses.[29] There were even wholesalers who operated between wholesalers and retailers. Truck jobbers bought goods from grocer jobbers at the wholesale markets and warehouses and delivered these goods to grocery retailers who were not conveniently located to wholesale centers.[30] This service was particularly helpful to independent grocers in suburban locations. The filtering-down system of the independents spread the entrepreneurship of free enterprise into many hands.

The filtering-down system of food distribution, however, had certain diseconomies. Each business in the three markets had to add on a margin of profit to survive economically. As food goods passed from the primary market to the tertiary market, the consumer was buying groceries that had been marked up three times, not including the markup from the original food source, such as the farmer. The independent system allowed many people to start their own businesses and be their own entrepreneurs. Yet, some business people realized that a high-volume trade managed by a few hands was more profitable than the lower volume sales of many individual businesses. The chain store owners saw duplication and inefficiency in the traditional wholesaling system. In their eyes, there were too many wholesalers who reproduced unnecessary overhead costs, such as management, equipment, and building properties. The chain store owners wanted to minimize not only the number of contracts that they had to negotiate but also the number of wholesalers with whom they worked. By streamlining the food acquisition process, grocery chain store owners sought to increase the velocity of their trade as well as reducing overhead costs.

The grocery chains circumvented the traditional wholesaling system by working directly with mass food producers. This move enabled the chain companies to reduce transaction costs and uncertainties. By specializing in certain lines of goods, chain store owners made contracts with manufacturers for several months or a year's supply instead of the small volume purchases made by independents with wholesalers. With grocery chain stores working with a large volume of trade and long contracts, food manufacturers were able to calculate closely their contract costs.[31] The chain store companies reduced food buying costs not only by avoiding contracts with middlemen wholesalers but also by being able to obtain more precise, stable prices from food manufacturers.

The profits realized from bulk buying had enabled chain store companies to reorganize and to restructure their economic relations in the marketplace. The grocery chains reinvested some of their financial gains into their company management in order to reproduce their market advantage. Buyers who specialized in understanding certain product lines were hired and developed so that the company could maximize volume sales and thereby reduce unit costs.[32] These buyers kept abreast of what items customers would or would not buy, and by entering into contract negotiations with this knowledge, buyers were able to reduce contracted items to goods that were proven sellers while avoiding low-turnover merchandise. Independent grocers lacked this advantage because they had to manage their stores as well as make wholesale purchases, and they were unable to become as skilled in wholesale buying as chain store buyers. Increasingly, chain store companies were able to bring specialized merchandising knowledge to address a given problem at a given time for the maximization of profits.

After the inception of mass food producers in the nineteenth century, mass retail distribution had finally become a parallel corporate force. Mass food producers, such as Quaker Oats and the Campbell Soup Company, had benefitted from large-scale production and reduced their unit costs. By dealing directly with farmers and minimizing their need for wholesale jobbers, mass food producers were able to reduce significantly their overhead costs.[33] Grocery chain stores had now accomplished the same feat. Both in manufacturing and retailing, mass volume food corporations were circumventing the traditional wholesale system of American trade.

The chain stores had to organize new physical facilities as they displaced the traditional wholesale system. Just as the mass food producers had done, some grocery chains created their own warehousing system to store contracted goods, and they became adept at routing food items to their retail stores. Chain store warehouses were often located as a hub to the stores in the chain. This strategy minimized time and transport costs between stores and the warehouse. If one section of a city was expanding more than other parts, grocery chain executives preferred to locate their warehouses in the areas that responded to this suburban movement, because their newer stores would likely follow. This logic was contradictory to the traditional approach of locating a facility in a warehouse district. The hub approach was also used to serve geographic regions in order to reduce costs. Chain store warehouses were designed to be smaller than previous facilities. In the nineteenth century wholesale warehouses were large, because those buildings served large areas in which the means of transporting of goods were poor. With high turnover in their stores, grocery chains wanted their warehouses to be only large enough to parallel the turnover of goods in stores served by the warehouse facility.[34] As a result of these requirements, the grocery chains located and designed their facilities differently from independent wholesalers. Slowly but surely, the wholesale grocers' warehousing system was being replaced by the grocery chains that were increasing their retail sales and using their warehouses efficiently.

The grocery chains and food manufacturers were similarly eliminating the traditional wholesaling system, but conflicts began to occur between these two corporate food interests. Initially, food manufacturers preferred contract relations with chain stores over those agreements made with independent wholesalers. They sold their goods to chain stores at lower prices than to independent wholesalers, but the reduced number of contract agreements and an ensured volume of sales meant that the food manufacturers' overhead costs for managing these contracts were reduced significantly. Food manufacturers found this contract arrangement to be very profitable as long as their recommended wholesale prices were followed by chain food retailers. But the grocery chain stores saw it in their interest to provide the lowest possible retail price in order to sustain company growth. The A&P Company had made a wholesale agreement with the Cream of Wheat Company, but in 1915, A&P refused to agree to a price increase announced by the cereal company. It was important for Cream of Wheat to gain price control over their product. If A&P were able to lower the price of their product, independents would soon have to lower their prices as well or reduce their purchase orders and then sell the cereal at a price higher than the grocery chains. The Cream of Wheat Company was fearful that their wholesale prices would eventually be dictated by grocery chain companies, potentially eliminating independent grocers through market competition. As a result, the cereal company saw that it had two choices, either to lower its wholesale price or to stop shipments to A&P. The Cream of Wheat Company chose the latter alternative, and A&P sued under the 1914 Clayton Act, antitrust legislation intended to forbid restraint of trade. In court, Cream of Wheat won the case, and the A&P Company was prevented from dominating the corporate world of food manufacturing.[35] It became clear to the food industries that chain store companies wanted to dominate not only the independent retail trade but also the profit margins that could be extracted from mass food producers.

To capture control of wholesale prices, grocery chains began to manufacture their own food product lines. The A&P Company decided to organize to manufacture food soon after losing its court case with the Cream of Wheat Company. A&P management wanted to thwart what they saw as monopolistic practices by the food manufacturers. These manufacturers bore the same fear against A&P and other grocery chains.[36] In the 1920s a wide variety of food product lines were being offered by A&P, National Tea, Kroger, and other companies.[37] Many grocery chains had their origins in the tea trade and were accustomed to making tea blends and selling them as a company product. The grocery chains saw the opportunity to gain a retail market advantage by eliminating another overhead cost by manufacturing its own food goods. The big grocery chains had now positioned themselves to deal directly with food sources, such as contracting with farmers or buying raw materials in the commodity markets. Although they were unable to manufacture every item that was sold in their stores, grocery chains attempted to manufacture or process every food good that was profitable for them to manage. Baked goods, canned fruit and vegetables, coffee, butter, eggs, cheese, and smoked meats were product lines found with company labels in the chain store. The grocery chain companies adopted the basic policy to control as much of the food distribution system as was economically feasible.

The chain store product lines included a psychological factor, for both the grocery chains and customers. As the founders of grocery chain stores worked to make their companies grow, they took pride in their efforts. The product lines were an extension of their desire to succeed, and the A&P Company policy typified this endeavor:

Always to:
Do what is honest, fair, sincere, and in the
best interest of every customer.
Extend friendly satisfying service to everyone.
Give every customer the most good food for her money.

Assure accurate weight every time—
16 oz. to each pound.
Give accurate count and full measure.
Charge the correct price.
Cheerfully refund a customer's money if for
any reason any purchase is not satisfactory.[38]

Such company ethics instilled pride within a grocery chain, from president to store clerk, but these ethics were grounded on bedrock profit-making principles. Being honest, giving friendly service, and returning money to an unsatisfied customer were not only ethical guidelines but also means to minimize customer disturbances. With such policies, grocery workers sustained a constant set of behaviors that did not interfere with a store's volume of trade. Chain store owners knew that if their employees' personal behavior was not directed and held constant, customers would be lost, and store expansion and locations would then be destabilized. Policies to give the most food for the money, accurate weight, full measure, and correct price were economic controls needed by management. It was critical for grocery chains to control the flow of goods through the huge number of stores operating within their chain system. By ensuring that store employees were accurate in their customer service, chain store management could calculate more accurately the supply and demand for their goods. It paid grocery chains to be accurate about their sales in order to plan strategically for increasing the volume of their sales, from new food products that they could manufacture to new product lines to be purchased from wholesalers. Company customer policies were, metaphorically, welded joints that prevented the leakage of retail trade in a consumer pipeline.

Chain store policies, store design, and store brand food products gave customers a sense of assurance when they shopped. Lower prices for quality goods in a well-designed store is what shoppers wanted. Attention to these details gave customers the confidence to buy chain store product lines, and as a result, many people became devoted to purchasing the chain store's own food brands. Customers were treated fairly by grocery chains in the selection of product lines on the shelf, because other brands were offered for sale. The grocery chains tested food products for quality in advance, and poor products were rejected. At the same time, such testing enabled chain store companies to understand their competition and to improve their own company products. With chain stores increasingly controlling the price and quality of their food goods from beginning to end, shoppers were attracted by the security of buying goods at a consistent quality in a store that was neat and clean.

The systematic control and integration of food distribution by chain stores was furthered by changing conditions in American society. The vast growth of these companies in the twentieth century was due to the nation's great increase in population. The population of the United States was increasing with the large immigration movement and improving health standards. Within this population boom, the urban-rural population composition was changing as well. By 1920, more people lived in towns and cities than in rural areas. This population movement assured grocery chain companies of an expanding market within more confined geographical bases. At the same time, technological advances were spurring the growth of grocery chains. In the nineteenth century, the railroad and telegraph made it possible to bring currency and manufactured food products into the nation's hinterlands. These same technologies enabled grocery chain companies to operate regionally. Food products in warehouses could be received and delivered to company stores more efficiently using the railroad for shipping and the telegraph for communication. Eventually, the truck and telephone allowed for even more efficient means of local transportation and communication. A phone call from a chain store to the warehouse and a delivery by truck was faster than a telegraph wire and a horse-drawn delivery wagon. Finally, the structure of the American family was changing, especially in the 1920s. Women were entering the work force, and they no longer spent long hours processing food or cooking as they did before World War I. As a result, American families were depending more on processed foods, which they could buy economically.[39] These socioeconomic conditions provided the basis for chain stores to structure their means of production. Grocery chains were more able to build many stores, to increase their economic leverage in wholesaling, and to develop their own food lines because advanced technologies were serving more people who lived in concentrated areas and who were increasingly part of the labor force. Independent grocers were also sustained by these national trends, but grocery chain companies were better organized to exploit these economic opportunities.

The chain store system of building on the nation's market potential began to have its effects on independent grocers and wholesalers. The traditional wholesale system was unable to compete with the chain store system. It was a fragmented network of many wholesalers and retailers who were unable to do bulk buying in the same volume as chain stores. Because grocery chains were more flexible in their ability to build new stores, suburban expansion by the chain stores was felt most by independent grocers. They tended to be confined to more central city locations, which had a higher tax base, and their stores were located on properties that were often valuable for more profitable commercial ventures. Simultaneously, low profit margins made independent grocers less able to expand and more threatened by displacement through urban development than were chain stores.

The American small town was affected significantly by the grocery chains. The most obvious threat was to the local grocery store, whose business operation was not significantly different from its predecessors in the late nineteenth century. Although small town stores were initially uneconomical investments for the grocery chains, improved roads and rail connections made the chain store a profitable venture.[40] With only two or three grocery stores in town, it was often inevitable that a chain store forced at least one local store out of business while hurting the other stores, because the chain store was able to offer goods at a lower price. The external effects of a chain store in a small town were often significant. The local independent grocer depended on local merchants, whereas the chain stores did not. Chain store management was able to afford the best business locations in town while independent grocers could not.[41] The town grocer usually bought building insurance from a local agent, and if a loan was needed, the local banker was available. The independent grocer bought a delivery truck from a local dealer. Small town businesses supported one another, but the chain store did not need local support. With centralized management and purchasing, grocery chains bought support services and equipment just as they obtained food products, through bulk buying. Minimizing the number of contracts for a maximum number of stores, from buying insurance to trucks, meant reduced overhead costs to grocery chains. For large highly organized chains, minimal local labor was needed to set up a new economy store because the equipment was predesigned and often installed by company employees.[42] Just as they had avoided wholesalers, company chains bypassed the business community of small town America. To many local business people, the grocery chain store was shipping its profits out of town instead of supporting the local economy.

Chain store advocates argued that the chain store system did not economically damage small town America. They presented a typical case. A dollar spent in a typical independent grocery store was divided approximately into 81 cents for the costs of merchandise, 17 cents for the store's operating expenses, and 2 cents for profit. In sum, 19 cents remained in the community, whereas 81 cents left. In a chain store, a shopper would pay 90 cents, 10 cents less, for the same item that cost a dollar in the independent store. From that 90 cents, the chain store's gross profit was divided into 73 cents for the cost of merchandise, 16 cents for the store's operating expenses, and 1 cent for profit. However, operation expenses and profits were distributed differently for chain stores. Twelve cents of operation costs were local, whereas 4 cents left the community to cover the chain corporation's administrative expenses, and the 1-cent profit also left the community. The combined retention of capital in the community from a chain store was 12 cents for local expenses and 10 cents customer savings for a total of 22 cents. Thus, a chain grocery store allowed more money to remain in the community (22 cents) than an independent grocer (19 cents).[43] The chain store advocates were arguing that small town America was better off with the new system than the traditional independent system.

The chain store advocates, however, ignored the repeated flow of profits into chain stores rather than into the independent establishments. What happened to the ten cents of savings? With a continuous flow of capital, customers either bought more goods from the chain stores or did not buy at all. But independent retailers and their employees were customers too. The local grocer, hardware retailer, druggist, department store owner, shoe store owner, and other independent storeowners depended on mutual shopping support. The customer who saved at the chain store was often an independent business employer or employee. At the same time, chain store employees also sought out lower prices, and as a result, managers and clerks created mutual economic support among chain stores by attempting to achieve savings. With profits flowing more into chain stores, an independent, such as a grocer, was not able to afford as many loans, to buy as much insurance, to make as many store improvements, to hire as much local labor, and to pay for other business matters as they were able to do before the chain stores came to town. The chain store advocates argument that three more cents were left in town when people shopped at a chain versus an independent store made sense only as long as independents were able to remain in business. By eliminating competition, chain stores were eliminating buyers who worked in the independent retail sector. The resulting unemployment meant that small town people migrated to cities, found some other local job, or remained unemployed. Many independent business owners were forced to become employees instead of owners. The resulting savings to customers through chain store shopping began to transform local control of business and labor relations in small town America.

The entrance of the chain store into small town America also disturbed local conceptions of a grocery store's purpose. Traditionally, the general store, and then the grocery store, had been a social institution, a meeting place for the community. But the logic of the chain store was contradictory to community habits. The chain store, especially A&P's economy model, had been designed as a consumption factory, and loitering was antithetical to its designed purpose. Although local managers were friendly to customers, benches inside or outside of the building were eliminated in small town chain stores. The policy of preventing the use of the store as a community center reminded the locals that the chain grocery store was devoted to extracting profits and had few community commitments. Chain stores of all types were in the process of restructuring the economic and social life of small town America.[44]

The chain store system was significantly deteriorating the traditional system of American retail distribution. Grocery chains were passing the secondary market of wholesalers and making inroads into the primary circuit of food manufacturers and brokers. With their ability to do bulk buying, chain store companies were able to circumvent the traditional market avenues for wholesaling, and because they were unable to control primary market prices, grocery chains began to manufacture and process their own food brands. The consequences were highly evident to independent grocers who found it exceedingly difficult to compete with the lower prices of chain stores. As American cities grew, grocery chains were more financially able to establish new stores in suburbia than the independents. Small town America felt the impact of chain stores as local businesses were unable to compete and were forced to close, and this problem was compounded by the fact that chain stores did not depend heavily on local business services to sustain their trade. By the 1920s, the chain store as a retail force had become so powerful that it was replacing the traditional system of independent retail businesses. In 1930, Senator Hugo L. Black, later a Justice of the U.S. Supreme Court, said:

Chain groceries, chain dry-goods stores, chain clothing stores, here today and merged tomorrow—grow in size and power. We are rapidly becoming a nation of a few business masters and many clerks and servants. The local man and merchant is passing and his community loses his contribution to local affairs as an independent thinker and executive. A few of these useful citizens, thus supplanted, become clerks of the great chain machines, at inadequate salaries, while many enter the ranks of the unemployed. A wild craze for efficiency in production, sale and distribution has swept over the land, increasing the number of unemployed, building up a caste system, dangerous to any government.[45]

THE ANTI-CHAIN MOVEMENT

Independent business people in all facets of retail trade realized that they could not allow chain stores to continue at this rate and still remain in business. Independent retailers and wholesalers decided to fight back on both the business and legislative fronts.

Independent wholesale grocers began to organize and use economic pressures against grocery chains, with limited success. Wholesale grocer associations in California and Texas were challenged by court orders for pressuring manufacturers not to sell directly to chain stores. In 1924, the Federal Trade Commission issued a complaint against the Arkansas Wholesale Grocers' Association for telling its members to threaten a boycott against food manufacturers who sold directly to chain grocery stores. A wholesale trade paper published a list of manufacturers who dealt directly with chains, and the list of undesirable manufacturers was intended to tell independent wholesalers which manufacturers they could pressure by reducing or stopping their orders. The courts had disallowed many of the wholesale grocers' tactics.

Chain store owners wanted to prevent any more guerilla movements against food manufacturers. Food manufacturers were uneasy because independent grocers and wholesalers still constituted the majority of their business. To counter the wholesalers' tactics, the chain stores organized their own associations to deal with food manufacturers. Chain store owners in California formed the Western State Chain Grocers' Association in 1921 and formed a task force to meet individually with manufacturers. At first, the chain store association was unable to gather support from the manufacturers. But the organization grew from representing 685 stores in 1921 to 1,621 stores with twenty-six members of the association in 1922. Food manufacturers were unable to ignore the potential buying power behind the chain grocery association. Manufacturers began to respond by changing their company policies to permit them to sell directly to chain stores. Although some manufacturers were reluctant to yield, eventually most of them agreed to the change.[46] Independent wholesaler associations saw that they were losing on the business front, and they decided to engage in a different kind of frontal attack.

Independent wholesaler associations joined with independent retailer associations to gain support for anti-chain bills in state legislatures. As early as 1922, the National Association of Retail Grocers openly suggested in its convention that the number of chain stores in any community should be limited by law. The independents sought to have corporate chain companies taxed so that their comparative advantage against the local retailer would be neutralized and even eliminated. Between 1923 and 1926 only 5 anti-chain bills were introduced in state legislatures, but from 1927 through 1930, 169 bills were put before state governing bodies. Anti-chain lobby groups created a wave of legislative discontent between 1931 to 1935 by supporting 728 bills that were introduced in state houses.[47] Independents came to see the legislative process as the primary means to fight against the chain companies.

The basic legislative strategy was to impose a chain store tax. The first tax statute was enacted in Maryland in 1927, and the law required not only a tax but also, and more critically, provided that no chain could have more than five stores in a county. The Maryland tax was declared unconstitutional, and many others like it were declared invalid. Some states introduced tax legislation on a fixed rate tax per store in excess of a designated number of stores, usually one or five. More aggressive bills included a graduated tax structure. In Kentucky, grocery chains with less than five stores were taxed the same as independents, 1/4 of 1 percent of gross income, but a chain operating with five or more stores was taxed at a higher rate of 1/2 of 1 percent of gross income. Independent retailers and wholesalers were helping state politicians to design legislation that would neutralize and even erode the competition from chain stores.

The anti–chain store tax bills had limited success. Although many proposals were introduced in state capitals, only ten bills became statutes. These ten laws were challenged by the chain store interests, and the courts invalidated six of these statutes. The basic difficulty that independents faced was finding sufficient legal grounds to support differential treatment of chain store retailers versus independent retailers. The independents needed favorable court rulings, because the chain store interests continued to challenge their legislative efforts.

Revisions in initial chain store tax statutes were made in some state legislatures as a response to court decisions. In 1929, North Carolina passed a bill to tax chain stores. The grocery chains sued on the grounds that the statute was unconstitutional, and although the North Carolina Supreme Court had invalidated the state's 1927 tax statute, it now supported the 1929 revised law. The Court decided that a tax law that classified businesses differently, such as chain stores versus single stores, was not arbitrary or unreasonable. Eventually this case went to the U.S. Supreme Court in 1930, and the Court upheld the North Carolina ruling. This case laid the foundation for the landmark case on chain store taxation. The Indiana state legislature enacted a chain store statute with a graduated tax rate. A single store paid an annual license tax of $3. Chain stores, however, paid $10 annually per outlet for operating two to five stores, $15 per year for six to ten stores, $20 for eleven to twenty stores, and $25 for each additional store above twenty. Although the chain interests did not consider the tax to be severe, they were fearful of the graduated rate principle being adopted, because other states could enact a similar law with a heavy tax burden. The chain interests immediately sued the Indiana State Tax Board. Decisions and appeals ensued, with the case eventually reaching the U.S. Supreme Court. In 1931 the Supreme Court supported the Indiana statute that chain stores could lawfully be taxed differently and on the basis of a graduated rate.[48] The independents were building an arsenal of legislative weapons with which to attack the chain stores. Chain store advocates reacted to what they viewed as the political interests behind these taxes and court rulings. As managing director for the Institute of Distribution, which was supported by chain store interests, John Nichols said:

It must be recognized at the outset that the so-called "chain store tax" was a social rather than a fiscal measure . . . the enactment of all such laws was the purpose of . . . a certain class of jobber, broker, and wholesaler; the political agitator and the professional propagandist to cripple or to destroy the chain store through discriminatory taxation for self gain.[49]

The idea of state taxes on chain stores created the potential for local taxes. Like the states, cities needed sources of tax revenues, especially because the depression in the 1930s had hurt many local businesses, whereas the chain stores remained economically strong. Portland, Oregon, was the first American city to enact a chain store tax ordinance, and it was designed with the Indiana decision in mind. A single store paid $6 annually; this rate progressed to $50 per store for chains that operated more than twenty stores. The chain store interests helped to attack this ordinance by organizing a signed petition to have the tax voted on in a public referendum, but the chain store interests lost the vote by a small margin. By 1933, cities in fourteen states had enacted some local tax on chain stores. But some cities became greedy. Hamtramck, Michigan, and Maplewood, Missouri, both passed graduated tax ordinances that charged an annual tax of $1,000 for each store over three in a chain company. The Hamtramck ordinance was challenged immediately by the

Kroger Company, and the Circuit District Court found that the city ordinance tax rates were discriminatory. City ordinances continued to be enacted throughout the 1930s, but the chain store interests continued to battle against these ordinances, which they saw as tactics for tax gouging by cities.[50] Most of these ordinances were primarily enacted in states east of the Mississippi, and especially in the South. Independents were making their presence felt at both the city and state levels, and the chain store interests were on the defensive.

In addition to city and state taxes, independent retailers and wholesalers pushed for state fair-trade laws in the 1930s. The aim of this legislation was to put a price floor under the retail prices charged for a manufacturer's brand products. The specific controls were put into contract agreements between manufacturers who were enabled to set a minimum resale price with buyers. By 1937, forty-two states had enacted such laws, and although chain store interests had challenged these laws in court, the U.S. Supreme Court decided in 1936 that such contractual price controls were legitimate, and Congress recognized the legitimacy of these fair-trade laws by passing the Miller-Tydings Act in 1937. Yet, chain store grocery associations worked with food manufacturers and convinced them that chain stores would sell more of their products if manufacturers chose not to include minimum retail prices in their contracts with the grocery chains. Although price controls were used for other retail businesses, such as the druggist trade, the grocery chains were able to avoid the price maintenance controls allowed in fair-trade laws.[51]

The independent retailers and wholesalers wanted legislative action that was more encompassing than what they had seen on the city or state fronts, and they campaigned vigorously for federal legislation. They found a staunch advocate in Wright Patman, a Texas member of the House of Representatives. Being from the economically depressed, northeastern section of Texas, Patman was acutely aware of the effects that chain stores had on business people in his legislative district. He undoubtedly received election campaign support from independent retailer and wholesaler associations, but his disdain for chain stores was just as vehement as the disdain felt by his political supporters. He was "the" anti-chain crusader in the U.S. Congress. With the help of Senator Joseph P. Robinson, Patman forged a legislative bill, and in June, 1936, the Robinson-Patman Act took effect.

The Robinson-Patman Act attempted to limit the interstate commerce of chain stores that state legislation and court decisions could not easily address. This federal legislation was in response to what the U.S. Congress saw as inadequacies in the Sherman and Clayton Anti-Trust Acts, which were designed to prevent monopolies and restraint of free trade. The new act attempted to address the practices of unfair price controls, false business agents, and advertising allowances.

The act made it unlawful for sellers to discriminate in price between buyers when such discrimination could lead to a monopoly. This control aimed to curb price control agreements between manufacturers and chain companies. Some manufacturers had agreed with some chains to sell a well-known product at wholesale and retail prices at which both the manufacturer and the chain sold the product at a loss. This loss-leader tactic drew customers to the store, where they then bought other items. The chain store was eliminating competition through this tactic, and the manufacturer recouped losses and made profits by selling the same product at a fixed price to independent wholesalers. At the same time the manufacturer was gaining advertising exposure for its product, giving an advantage over other manufacturers who did not use this price reduction tactic.[52] The U.S. Congress sought to control contractual agreements between manufacturers and chains that were aimed at eliminating competition through such schemes.

The legislation was designed to eliminate brokerage payments to a puppet agent who actually worked for and was paid by a buyer who operated a retail business. Only a broker who was a bona fide third party could now collect commissions. A broker traditionally acted as a go-between, for example between a grower and a grocer. In this particular example, the act was attempting to stop a grocery chain from using a company employee as a broker. This strategy enabled a grocery chain to gain access to goods as a wholesaler and to keep brokerage fees. Independent brokers argued that free competition was being eliminated, because the chains were using "pseudo brokers," preventing in principle equal brokerage access to buyers. Any broker should be able to offer services to any buyer, but the chain stores had eliminated a legitimate broker's right to offer services. At the same time, a broker who was employed by a grocery chain but charged a brokerage fee to a grower as a buyer was not a true broker. Brokers argued that you could work for a buyer or a seller, but to work for both parties was unethical. Brokers argued that the only fair way for them to operate ethically "between" buyer and seller was to be unbiased agents whose services were purchased openly by either business party. The overall effect was that "pseudo brokers" were eliminating the need for legitimate brokers, and more importantly, chain companies were dismantling the secondary market of wholesaling. The Robinson-Patman Act was adopted by the U.S. Congress as a legislative control on brokerage intended to preserve the wholesale system of independent brokers who clearly represented a seller or a buyer.[53]

The last major legislative change that affected corporate chains was advertising allowances. Due to the volume of their trade, chains received such allowances from food manufacturers who wanted to advertise their products. Although manufacturers had used other means, such as magazines, to advertise their products, retailers were directly attuned to customers and were able to make sure that promotion was geographically distributed by means of their stores. Food manufacturers felt the best way to promote their products was in the grocery store itself. Active stocking as well as counter and window displays of their products were the preferred tactics. The problem was that independent retailers were not receiving such allowances, because their volume of trade was significantly less than the chain companies. The Act now required manufacturers to provide such allowances on a proportional basis that was equal and available to all buyers.[54] Thus, the U.S. Congress was trying to prevent chain companies from having a competitive advertising edge over independents due to their economic leverage through bulk buying.

The Robinson-Patman Act embodied many of the actions that independent interests had wanted to take against the chain companies, and the chains objected. No chain was as emblematic of the independents' frustrations as the A&P Company, and their advertising and brokerage fees attracted the greatest congressional attention. During a committee hearing in July 1935, the A&P Company admitted to receiving $6 million in brokerage fees. Yet other grocery companies, such as Safeway, Kroger, and Independent Grocers Alliance, had received such fees. Chain store advocates argued that the chains' competitive advantage was minuscule. In the case of A&P, the company's gross profits were $842 million with a net profit of $16.7 million. Moreover, the $6 million for advertising was spent for that purpose. On a percentage basis, A&P's net profits were only 2 percent of gross profits. Chain store advocates argued that proportional advertising allowances were impractical as a means to promote products. With independent grocers buying only a small number of food units from an independent wholesaler, the proportional allowance that the grocer received from a food manufacturer would be too small to pay for advertising costs. The argument against brokerage fees was countered by the claim that grocery chains were already functioning as wholesalers because their bulk buying required them to create a warehouse system at least equal to if not greater than those facilities provided by wholesalers. The brokerage fees helped to pay for the chain company's warehouse facilities and operations, costs that independent grocers did not have.[55] Chain store advocates saw the Robinson-Patman Act as an attempt by independents to neutralize the business efficiencies utilized by the chain companies.

The growing tide against the chain stores was too great for its proponents to allow business to continue as before. Chain store taxes, fair trade laws, and the Robinson-Patman Act gained political support from a growing anti-business sentiment. Before the Robinson-Patman Act had passed, the chain store interests had organized the American Retail Federation (ARF) to serve as a unified voice for chain distributors on economic problems and national legislation. The New York Times accused this new group of being a superlobby designed to influence politicians in Congress. The newspaper attacks that followed were so damaging that the organization was politically neutralized until after World War II. The ARF was characterized by the newspapers as a means to unify the influence of significant large business interests. Big business, however, was blamed by many people for the country's great depression, and although chain stores were financially hurt by the depression, the general public saw these interests to be far more prosperous than the independent store owner. Perceived chain store advantages and abuses were constantly being challenged with law suits between chain corporations and their opponents.[56] Although chain store corporations had suffered a growing number of setbacks, there were changes on the political horizon, both state and federal.

Most of the chain store taxes were passed by states located east of the Mississippi River, and in the western United States, California was a significant battleground in which the chain interests gained some momentum. A chain store tax was put on the state's public referendum in 1935 with an election to take place in November 1936. The Robinson-Patman Act had just been passed in the summer of 1936, and the state treasury had a big deficit that needed to be paid. A chain store tax seemed inevitable. Knowing that they had to act quickly, chain store owners organized into the California Chain Stores Association. The association realized that there was no time to handle internal dissent on issues or to manage a political battle by themselves. Acting quickly, the association hired an advertising agency, Lord and Thomas, to manage their political campaign, and chain store executives did not interfere with the firm's campaign decisions.

The battle plan designed by the advertising agency was to go on the offensive and to get off the defensive. Accusations by independent merchants were ignored, both to focus on their own campaign and to avoid arousing sympathy for the underdog. The campaign was structured to illustrate who benefitted from the chain stores. A key element of support came from farmers, and a local farming crisis emerged. The California Canning Peach Growers Association notified the chain store campaign that the peach industry was suffering from an underconsumption of canned peaches, and with a new crop about to be picked, peach farmers would suffer great financial losses due to the surplus. Through the national chain store association, a nationwide drive was launched to absorb the peach surplus and to promote peach sales. The outcome was that peach growers made a substantial profit. The same dilemma occurred with dried fruits, and chain store owners responded. These economic responses gave chain store interests part of the political support that they needed, especially from rural areas. Finally, only six weeks before the vote the full attack began with chain store employees who voluntarily canvassed neighborhoods to get out the chain store vote. They actively promoted the cost savings that chain stores provided customers. By organizing, the California chain store companies won the vote on the tax referendum.[57] The California experience taught chain store interests that they could win their political battles if they effectively organized their resources.

Although the independent retailers and wholesalers had achieved congressional success with the Robinson-Patman Act, they wanted even tighter controls over chain stores, but chain store interests were ready and had allies. In the spring of 1938, Wright Patman introduced a tax bill aimed directly at chain stores. Although a number of states had enacted statutes with graduated tax rates on chain stores, many states had not. Independent interests now wanted a comprehensive attack that the chains could not escape. U.S. Supreme Court decisions now allowed chain stores to be classified differently from single stores and to be subjected to a graduated tax rate. The independent interests had accomplished their objectives with taxes in the courts, and they now wanted those court decisions to be backed with federal legislative force. But Patman's proposal was opposed strongly and became known as the "death sentence" bill. The tax structure was so oppressive that it would have eliminated the chain system of business altogether. Congressman Patman did not help himself as he made unfounded assertions, such as that food costs were higher where chain stores dominated trade. It was a point that he was unable to substantiate to his critics. The bill was defeated, and although Patman attempted to reintroduce the bill to the House Ways and Means Committee, his efforts were unsuccessful.

The anti–chain store tax movement was defeated in the U.S. Congress for reasons beyond their attempts to pronounce a death sentence on chain stores. There were other political interests who felt that chain stores were now more advantageous to them than the independents. Labor unions preferred chain stores, because they were more able to organize contracts. With a chain store, many union members would be covered with a single contract, but with independents, many contracts had to be negotiated. Real estate interests tended to back chain stores, because the chains could afford more expensive properties and were good credit risks on their mortgages. Farmer groups were willing to support the chain stores, because the chain companies had promoted the sale of their crops when there was a surplus. Manufacturers supported chain stores, because chains were high volume, consistent buyers who did not create collection and credit losses. Consumer groups supported the chain system, because chain stores offered lower prices than independents. In contrast, the anti-chain groups consisted primarily of independent retailers and wholesalers. The collective support of the pro-chain interest groups outweighed the efforts of the anti-chain movement that was supporting a federal graduated tax on chain stores.[58]

The conflicts between chain stores and independents were bitter. The anti-chain movement began in the 1920s and carried on through the 1930s. Although the chain interests had battled in court and in legislatures across the country, they had lost many battles. But by the mid-1930s chain interests were beginning to fight back successfully.

THE CHAIN STORE AGE

The chain store system radically changed business operations in the grocery trade, because the cost saving techniques attained through mass production also applied to mass distribution. The benefits of mass distribution in the nineteenth century initially helped the shopkeeper to buy wholesale goods that were delivered quickly and were packaged in units that customers wanted. But as ambitious retailers saw and learned how the economic advantages of mass production could be applied to retailing, they changed their business strategies. Bulk buying enabled such retailers to lower their overhead costs substantially, and their sale volumes were simultaneously increased by redesigning the store into functional components. Cash-and-carry, along with self-service, reduced the labor power needed to operate a store. The grocery store was transformed from a shopkeeper's domain that was a community social institution to a factory of consumption designed by economic reasoning.

The growth of the chain store followed critical trends that were evolving in the nation. Better transportation and communication systems enabled businesses to organize at a corporate level rather than remaining as a single enterprise at a given location. As a result, grocery companies evolved from merely local businesses to corporate chains. The velocity of American business was increasing, and in the retail sector the chain store system became the dominant force.

The public, however, began to realize that economic efficiency in chain stores was not optimizing social aims. Communities were disrupted by the transformation from the traditional shopkeeper and wholesaler systems of trade to the chain concept. The American notion of free enterprise was that an individual could enter business, and with responsible hard work, succeed. But many responsible business people were unable to compete, because they could not overcome the economies of mass distribution built into the chain system. Americans enjoyed the better-designed chain stores and their lower prices, but they could not ignore the responsible independent merchants who either were closing their stores or were struggling to stay in business. The chain system was transforming the nation's retail sector from a community of independent business people to a team of employees headed by a small management group. Independent business people were losing this business war in which they hoped to remain owners rather than become employees. Their outcry was that the chains were monopolistic and unfairly profited at the expense of small businesses and the principles of American free enterprise.

The anti-chain movement that ensued in the courts, state legislatures, and the U.S. Congress was inevitable. Many independent retailers and wholesalers were unwilling to stand by and see their life's work in business decimated by chain businesses. The depression of the 1930s made resentment against the chains even deeper, because many Americans blamed big business for the nation's economic plight. Of all types of retail chains, the grocery chains had the largest sales volume in the nation, and large corporate chains, such as A&P, Kroger, and Safeway, were in the middle of the legal fight. Although independents were to achieve some success on the judicial and legislative battlefields, they were unable to defeat the corporate chains. Although warfare was inevitable, it was also costly. Statutes and court decisions did eliminate abuses by both parties and stabilized business somewhat. Still, the economic force of the chain stores continued to grow, and these means of business warfare ultimately had limited effects.

To end the warfare, a business solution was needed that recognized not only that chain stores would continue to succeed economically but also that independents would not give up their fight. A new retail system needed to be introduced that enabled independent businesses to operate alongside corporate chain stores. The solution that had emerged slowly was that independents were capable of organizing themselves as a chain. This new economic strategy and changes in the American way of life created the stage for the next major change in the retail grocery trade, the supermarket.

Chapter 4

THE SUPERMARKET EVOLUTION

A supermarket is difficult to define because its meaning has changed over the years. East Coast grocery operators used the term to describe the large self-service markets that opened in Los Angeles during the late 1920s and early 1930s. The first user of the term *supermarket* in a trade name was Albers Super Markets, which opened its first supermarket in 1933. In the 1930s, the grocery trade defined the term this way: "A Super Market is a highly decentralized retail establishment, either wholly owned or concession operated, with adequate parking space, doing a minimum of $250,000 annually. The grocery department, however, must be on a self-service basis."[1] Over the years the dollar volume specification has changed, but this definition is generally applicable for today's supermarkets. Retail grocers, both large and small, accepted—often reluctantly—the economic logic within this definition of the supermarket and its consequences.

The coming of the supermarket was not so much a physical design revolution as it was an economic evolution shaped by business management, urban growth, and technological innovations. The grocery chain corporations had adapted many of the business techniques of mass food production and applied them to mass retail distribution. The major shift was that a grocery company was shaped by a corporate structure with specialized departments that could analyze separately the business's functions and could introduce more efficient, profitable business techniques. To assemble and pay such an army of expertise, the grocery company had to produce a huge volume of sales. The traditional independent grocer was unable to compete with a chain company's ability to buy more products at a lower unit cost or to afford a professional management staff. To operate on a larger business scale, independent grocers realized that they needed to join together if they were to survive economically against the corporate chain stores. The nation's population growth in cities accelerated the trend toward larger stores with high sales volume. As these trends kept pace with industrial growth, technological advances were also introduced to supplement customer service. Together, these conditions led to structural changes in the retail food trade, which, in turn, helped forge the supermarket as a tool for retail consumption.

The grocery chain store of the 1920s gave way to supermarkets in the 1930s, but only after the retail grocery business made major structural changes. First, most independent grocers organized as affiliated independents in order to compete economically against corporate chains. This change meant that most of the nation's store operators ran their retail business on the principle of bulk buying with the potential for high-volume sales. Second, all grocers became increasingly aware that a store's layout and design were directly related to retail sales, and they became more astute in the systematic design of their stores. Third, as corporate chains and affiliated independents began to dominate store ownership, they eroded the economic influence of small, independent grocers, green grocer stores, and butcher shops. As a result, grocery stores were increasingly controlled by a small management class with an available class of trained butchers and clerks that could supply a large store. Fourth, food manufacturers began to market an increasing variety of food products, which required more shelf space than a small grocery store could provide. In fact, grocery companies realized that they could manufacture these products themselves, and this trend created an internal demand for more shelf space. Fifth, consumers changed as they began to purchase automobiles and refrigerators. They wanted to buy more food goods in one shopping trip. All of these changes were important steps toward the eventual development of the supermarket.

THE AFFILIATED INDEPENDENT AS A RESPONSE TO CRISIS

Independent grocers soon realized that they could not ignore the corporate grocery chains, and as small retailers, they had to respond. During the 1920s, the grocery chains were expanding tremendously, opening new stores all over. Some independent grocers began to organize as affiliated independents in order to stave off the economic onslaught of the corporate chains. Their logic was relatively simple: "If you cannot beat their methods, use them." The main method that independent grocers and wholesalers wanted to achieve was the ability to do volume buying of goods from food manufacturers to lower per unit costs. It was necessary for independent grocers to reorganize to benefit from the economic advantages enjoyed by the corporate chains.

There were many ways in which independents became organized, but three basic formats were prevalent. Called voluntary chains in the 1920s and 1930s, they were retail cooperatives, wholesaler-sponsored groups, and voluntary syndicates.

In retail cooperatives, independent retailers informally joined together to do cooperative buying and selling. One type of cooperative, such as Associated Grocers of Chicago, operated primarily as a buying pool with some cooperation in merchandising and advertising. These retailers bought through any source of supply rather than through one wholesaler. Another kind of retail cooperative, such as the Frankford Grocery Company of Philadelphia, operated as a cooperative advertising and buying group while also functioning as a wholesaler. Some retail cooperatives, such as the Advertising Retail Grocers' Association of Canton, Ohio, included retailers who operated as an advertising and buying group, and they coordinated their buying through cooperating wholesalers. In each of these cooperative types, retailers maintained ownership of their stores while reducing their wholesale costs through large volume buying.

Some independent wholesalers organized their own retail groups. Some wholesalers primarily supervised and controlled merchandising and store management. At the same time, they secured most of the wholesale purchases for their retail members. Organizations, such as Voluntary Food Stores of Chattanooga, Tennessee, provided standardized store signs and coordinated advertising for which participating retailers paid. In wholesaler-sponsored groups, independent wholesalers found that they were able to increase their volume buying through assured retailers. In some cases, such as the National Grocery Company of Detroit, the wholesaler also participated in ownership and profits with the affiliated independents.[2] This strategy enabled them to survive the loss of business to corporate chains that bypassed them to buy directly from food manufacturers.

Some wholesalers organized independents into wholesaler groups that were called voluntary-syndicate chains. Store owners participated in a franchise plan with a national name, a trademark, and a private brand of foods. Company management coordinated their affiliates to operate under a unified set of buying and store operations. Some voluntary syndicates began to accumulate the organizational strength of well-known corporate chains, such as A&P and Kroger. In 1920, Smith M. Flickinger, a wholesale grocer, conceived the idea of organizing a group of retailers with their wholesaler in promoting their own brand, having a common name, and advertising collectively. He founded the Red & White affiliated independent using these principles and, by 1930, Red & White had 4,500 stores in the United States. Also in the 1920s, J. Frank Grimes, a certified public accountant who audited the books of many wholesale grocers, foresaw the chain store problem, and he organized wholesalers with their retailers into the Independent Grocers Alliance, or I.G.A. By 1930, I.G.A. had 9,000 retailers. Grimes' approach was for the corporate arm to manage a voluntary syndicate. This approach meant that corporate headquarters made contract arrangements for its wholesalers under the banner of the affiliated independent. The result was that the syndicate arrangement reduced bulk buying costs significantly more than any one wholesaler who had organized a voluntary syndicate. Large affiliated independents, such as Red & White, adopted a similar approach. Operating at a large volume of sales, voluntary syndicates were more able to establish their own food brands and advertise them.[3] I.G.A. and Red & White were operating under the same management principles as the large corporate chains, such as A&P and Kroger, and were becoming national competitors.

The wholesaler-sponsored groups, which included voluntary syndicates, eventually became the most common type of alternative to organize affiliated-independent stores. A primary reason was that wholesalers already had existing connections with food manufacturers. By increasing their volume buying for a known quantity of stores, wholesalers only had to get a price agreement for a larger order. In contrast, retailers were unaccustomed to dealing directly with food manufacturers, and as a result they were less organized in responding to food manufacturers who had their own ways of doing business.[4] Regardless of the alternative taken, independent grocers who feared the corporate chains joined an affiliated independent that was being organized by nearby retailers or wholesalers in order to cut their overhead costs through larger volume buying of manufactured food goods.

As the corporate chains increased the number of their grocery stores, there began a parallel increase in the variety and number of affiliated independents. Before 1920, probably less than forty groups existed, and growth in the early twenties was moderate.[5] Independents first formed cooperative retail groups as a response to the corporate chains. This informal alternative of joint buying was a cautious step in which business people of similar interests thought that they could make a modest change in their operations to counter the corporate chains, and this approach was the dominant organizational method in the early 1920s. To a lesser degree, independent grocers organized as retailer-owned wholesalers and operated their own wholesale warehouses. Although the grocers were stockholders in this type of organization, the slow growth of this approach was likely due to the necessary up-front capital needed to build or to lease a warehouse facility as well as to pay a manager to administer it. Most independent grocers were not financially able or willing to invest heavily in a wholesale operation. Yet, the approach was sustained by a small number of retail grocers. After 1925, the voluntary group sponsored by a wholesaler was significantly the most used alternative, and the reason was most likely economics. Some wholesalers opened their own stores under this system, but the most practical approach was for wholesalers to recruit independent grocers to join their affiliated independents. The built-in practicality was that property relations remained the same. Wholesalers retained their warehouses and the grocers kept their stores. Yet, this arrangement meant that these two parties had to cooperate and to trust one another. With the traditional animosity between wholesalers and retailers, retail grocers were more willing to work with other retailers in the beginning, but in the 1920s, they realized that wholesalers could provide skills and working relations with food producers better than they could do on their own. Regardless of the type of organizational model used, independent retailers recognized the necessity of combating the large corporate grocers by joining affiliated independents. By 1930, the number of stores belonging to affiliated independents exceeded the number of stores in corporate chains.[6]

Although they had some success, affiliated independents still lagged behind the corporate chains in efficiency in both their management and store operations. By introducing corporate methods into their newly formed organizations, many affiliated-independent members—both wholesalers and grocers—still clung to their independent ways of doing business while introducing some corporate methods. These merchants were ultimately compelled to understand what made the other's business run efficiently.

A basic wholesaling problem was the location of warehousing. When the corporate chains located a new store, part of that decision was related to the distance between the store and the warehouse. For example, in the early 1930s, "90 percent of the sales of the chain store's warehouse are within 75 miles of that warehouse." In comparison, independent wholesalers had to travel 150 miles to achieve 50 percent of sales from their warehouses.[7] This warehouse location problem varied with the type of affiliated independent that was organized. The cooperative retailer groups had to find the independent wholesalers who were most centrally located to them; these retailers could not optimize travel costs of goods from the wholesaler's warehouse as the corporate chain had done. Both retailer-owned wholesaler groups and wholesaler-sponsored groups, however, were able to plan for their wholesaler warehouse locations. Obviously, retailer-owned affiliated independents located a warehouse facility that was most central to all members, but they inevitably had to ask: "Who can be a member?" If independent grocers wished to join such an affiliated independent, their stores could not be so close to current members as to cause too much competition, which would lower profits. At the same time, a member store that was distant from the affiliated independent's warehouse represented an overhead cost shared by all. These constraints also existed for the wholesaler-sponsored voluntary group except that the wholesaler decided who could join the affiliated independent. Bulk buying allowed retailers to lower their overhead costs, and choosing a good location for a wholesale warehouse also resulted in savings, because the cost of any food item for the grocer included both the expense to produce it and the cost to ship it to the store.

Affiliated independents had to reorganize their stores to present a unified image and design that led to increased sales volume. A common complaint corporate chains made about many independent grocers had been that their stores were dirty and poorly designed. In refurbishing a store, a wholesaler-sponsored affiliated independent was the most effective, because this organizational type had a clear chain of command like a corporate chain. The wholesaler could more easily centralize decisions over store changes than could retailer groups who used the slower committee method to advise retailers or who hired someone to supervise store renovations. Initially some wholesalers attempted to rearrange their member stores into a unified pattern without understanding the underlying principles of store design that attracted more customers. Retailer-controlled affiliated independents were just as ineffective, because they attempted to minimize changes or to introduce uniform design controls without knowing whether or not such changes would increase retail sales. Affiliated independents initially saw image and design as a visual way to unify the identity of their stores, but they were unable to link design changes to profitability.

Eventually affiliated independents recognized fundamental design principles. They learned about these guidelines by studying the designs of corporate chain stores and by reading design articles in their trade journal, *Progressive Grocer*. The major design changes that independent grocers had to make in their stores were related to product exposure and store layout. For exposure, the customer needed an unobstructed view of the store from the exterior. People needed to identify not only that the building was a grocery store but also the variety of products to be bought. Store front windows were often cluttered with too many signs, and window displays sometimes blocked the customer's in-depth view of the entire store. To enable people to sense the variety of goods and quality of the store, brighter lights were needed, because more illumination promoted cleanliness, discouraged thefts, and attracted customers. Promotional products needed to be put into open displays so that customers could see and touch the merchandise. Storage in stockrooms had to be reduced significantly in order to put as many goods as possible in front of the customer. The independent grocer had always stacked goods up the entire height of sidewalls and placed them behind counters. To allow customers to service and to choose goods themselves, the traditional counter had to be discarded and shelves low enough that a customer could reach any item for sale had to be provided.[8] Store redesign was a psychological tactic to attract customers to the store and make them comfortable during their shopping.

Product organization and store layout were major concerns. Merchandise had to be more systematically organized than before if self-service was to be introduced. Under these conditions, all merchandise needed price tags, and the customer circulation through the store needed to be more systematic. Goods were reorganized into departments much like department stores had done. Most critically, store owners had to adopt a strategic design for customer movement. Food departments had to be arranged in a circulation pattern to maximize exposure and purchasing from one food department to the next.[9] Some professional analysts felt that fruits and vegetables should be positioned near the end of the shopper's buying circuit, because these items have the most tempting appetite appeal, which meant these goods had the highest impulse buying potential. In organizing merchandise and shopper flow, a market analyst for the affiliated independents recommended:

The natural circulation then is down the right-hand side of the store past the exposed merchandise and past the refrigerator to the meat counter, then to the fruit and vegetable display, where possible purchase of fruits and vegetables can be made while waiting for meats to be cut; next to the bread counter, up the left-hand side of the store, to the work counter [cashier], and out.[10]

To implement these changes the management in affiliated independents had to train store owners and then help them to make the needed changes. With their centralized management controls, the wholesaler-sponsored chains were best prepared to reorganize retailers. Far-sighted wholesalers provided their retailers educational programs that enabled them to learn basic techniques used by the corporate chains to increase store productivity. Topics such as store design, training store personnel, principles of stock turnover, advertising, accounting, management, building maintenance, and financial policies were covered. To help retailers reorganize their stores, the wholesaler's salespeople would visit and remain at a store to redesign and reconstruct their stores while simultaneously reinforcing the training provided at the introductory educational program.

A major task for affiliated independents, such as Red & White and the Independent Grocers Alliance, was to restock stores with food goods more systematically than the store owner had done as an independent grocer. Most independent grocers had carried a wide variety of brands of a given item, but they had not analyzed stock turnover. One reason for this neglect was that many independent grocers still had the old country store mentality of maximizing profits per sales item. If store owners wanted to think in terms of net profits per square foot of store, they had to analyze stock turnover. A food product had to earn enough profit and turnover to deserve a place on a grocer's shelf. If a grocer carried seven brands of catsup and 90 percent of the store's trade was with three brands, the other four brands were only doing 10 percent of catsup sales. The grocer was better off using the shelf space previously devoted to the four low-turnover brands for stocking the other three brands or for another food product. Personnel from the chain's headquarters had to help store owners to cut down brands, to organize a sale of dead food stocks, and to establish how much of a product should be bought in a given time period.[11] These principles for conversion were designed to help a store owner to increase the velocity of trade within the store's spatial limits.

Affiliated independents began to benefit from corporate chain techniques beyond the initial principle of bulk buying. One key method that corporate chains had used was the loss-leader sales item. They sold well-known food brands at a loss in order to draw customers into their stores. From 25 to 30 percent of their food lines were sold at a loss, but the deficit was recuperated from the remainder of their food stock. Many store owners were fully aware that corporate chains used loss leaders to capture customers that had traditionally shopped at independent stores. But this technique also depended on volume sales, and when affiliated-independent store owners cooperated, they were able to place newspaper advertising for all stores. This was an asset to all members that no single owner could afford.[12] To supplement existing product lines, some wholesaler-sponsored affiliated independents created their own brand labels, and this technique lowered food costs per unit and shifted much of the profit away from the brand name products over to the store brand. Bulk buying was the initial impetus for independent grocers to join an affiliated independent, but they soon realized that other chain store marketing techniques could increase the velocity and profitability of grocery sales.

Affiliated independents began to borrow corporate chain methods for co-ordinating physical requirements. Central management for some affiliated independents helped their store members as an exchange. If a store wished to be rid of one piece of equipment and was in need of another, central management for affiliated independents organized an equipment exchange. Management also salvaged large quantities of waste materials that no single store owner was able to do, and the savings in overhead costs were passed on to owners.[13] Management sometimes played a critical role in location analysis. An affiliated independent's management kept an eye on a store's profitability, because a store often lost profits due to its location. In these circumstances, management would recommend that the store owner change locations, and being aware of the larger picture, an affiliated independent's management knew of other store sites that were proven to be profitable. In some cases an owner did not fit well with local neighborhood changes. Accustomed to middle- and upper-middle-class trade, some grocers were not psychologically prepared or willing to provide trade for lower-class people. Management sometimes suggested a new location so that the owner could manage a store that matched the grocer's personal choice for clientele.[14] These techniques were typically beyond what independent grocers could do for themselves. Affiliated-independent management was able to provide continuous on-site supervision that allowed a store owner to keep up to date on new techniques or to fine-tune operations, such as having a food display expert evaluate a store's food presentation methods. Inevitably, the use of central management in an affiliated independent to articulate a store's design and location was becoming increasingly similar to corporate chain procedures.

Affiliated independents did experience problems between management and store owners. In some affiliated independents, especially groups controlled by retailers, store owners sometimes bought goods from other wholesalers.[15] Such purchases on the side kept the affiliated independent from

4.1 Spatial Competition Between Affiliated Independents and Corporate Chain Stores, Dresden, Ohio, 1930s (Courtesy of the Food Marketing Institute)

maximizing its ability to get lower purchasing rates from food manufacturers. When store members in the affiliated independent offered different prices for the same food goods, central management was displeased, because they were afraid that customers would become aware of these price inconsistencies and be dissatisfied with their stores. Both on-the-side wholesale purchases and price differentials made it difficult for the central management of an affiliated independent to coordinate advertising. They were less able to maximize the bulk buying of goods and to promote set prices. Wholesalers also created problems for retailers by encouraging store owners to buy more food goods than they needed. An independent wholesaler's objective was to maximize sales, but this aim was hardly in the grocer's interests. Retailers had to maximize the turnover velocity of all goods, and ultimately, it was not in the chain's interest for the grocer to buy more goods than could be sold. Wholesalers who joined affiliated independents learned that they also had to forsake many of their previous independent practices just as their retail grocers did.

The overriding dilemma that affiliated independents had to conquer was the inefficient set of administrative functions that existed between retailers and wholesalers. An affiliated independent needed to work as a team with quality management personnel, because their organizational structure placed greater demands on coordination than that of the corporate chains. An A&P or Kroger corporate manager was able to make an executive order, and all store supervisors were company employees who had to comply. In contrast, store members in an affiliated independent remained property owners and often acted independently. Affiliated independents combated this coordination problem in their contracts with store members, and although sometimes specifying loose controls, those affiliated independents using tight policies with ironclad clauses exercised the greatest amount of systematic control over their store members. When these controls were based on what made retailers successful, central management experienced few problems. More progressive affiliated independents such as Red & White supplemented contract agreements with educational programs for their grocers to demonstrate why unfamiliar wholesaling policies were used.[16] The affiliated independent's contract was its substitute for the corporate chain store manual. But contracts only worked effectively when retailers and wholesalers actively cooperated. Corporate chains had fewer coordination problems in administering their stores than did affiliated independents whose members were accustomed to deciding issues independently.

Although affiliated independents faced numerous problems, they did have some advantages over corporate chains. Their basic assets were flexibility and legal status. They could avoid restrictive chain store legislation, which enabled them to keep their doors open and to sustain certain market segments.

Flexibility resulted from affiliated independents combining positive elements from the changing times with successful practices from the past. By joining an affiliated-independent group owners received more than savings in over-head costs through bulk buying. They were able to profit by adopting techniques that corporate chains had developed over a long span of time and at great costs. When management for an affiliated independent systematically organized and taught these corporate chain methods to their new members, each store owner reaped immediate benefits that could not only save a store but also make it profitable. Many store members also found that they were able to specialize in their grocery trade as they had done in the past. The corporate chain stores were geared to offering a standard set of brands at the lowest price. There was little or no adaptation to local circumstances. In contrast, many grocers who joined affiliated independents were accustomed to servicing primarily the middle- or upper-class trade.[17] Some of these grocers catered to the tastes of their ethnic neighborhoods. Although the food brands they carried became more limited for more efficient wholesale purchasing, these store owners were able to sustain market segments that the large corporate chains such as A&P, Kroger, and Safeway had avoided. Changing some practices and remaining the same in others allowed affiliated independent stores to become more efficient and still remain somewhat independent.

A structural reason why these flexibilities proved to be workable was the economics of volume buying in wholesaling. The corporate chains had a definite economic advantage over affiliated independents by having more stores in their system. With their huge size, corporate chains received lower prices from food manufacturers than did other grocers, but the advantage was not that great. As a chain added more stores, wholesale prices decreased at a decreasing rate. The wholesale buying advantages of a corporate chain with a thousand stores was negligible over a chain with only fifty stores.[18] Food manufacturers were able to reduce their prices only so much, because these companies had to sustain their own profit margins and pay for their own overhead costs. Moreover, there were some food producers that did not give price concessions for volume buying, and for these goods all grocers, independent or chain, competed on equal terms. These elements of wholesale economics in the grocery trade meant that an affiliated independent did not need to become particularly large in order to overcome the volume buying advantages of the corporate chains. These economic conditions made it possible for an affiliated-independent group, even a small one, to become efficient quickly through the use of corporate chain methods while continuing to orient their stores to a particular class or culture of clientele. Although affiliated independents usually had small stores, volume buying was to become essential when they later built supermarkets that depended on high volume sales and low prices.

The affiliated independents were able to avoid both state sales tax legislation and federal legislation designed to limit the economic growth of corporate chains. It was the unaffiliated independents, both wholesalers and retail grocers, who promoted such taxes and controls, because they were being forced out of business. The tax legislation was geared to how many stores were owned by a company. In large corporate chains, company ownership was in the thousands of stores, but most affiliated independents did not own stores, only the individuals who were participating members were owners. Because the tax legislation was aimed at taxing the corporation rather than the store owner, affiliated independents largely escaped the effects of chain store taxation. In some cases, owners of small corporate chains dissolved their companies and joined affiliated independents to avoid taxation.[19] Rather than being reactive as they had been in the past, affiliated independents supported such tax laws and the Wright-Patman Act as a political offensive against the corporate chains.[20] Affiliated independents in the grocery trade were increasingly operating their wholesaling operations and retail stores with the same economic efficiencies introduced by corporate chains. Yet, affiliated independents did not create public opposition to their businesses as did A&P and others, because their stores were typically owned by local grocers.

Grocers who joined affiliated independents responded to the economic crisis created by the corporate chains. Many of these business people survived the transition from an independent to an affiliated-independent member, but there were structural changes that severed their trade from traditional ways of business.

RECONSTRUCTION OF THE GROCER CLASS

By the 1930s, an overwhelming majority of grocery stores in the nation belonged to either a corporate chain or an affiliated independent, and this movement brought an end to the shopkeeper's age. Grocers were no longer self-reliant or specifically organized to meet the needs of a local community or neighborhood. With the arrival of the corporate chain, the local grocer became a company employee who supervised the selling of goods through the company's store, which was designed to maximize trade volume per square foot of building space. As grocers joined an affiliated independent, their business reasoning was transformed into the same systematic means for conducting business. The economics of a chain system had overtaken the economics of the individual storekeeper. The major consequence was that corporate management was substituted for the individual store owner.

Corporate management resulted in new forms of property relations. Corporate chain companies such as A&P owned the means for retail distribution, and grocers in their stores were the equivalent of factory foremen and workers. As the corporate chain store eliminated the independent store, a group of paid workers replaced a small merchant with workers. The corporate chains were centralizing store ownership into fewer hands as non-affiliated independent grocers were forced out of business. Affiliated independents remained in control of their store properties, but they had less control over their product inventories as wholesalers played a greater role over what food goods should be on the grocer's shelf. Stores in affiliated independents were redesigned physically to meet physical demands that were congruent with reasoning that complied with chain store retailing demands. Under corporate management, property relations were centralized or remolded to meet the demands of a chain system.

Chain store methods affected the grocer's social class in a variety of ways. Unsuccessful independent grocers either left the business entirely or went to work for a chain store. In the latter case, their status was changed from an employer to an employee. In some circumstances, a grocer's class status was mixed and remained the same. A few grocers operated hole-in-the-wall stores in which the back part of the store was used as the owner's home. Most of these stores were owned by men who were factory hands or workers elsewhere, and during the day their wives and children managed the store. With little investment, these hole-in-the-wall stores neither expanded nor closed, because they were unaffected by their competition due to their low volume of trade and low overhead costs of space and labor. In contrast, top-flight independents had large stores that generated a sufficient volume of trade to compete with the chain stores.[21] Racial discrimination was prevalent. Like other businesses, corporate chains did not attempt to use African-Americans as store managers. Even when African-Americans owned their own grocery stores in the South, other southern independents who formed an affiliated independent did not allow their fellow African-American grocers to join. As a result, African-American grocers in the South had to organize their own affiliated independents. In contrast, African-American grocers were accepted in affiliated independents in the North and Midwest.[22] Economically and socially, the chain system was used both to change and to sustain a grocer's socio-economic class.

The emergence of the chain system created divisions among grocers that had not existed in the past. Before chain stores, independent retailers had mainly seen their conflicts associated with wholesale jobbers. Getting the best price for food goods from wholesalers was their major concern. Direct competition with a categorically different type of retailer had occurred with stall merchants in public markets. Although competition did exist between stall merchants and grocery stores, there were no drastic shifts in one retailer capturing the other's business. Corporate chain stores made their economic presence felt, by forcing independent grocers either to change their business methods or to close their stores. Merchants who formed affiliated independents significantly changed their retail business from competition between small merchants to competition with grocery chains.

There was a general feeling and fear among many business people and politicians that the corporate chains would monopolize the grocery trade, but they did not. In 1929, corporate chains had captured 39 percent of the grocery store trade, and in the 1930s and 1940s, the percentages dropped.[23] The major reason why corporate chains never monopolized the grocery trade was that independent retailers and wholesalers were able to organize as affiliated independents more quickly than corporate chains could expand. Potential members of affiliated independents had already developed their local clientele, and when they adopted chain store techniques, corporate chains met stiffer competition. At the same time, corporate chains were able to grow only so fast. New store sites and a larger pool of trained grocers were needed for them to install new chain stores. The economics and time demands of expansion in corporate chains were greater than the resources needed to refit grocery stores and for their owners to function as affiliated independents. Affiliate members had the necessary grocery store sites and experienced labor force in place. As a result, they were able to capture the corporate chains' assets of more efficient business techniques, whereas the corporate chains were less able to exploit or to eliminate the affiliated independents' labor pool and business sites. With voluntary syndicates competing at the same level with national corporate chains, warfare among the business class of grocers reached a new level, but as the twentieth century progressed, the fully independent grocery was losing the battle to remain a viable form of business.

PRECONDITIONS TO THE SUPERMARKET'S EMERGENCE

The chain store system was certainly a precondition that shaped the supermarket, but it was not the only one. Food production developments, changes in urban transportation, and reactions from large independent grocers also set the stage for the supermarket as a viable spatial design mechanism for food retailing.

As an input to mass retail distribution, the organizational expansion of food companies began to influence the grocery store. Companies that processed perishable goods, packaged food, or manufactured these products, were driven by economic growth. Corporations such as Armour, United Fruit, National Biscuit (Nabisco), and Campbell were able to expand in two basic ways. First, markets could be expanded. Many food companies increased their production not only throughout the United States but also abroad. The other strategy was to create new food products or make lesser known goods available to consumers. Food manufacturers began to make increasingly different types of cereals, beverages, soups, and other items. For perishable goods, meat companies began to develop foods from by-products that were previously discarded. Fruit companies sought to expand trade beyond apples and oranges to more exotic fruits. Expanding markets and developing new products usually resulted in food manufacturers and processors investing more into their plants and transportation facilities.[24] To expand geographically, to create more food products, or to make available more food goods, food companies had to change their organizational frameworks.

The basic approach around which major food companies reorganized for economic expansion was vertical integration. This integration was aimed at the strategic planning of production, marketing, and purchasing through administrative management. Developed mainly through the last quarter of the nineteenth century until the 1920s, these three functions were developed separately, and had different administrative requirements.

Food production was first brought under control. As mass production techniques were introduced, factory consolidation was necessary because machines could replace labor while sustaining manufacturing levels. Some food companies closed down some factories and concentrated their production in a few modernized factories fitted with continuous process machinery. In some cases, integration was done through company mergers. When companies merged and became a single corporation, factories and facilities that duplicated production or processing of food goods were eliminated. Centralized management determined which plants had the best locations for distribution and were best suited for expansion and modernization.[25] Increased production increased the pressure on food manufacturers to expand.

After reorganizing production, corporate management in food companies expanded into marketing and then into purchasing. The efficiencies gained in factory outputs began to exceed the companies' ability to sell their products. Regional and foreign offices were created by larger companies in order to develop new markets, because food manufacturers often found that the means to market their goods were inadequate or non-existent. Although wholesalers and other middlemen helped to advertise the food companies' goods, they were not prepared to develop the sales of a single company. Food companies replaced independent wholesalers as they established their own regional distribution centers. Managing production and marketing led to increased and more predictable trade, but food companies had to gain control over purchasing so that there would be an adequate supply of food resources to fulfill the planned demand for manufactured or processed foods. These companies often built their own purchasing establishments and began to supply and transport their own materials.[26] With purchasing and marketing pivoting about production, food companies necessarily had to restructure their organizations to manage these added functions.

The ultimate aim of food manufacturers, like many other American corporations, was to manage their input and output—from purchasing to production and finally to marketing. Middle management was needed to administer this organizational integration through these three functions, either centrally or regionally. Each function began to be separated into divisions, such as the production of different food types, and middle management specialized in making such divisions more efficient and profitable. Top management began to coordinate middle management so that efficiency in one function helped to improve the others. Whereas purchasing, production, and marketing had often been independent businesses, vertical integration was a more efficient way to produce a volume trade with profits, and it required a corporate management system that depended on middle management to administrate specialized tasks.

The economic aims of food manufacturers and their organizational restructuring began to nurture a retail distribution system that was similar in structure to their own wholesale systems. For a food manufacturers, the most economical relationship with wholesalers and retailers was to have a single order in which a large volume of goods was bought in every one of its food product lines. Food companies wanted to maximize diversity as well as volume, and large single orders minimized management costs. It was in a food manufacturer's interest that grocery firms be organized efficiently to manage a simple contract for a variety of food products. As corporate chains and affiliated independents became larger, top management increasingly developed middle-management positions that specialized in wholesale and retail functions. Management for corporate chains and affiliated independents pursued not only increased sales but also inventory controls and a better accounting of food products that performed well. Such knowledge helped grocery management learn what mix of food products would increase retail sales. This knowledge also relayed important information to food companies. Food orders were becoming more reliable market predictors for food companies, because the use of corporate techniques in grocery stores had reduced retailing inefficiencies caused by ill-designed stores, inadequate advertising, poor stock inventories, and other shortcomings. As corporate chains and affiliated independents improved the management of their stores, food manufacturers increased their ability to predict how much food products they needed to produce.

With food manufacturers, corporate chains, and affiliated independents adopting similar corporate structures, there was ultimately a design misfit in the grocery store. Management guidelines redesigned the grocery store to increase the velocity of retail sales, but the typical store plan was physically too small to provide the variety of food lines that food companies wanted the retail grocers to sell. Volume sales in each product line for a diversity of products was not possible when floor space was limited. Ultimately, a grocery store with a greater square footage enabled food manufacturers to develop markets for diverse food goods.

For grocery stores to become larger, changes in transportation had to take place. The rush to the suburbs depended initially on a trolley line system that allowed for expansion. To bring groceries home, most Americans used a streetcar, walked, or used home delivery. Grocery store customers bought a limited amount of goods at one time, because they were unable to carry large parcels conveniently. People who depended on home delivery could have a large amount of groceries sent to their home, but there were two problems. First, home delivery service was more expensive than in-store shopping. Second, customers who ordered over the phone did not visit the store, and as a result they were often less aware of the products available and less demanding of food varieties and brands. Because customers wanted to carry few groceries or shorten the time for groceries to be delivered to their homes, they found that shopping at many nearby stores was more convenient than shopping at a few large stores that were more distant from home. The small size of chain stores fitted well with these customer constraints, but these limits began to erode.

In the 1920s, the private automobile became more common.[27] Grocery customers were increasingly able to drive to the grocery store themselves and to haul their purchases home. For customers, it was more economical to buy many groceries in one shopping trip than to make several trips. Automobile ownership also increased the volume of retail trade in cities and towns. More country people now owned automobiles, and they traveled to larger communities to buy groceries. Corporate chains and affiliated independents had some stores in small towns, and the automobile enabled them to gain greater access to the surrounding rural areas. The impetus for using the automobile for grocery shopping was also aided by the introduction of refrigerators in the home. In 1926 there were 205,000 refrigerators in households, and by 1936 the number had risen to 1,996,000. Home refrigeration changed American buying habits because it allowed consumers to store more food longer and make fewer shopping trips.[28] Some grocers responded by opening automarkets where the driver drove into the store and made orders at the cashier's stand, but this experiment ultimately proved to be unsuccessful.[29] The automobile was changing customer shopping habits in towns and cities, and those changes were beginning to influence the design of grocery stores.

The average grocery store was typically one narrow building slotted between others built in the same manner, but this design did not meet the demands of automobile trade. When developers built their speculative buildings on taxpayer strips along extended trolley lines, they normally used the same construction methods and plat layouts as if they had built on a city block. Structures covered the entire lot and were located up against the sidewalk. The only place that customers could park was along the street in front of the store. Sufficient parking was a growing problem and there was increased pressure upon grocers to provide parking space. In the 1920s, Safeway first considered the availability of on-street parking space when locating its chain stores. Although rare, some building speculators at this time began constructing taxpayer blocks with building setbacks and off-street parking. The lack of convenient parking in the city's center created traffic congestion and motivated people to shop at suburban stores where parking was available.[30] But the increasing public desire for parking space placed economic demands on the grocery store. Profit margins in corporate chains such as A&P were only 2-1/2 cents per dollar, and if parking space was added to a lot while the store remained the same size, the grocer's overhead costs increased. To pay for this added cost, customer volume had to be increased, and a larger grocery store was the most obvious way to do this. The customer's shift to the automobile for shopping set the stage for remolding site design and the size of grocery stores.

Corporate chains and affiliated independents initially ignored the increasing demands made by the automobile, but some non-affiliated, independent grocers heeded them. In nineteenth century American cities, the grocery store began to develop as a suburban alternative to the public markets in the central city. It was the convenience store of its age. Suburbanization also created economic pressures that forced stall merchants who were butchers and green grocers to leave the public market and open their own shops. Although grocery stores did sell some perishable foods, their major trade was in canned foods, dry food goods, and other items. Butchers and green grocers provided home delivery in addition to store service. But a customer had to make multiple telephone calls or take trips to the butcher, the green grocer, or the grocery store, and this commercial arrangement became less satisfactory as people began to use their automobiles for shopping. Some merchants realized that trips to separate stores were inefficient for the customer. As a solution, some grocers absorbed a neighborhood's butcher store and green grocer shop into their premises during the 1920s.[31] In this case, a customer saved time by shopping at one store rather than three stores. Butchers and green grocers who had moved from public markets to their own stores were jointly being driven out of business by big independent grocers and by chain stores, which sold limited amounts of meat, vegetables, and fruits. The economic pressures toward consolidation in food retailing were displacing the traditional butcher and green grocer and forcing them to seek employment in grocery stores.

The combination store was designed to combat the economic advantages of the chain store model. Non-affiliated, independent grocers who wished to survive realized that it was unwise to duplicate completely the physical design of the chain stores. Being equal in store design did not compensate for the bulk buying advantages that chain stores had introduced. To decrease their costs, independent grocers had to increase the overall trade volume in their stores, and the solution was to increase the store's physical size and food product variety. With all the traditional food shops under one roof, the combination store functioned like a department store. Clerks were assigned to different food departments and gave direct service to customers. Behind counters in their separate food departments, clerks recalled the tradition of merchants with separate stalls in public markets. In the combination store, however, clerks were employees, not employers. In some cases, combination stores provided self-service shopping, and cash-and-carry was one way to reduce overhead costs.[32] Customers were able to optimize the mix of goods and services that they wanted in one place. Customers who shopped mainly at one store often supplemented their shopping at other food stores, and combining all the different types of food retailing into one building enabled

4.2 Neighborhood Independent Grocery Store, Provincetown, Massachusetts, 1942 (Courtesy of the Library of Congress)

these customers to reduce their food shopping to one trip. When able to do one-stop shopping in one big store that offered good prices, customers were psychologically disinclined to shop at a variety of grocery stores, including the smaller chain stores. The competitive aim of the combination grocery store was to offer a complete range of goods and services at one location.

The combination store was a temporary trend in food retailing in urban areas where transportation was a constraint. People came to this type of store by streetcar, on foot, or by car. The only parking that was made available was along the street. Transportation in American cities was in transition during the 1920s. Many people in cities, especially large cities, continued to rely on public transportation, but public transit systems were gradually giving way to the automobile. For a large combination store to sustain a high volume of trade, grocers had to address the problem of adequate parking. The combination store was an architectural means to handling volume trade, but it was not a long-term solution that addressed the site design requirements created by automotive traffic.

The combination store's success, however limited, depended on inexpensive architectural space. With low profit margins, these stores had to locate on low-priced lots, such as a suburban taxpayer strip. Just as crucial was having an inexpensive building. Architectural engineering had advanced during the nineteenth century, permitting the construction of skyscrapers. Most one story buildings were still built with load-bearing walls, but increasingly, steel columns and trusses were used to create wider and more open interiors than were possible with a wood structural system. Concrete technology was beginning to develop, and its use for post-and-beam systems for interior spaces with exterior load-bearing walls was becoming more prevalent. When circumstances made it economical to use these building systems, developers used them for speculative commercial buildings in suburban locations. In these structures, developers allotted limited street frontage for each store and used lot depth to increase square footage. When non-affiliated, independent grocers created combination stores, their architectural alternatives varied, but a common way to make a store larger was to rent or to buy two or more of the adjacent shops. In some cases, the facade was redone to create a unified front. In southern California with its great dependence on the automobile and low population density, freestanding buildings were constructed to house the combination grocery store.[33] Cheap space was critical to having more space, and advancements in architectural engineering enabled the construction of bigger structures for less money. Building technology thus played a part in making the combination store a commercial possibility.

The advancement of organizational development in food production and distribution, changes in urban transportation, and the arrival of the combination store set the mold for the supermarket to become a design alternative for food retailing. These systematic changes increased pressures to shape a new store design that addressed these new demands.

4.3 Dillons Combination Store, Kansas, 1920s (Courtesy of Dillons Stores)

EARLY EXPERIMENTS

Even though the grocery trade had advanced from being entirely independent retailers to the chain system, store design changes were modest.
Both corporate chain and affiliated-independent stores were redesigned for
greater internal efficiency, but the size of buildings remained essentially the
same. The internal restructuring of stores had changed customer flow through
the store, and many establishments were somewhat departmentalized. But
until the emergence of the combination store, such organizational divisions
were highly limited. The chains' redesign of the small store did increase the
velocity of trade, but volume selling was ultimately limiting. Small stores were
oriented to highly localized trade areas and were subject to nearby population
changes. These limits, plus the external pressures brought about by changes
in food manufacturing and by the growth of the American city, led to the
realization that the design of the small grocery store was inefficient.

Experimental designs for grocery retailing in southern California and the
Southwest foretold future changes. Although the chain store movement had
taken hold in the 1920s, its influence was primarily on the East Coast. The
citizens of Los Angeles were more dependent on the automobile than their
eastern counterparts, whereas development was less dense than in the East.
With a city growing outward, land costs per acre were relatively low. All these
factors encouraged business people to construct or to use freestanding buildings, which were larger than the typical grocery store. Ralphs Grocery Company and Alpha Beta Food Markets were early leaders. These stores were
organized by food departments, and sales were done on a cash-and-carry
basis. The main difference was the size of these stores. As far back as the
1920s, Ralphs Grocery was building new, large stores that cost $100,000 per
unit. In Pomona, California, Alpha Beta leased the 12,000-square-foot Buick
Garage building. Houston, Texas, was just beginning to grow in its spread-
out pattern, and Joe Weingarten, Inc., and Henke and Pillot built large grocery
stores that included parking lots in front. Miller's Super Markets of Denver,
Colorado, built a 6,250-square-foot store in 1931, and in Detroit, Wrigley
Super Markets opened a large store in 1928. It failed economically one year
later.[34] Where land or rent was cheap, the larger store was beginning to make
inroads into the local grocery trade.

The new supermarket had its greatest economic impact in the Los Angeles
area. In the late 1920s, the city's first supermarket opened, and by 1937,
260 stores were in place. Most importantly, these supermarkets captured 35
percent of sales in Los Angeles, as compared to 21 percent for all corporate
chain and affiliated-independent stores and 44 percent for non-affiliated,
independent grocers.[35] The economic inroads of the early supermarkets in
southern California, however, were ignored by corporate chains and affiliated
independents.

The supermarket made its presence known on the East Coast through the

4.4 Henke & Pillot Supermarket, Houston, Texas, 1922 (Courtesy of the *Progressive Grocer*)

innovative efforts of one man. Michael Cullen was working for a branch of Kroger Grocery and Baking Company in 1930 as a branch manager in Herrin, Illinois. Cullen anticipated the design shortcomings of chain stores and he submitted a written proposal to the company's vice-president for a super-market system. Cullen's request for a meeting with the company president was denied. He resigned and went into business for himself to implement his idea.

Cullen's plan was simple. Prices can be made lower by increasing sales volume, and to increase sales volume, a large store is needed. To reduce costs, he planned to sell three hundred items at cost, two hundred items at 5 percent above cost, three hundred items at 15 percent above cost, and three hundred items at 20 percent above cost. These price margins were considerably lower than chain store standards, and to maintain profits, the design of the store had to change radically.

The supermarket had to maximize physical size while reducing its overhead costs. Cullen planned for his supermarkets to be from 5,200 to 6,400 square feet as compared to chain stores that were often only 500 to 600 square feet in size. At the same time, Cullen needed to have five stores not only to reduce wholesale costs through bulk buying but also to eliminate the need for ware-housing. Food goods were sent directly to the stores.[36] Making the store bigger resulted in a simpler stream of goods with reduced overhead costs. When a warehouse was eliminated, building insurance and labor to run the facility were also eliminated. The supermarket principle put the warehouse on the grocer's aisle rather than apart from it. Increasing the floor space of the store ultimately reduced building cost per square foot. A building that is 40′ × 150′ has 6,000 square feet and 380 feet of exterior wall. The typical chain store was 20′ × 30′ with 600 square feet and 100 feet of external wall space if the store was freestanding. With ten chain stores being equal in size to one supermarket, these stores produced 1,000 linear feet of exterior wall compared to the supermarket's 380 linear feet. With exterior walls being a large portion of a building's cost, the potential savings in constructing one supermarket versus ten chain stores was immense. Of course, many chain stores shared party walls when part of a building complex, but even consid-ering this limit, a supermarket was still more efficient than the typical chain store in terms of its exterior footage of wall space. With fewer stores of greater size, building insurance and labor costs were significantly reduced. At the same time, transport costs from warehouse to store were eliminated when food goods were shipped by manufacturers to the supermarket. With small stores, corporate chains and affiliated independents were constantly trans-porting goods from the warehouse to the store, because the old system of back-room storage had been greatly reduced. The underlying economics of store size allowed Cullen to reduce building overhead costs that had not been recognized before.

Cullen opened his first supermarket in 1930 in Jamaica, New York, and other stores followed. Named King Kullen, his first store was located in a converted garage. His principle was to lease a large, cheap space near a city's business center. Yet, he wanted his store sufficiently distant from the business section so that customers were able to find on-street parking spaces. Cullen used newspaper advertising where he flagrantly posed his store as the price wrecker with prices that could not be beaten. Later stores that were opened were not only larger but also contained concessions, such as ladies ware, shoes, and house furnishings. Self-service and cash-and-carry were fully implemented to lower overhead costs. By 1932, Cullen was operating eight markets with $6 million in annual sales, and by 1935, he had fifteen stores. His meteoric rise as an independent ended with his death in 1936, but Cullen had demonstrated that the supermarket was a successful formula that could make economic inroads into the chain store trade.

Soon after the initial success of King Kullen, experienced businessmen Robert M. Otis and Roy A. Dawson joined with a grocery wholesaler to form a new grocery company that had an even greater impact than Cullen's efforts. Their tactic was to bring shoppers from a wide area and to capture customers by serving all of their needs in one shopping trip. In 1932, they opened the Big Bear store on the first floor of a two-story factory building in Elizabeth, New Jersey. It had 50,000 square feet of commercial space with 15,000 square feet devoted to the grocery store. The remaining space was used for a variety of departments such as auto accessories, hardware, drugs, and a soda fountain. Across the street customers were able to park their cars in a lot that had been leased. With its huge size, Big Bear had the hurried atmosphere of a large nineteenth-century public market, but it employed twentieth century business techniques. Max M. Zimmerman recalls:

The fixtures were of cheap construction, giving the layout a temporary bazaar-like appearance. Cheap pine tables were built and loaded with mass displays of merchandise. Piled high near the door, handy to the food department, were hundreds of market baskets. Customers were to be left free to walk about, and help themselves to whatever attracted them. With baskets loaded, they returned to the cashier's booth, paid for purchases and left. Surrounding the packaged food department were to be the concessions of meats, and fruits and vegetables, together with the non-food departments.[37]

Big Bear proved to be an enormous economic success. Of the 50,000 square feet of commercial space in the store, the grocery department accounted for 2.2 million dollars, over 56 percent of the store's sales. Part of Big Bear's profits were due to rental arrangements with its eleven concessions, which included various food goods, candy, cigars and tobacco, drugs and cosmetics, auto accessories, paints and varnishes, electronic goods, and a soda fountain. Concessionaires who operated these departments were charged about 5 percent of their gross sales in lieu of rent, and together their

4.5 An Early King Kullen Store in a Converted Automotive Garage, 1930s (Courtesy of the Food Marketing Institute)

4.6 King Kullen Store, 1930s (Courtesy of the Food Marketing Institute)

total fee in the first year was over $86,000 for rental space that had cost management only $15,000. The concession system was not unlike the stall merchant fees in the public market, and it proved to be a profitable addition to the grocery department, which was devoted to packaged food brands.

As with King Kullen, the proprietors of Big Bear emphasized newspaper advertising, and the results were phenomenal. With its low prices, the store's advertisements not only brought in customers but also attracted attention from coast to coast. Customers drove as far as fifty miles away to shop at Big Bear. Some retailers followed the example of King Kullen and Big Bear, and their names, such as Giant Tiger and Big Chief, duplicated in economic imagery what the original supermarket pioneers had explored. The low prices were so significant in these stores that they became known as cheapy supers.[38] With the national attention that Big Bear attracted, chain stores were no longer able to ignore the supermarket experiment.

REACTIONS

The impact of the supermarket was felt throughout the retail grocery trade. Non-affiliated, independent retailers and wholesalers, affiliated independents and corporate chains, and food manufacturers were astounded at the trade volume that one store could produce. Non-affiliated, independent grocers and wholesalers felt a special pain, because they had already been hurt economically by the rise of the chain system. Now, just as they had begun to adjust to this change, the supermarket appeared as a new threat.[39] Corporate chains realized that their bulk buying techniques with food manufacturers allowed them to establish a stable reduction in overhead costs that small independents and wholesalers could not match, but they had not anticipated that one supermarket could be so economically powerful as to neutralize the sheer number of their stores. The Big Bear Supermarket in 1932 generated a sales volume that was equal to one hundred A&P stores in the same New Jersey vicinity. King Kullen, which was much smaller than Big Bear, had a trade volume equivalent to ten A&P stores.[40] Affiliated-independent members disdained the supermarket with a mixture of feelings. They felt progressive by joining an affiliated independent and adapting to a new economic reality, but these grocers felt disheartened by having to face another major obstacle that could threaten their economic existence. Where all types of grocery retailers had seen the economic battleground between themselves, these grocers realized that they were now joined together by a new opponent, the supermarket.

Food manufacturers had faced many problems with grocery retailers. With chains varying in size, bulk buying wholesale prices varied, and as a result, grocers charged different retail prices. Food manufacturers lost their ability to stabilize the retail price of their food goods, and these price variations prevented manufacturers from promoting the price value of their goods. At the same time manufacturers were incensed that their products were sold under purchase value by corporate chains and affiliated independents as loss leaders to attract customers. Supermarkets made food manufacturers equally frustrated. Although the cheapy supermarkets typically did not use loss leaders, they sold many food items at cost to attract customers, recouping the profits in the sales of meats, vegetables, and specialty items. To customers, a manufacturer's food prices were increasingly seen as suspect, because with such price variations, it was logical to assume that food manufacturers and retailers were charging prices that were too high. At the same time, the corporate chains and the supermarket were a combined threat to lower prices that could put many retailers and wholesalers out of business. Food manufacturers also found large chains such as A&P to be ruthless and demanding about price discounts, and the supermarket system would only further reduce the manufacturers' margins of profit.[41] Food manufacturers were concerned about stabilizing retail prices and price discounts of their products to protect their profit margins.

All grocery retailers felt the economic impact of the supermarket. It was like a bomb. Those grocery stores that suffered the greatest losses were those businesses closest to the supermarket. Economy stores and combination stores were both devastated by the economic fallout created by the supermarket's presence. Many non-affiliated, independent grocers who had withstood the onslaught of the chain system were quickly eliminated by a nearby supermarket. Used to regarding the chain system as the critical threat, these independent grocers were now being put out of business by a different independent, the operator of this new kind of large volume store. The devastation to chain stores was more systematic. In 1933 as the supermarkets were beginning to have an effect, 20 percent of A&P's stores were unprofitable, and by 1937 the number had risen to 33 percent.[42] As the supermarket spread as an innovation, the small grocery store, which had lasted from early American history through the chain store age, was dying from economic inefficiency.

Reactions to the supermarket were political in the beginning. With supermarkets' reduced labor and overhead costs, there was a variety of responses. The Bronx King Kullen store was picketed by the Retail Grocery and Fruit Clerks' Union, which was affiliated with the American Federation of Labor. Picketers were protesting the fact that a supermarket that was equivalent in size to ten average grocery stores required significantly fewer workers to run it. Wholesalers who refused to stop selling food goods to supermarkets were blacklisted by grocers in New Jersey. Corporate chains worked in conjunction with affiliated and non-affiliated independents and put pressure on New Jersey newspapers to stop grocery advertising by Big Bear. Chain store papers and newspapers then provided editorials that proclaimed the unfair trade practices created by supermarkets. Newark, New Jersey, passed a license bill to restrict the number of supermarkets in the city. The Associated Grocery Manufacturing Association prepared a draft for a model state law to control the selling of products at or below their purchase costs. The American Wholesale Grocers' Association proposed a similar bill that prescribed cost controls at every level—production, wholesale, and retail.[43] Independents who opened supermarkets and began a chain were caught in the stream of anti–chain store legislation that was originally aimed at corporate chains, such as A&P, Kroger, and Safeway. The supermarket survived these political onslaughts by being a more economical vehicle for retail trade than the typical grocery store.

The supermarket was also helped by the nation's worst depression in its history. In 1932, 25 percent of Americans were unemployed, and people had little disposable income. Every penny counted and households saw supermarkets as a practical means to save money. They were willing to forego a nice store atmosphere for a crude store that offered lower prices. Supermarket owners were engaged in economic survival with their competitors, and the flow of customers into their doors was their biggest ally.

Executives at corporate chains and affiliated independents found it hard to accept the supermarket. In the beginning, they thought that this retail device was a gimmick that would disappear as soon as the depression was over. It was hard for them to believe that a store that appeared to be an overgrown country store or a warehouse was a rational solution to grocery retailing. These executives saw King Kullen, Big Bear, and other such markets as being loosely organized and crudely designed vessels for retail consumption. Corporate chains and affiliated independents, as well as some non-affiliated independents, had concentrated on fine tuning the operations of their grocery stores. Inventory analysis, customer flow, food presentation, store layout, wholesale procedures, labor analysis, and other concerns were issues that grocery companies had spent a great deal of time perfecting. The supermarket, however, was a paradigm shift. It required a large store with parking to handle volume sales, and self-service was a necessary criterion to ensure the velocity of trade. Unlike all stores before that had introduced self-service to a limited degree, the supermarket depended on it. Retail grocery executives had not foreseen this shift. Metaphorically, it was like the change from the motorized airplane to the jet. Management executives were perfecting the cylinder engine while King Kullen and Big Bear represented unrefined but workable jet engines. As a result, the supermarket's velocity of trade could not be matched by the limited capacity of the refined grocery store, such as A&P's economy store prototype. Although grocery management did not understand the supermarket's design, they were not blind to its overwhelming success.

Corporate chains and affiliated independents began to respond to the supermarket as a market mechanism to be designed instead of resisted through political means. Rather than making a dramatic shift, some corporate chains and affiliated independents introduced combination stores as a cautious step. A few grocers attempted to start their own supermarkets but made mistakes. Some leased large vacant buildings but failed to provide parking.[44] But the grocery companies, especially large corporate chains, had a staff of executives to analyze issues, and they responded to their mistakes and to change.

The resistance against the supermarket did not last as long as the fight of independents against the chain stores, because most store owners began to realize the benefits of converting. With anti–chain store taxes becoming prevalent in more states, a larger store made sense. Such taxes were assessed on the basis of store count rather than size, and consolidating many small stores into one helped to avoid such taxes.[45] Management in corporate chains and affiliated independents began to realize that change was needed. During 1934 in Cincinnati, Ohio the Albers Company was operating eight supermarkets, capturing 9.5 percent of the local trade. In comparison, A&P had fifty stores in Cincinnati, which were mainly their economy stores, and their local market share was only 7.7 percent. One Albers supermarket was economically performing to the equivalent of 7.7 A&P stores.[46] Many independents and small chains who had sufficient capital converted to the supermarket more quickly than big chains. Small chains, as well as affiliated and non-affiliated independents, realized that the supermarket was their future means of economic survival against the large corporate chains.

The corporate grocery chain giants awoke slowly to the threat of the supermarket, but finally they did react. A&P epitomizes this transition. John Hartford, president of A&P, waited to see how the supermarket trend would evolve, and his brother George, who was treasurer and chairman of the board, was cautious about making radical shifts that might incur economic losses. Although A&P had been known for adaptation, the company was also praised for innovation. The economy store was John Hartford's enormously successful brainchild, and undoubtedly he was reluctant to surrender to the notion that his invention was obsolete. At the same time George Hartford lived in a secluded world of financial analysis without fully realizing the consumer's preference for the supermarket. The two brothers had assembled the largest number of chain stores in the United States, and it was hard for them to admit that their road to success was leading them down the path to destruction. But the company's regional division managers saw the problem and began to experiment with the supermarket with little or no support from central management.[47] Those people in management who were closer to the economic battlefront saw the necessity of responding with a supermarket solution.

Experimentation by grocery chains was an attempt both to begin the supermarket approach and to minimize investments in a scheme that was flawed in design. When a large chain was planning to convert to the supermarket format, executive management wanted to achieve a standardized design that could be replicated manifold. In 1935, A&P's Central Western Division opened the company's first supermarket in Paducah, Kentucky. Fourteen

stores were then opened in Nashville, Tennessee, and on installing supermarkets in Cincinnati, A&P and Kroger competed directly with one another.
A&P tried many experiments. Still in 1935, A&P's Eastern Division opened
100 experimental stores, known as Baby Bears, in the Pittsburgh area. Some
supermarkets included concessions that were leased. In others, the warehouse
approach was tried, even using the ground floor of the company warehouse
as a market. This approach was eventually abandoned by A&P for new stores
designed to attract customers while retaining lower prices than their traditional
economy stores. After reviewing the success of the company's supermarket
experiment, A&P President John Hartford changed direction and began to
implement a speedy conversion to the supermarket approach. The change
was monumental. In 1936, A&P had 14,446 stores, which were mainly the
small, economy prototypes, and by 1941, A&P was operating only 6,042
stores, a 58 percent reduction. During the same time, A&P began to build
supermarkets, and by 1941, 29 percent of A&P's stores were supermarkets.
In five years A&P eliminated approximately 10,000 of its stores, mainly economy stores, and total sales increased from $864 million to over $1.3 billion
in the same five years. During the same period, Kroger, Safeway, and other
major chains made the same conversion to supermarkets and experienced
economic growth.[48] By first experimenting with and then converting to the
supermarket, large corporate chains such as A&P ensured their future success.
Although not the pioneer of the supermarket, A&P was often seen both as
the innovator and the economic powerhouse because of its fast expansion.
A chain executive recalled: "I don't know how it was in other places, but it
was A&P that invented the supermarket as far as we were concerned. I was
helping my dad in a small neighborhood grocery then, and I remember how
scared we were."[49]

INNOVATION AND CONFLICT

As the supermarket began to make its presence felt in American cities,
critical fixture innovations began to appear as refinements. The warehouse
approach was being abandoned gradually by all store owners in favor of a
modern, efficient store. The warehouse supermarket carried a large volume,
but it was unrefined in articulating customer service. Traditionally, canned
goods and packaged goods had been placed on shelves against the wall with
most floor displays being stacked. The gondola shelf system with cantilevered
shelves to serve two aisles, as used in supermarkets today, was introduced
in order to efficiently stack food goods within a customer's reach.[50] Because
supermarkets were so much larger than the traditional store, most food goods
were now stocked in the floor space rather than along the walls. The grocery
shopping cart was invented by Sylvan Goldman in 1937 for his Standard
Food Stores in Oklahoma City. Goldman had noticed that customers quit
shopping when their baskets became heavy. The cart alleviated this problem.

4.7 Early A&P Supermarket, 1930s (Courtesy of the Food Marketing Institute)

Most importantly, the cart was like a railroad car that allowed customers to maximize shipping purchased groceries from the cash register to their automobiles in the store's parking lot.[51] Eventually, two widths of a grocery cart became a critical dimension in determining the minimum width of a shopping aisle between gondola shelves. Both the gondola shelf and the shopping cart were innovations that established module dimensions on a micro scale that were multiplied and repeated for building larger supermarkets.

Beyond innovations in fixtures, the architectural design of supermarkets was a significant shift for the chains and independents. Supermarkets emphasized modern design found in the factory. Although Albert Kahn designed the Jack Cinnamon's Market in Highland Park, Michigan, he was primarily known for designing the highly efficient factory buildings for the Ford Motor Company that revolutionized modern factory design in the United States. The supermarket had become a factory for efficient retail consumption, and its appearance had to be efficient, progressive, and somewhat alluring.[52] Some grocery companies initially used Art Deco and Streamline Moderne, popular styles in the 1930s and 1940s. Glass became a prevalent feature of many store fronts, appearing more modern than the brick structures along taxpayer strips. Some smaller chain store owners were imaginative. Mirrors were used on interior walls, giving a sophisticated appearance. Instead of using only white, pastels and bright colors added variety in contrast to the starkness of many earlier stores.[53] Publix Supermarkets of Florida introduced the electric eye door that opened the door automatically for customers as they entered and exited.[54] Although a novelty, the idea of automation was congruent with the supermarket ideal of modern design and factory efficiency. The supermarket was beginning to fulfill the purpose of Taylorism, the scientific management of labor and space for economic gain.

The battles between food manufacturers and retail grocers continued, but the supermarket added a new battlefront. Corporate chains and affiliated independents continued to press for price discounts with food manufacturers who often cooperated. Large chains, such as A&P, often threatened to discontinue a food product if manufacturers did not concede to wholesale price discounts, and many manufacturers lost their product lines in chain stores for failing to concede to terms. These chain stores could offer their company brand to fill in any gaps caused by such conflicts.[55] New battle lines formed as corporate chains and affiliated independents attempted to bring in new product lines into the supermarket. When store owners brought concessions into the supermarket, the chain wars took a new tack. Competition was no longer just between A&P, Kroger, Safeway, I.G.A., and Red & White. At the arrival of the supermarket, these companies were beginning to compete with chains that specialized in drugs and variety goods, such as Rexall Drug and Woolworth. Milk companies had resisted inroads by the grocery trade, because they had always controlled retailing through home delivery. But the supermarket principle was an efficient, total food store, which included milk.

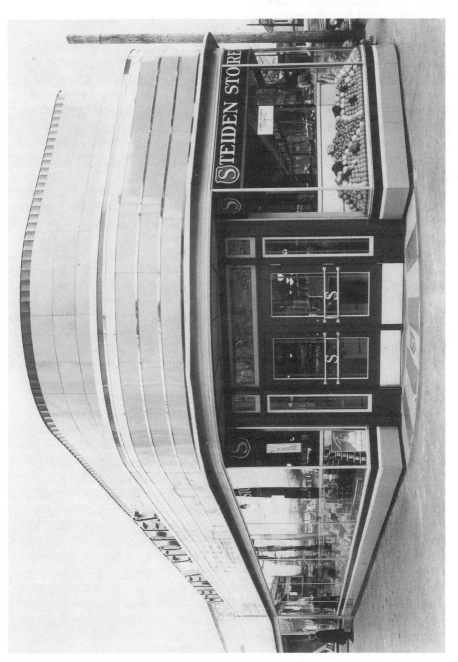

4.8 Streamline Moderne Style, Steiden Store, 1930s (Courtesy of the Food Marketing Institute)

4.9 Art Deco Style, Publix Supermarket, Winter Haven, Florida, 1940 (Courtesy of Publix Supermarkets, Inc)

Handling milk had traditionally been difficult due to the need for refrigeration, but that problem had been solved. Dairy producers still refused to sell milk to grocery stores, and they were unwilling to put milk into paper cartons. In time, several grocery companies started their own dairy operations to circumvent milk producers, and the feelings between grocery companies and the milk industry were filled with bitterness and some violence.[56] The supermarket was no longer a grocery store that dealt mainly in canned goods, produce, and limited meat selections. The supermarket was becoming an all-purpose food store that intervened in every aspect of the food industry and in some non-food products.

The supermarket met resistance from its retail grocery competitors, and those retailers who were committed to this new approach saw the need to organize in order to advance this system. In 1937, owners of supermarkets from across the United States joined together in New York City and formed the Super Market Institute. Their purposes were to educate each other; to study economic problems in the trade; to be a clearinghouse for information; and to promote relations with manufacturers, distributors, government, labor, and the public. But the most crucial move came from the Institute's new president, William H. Albers of Albers Super Markets. In his public address, he stressed the need for supermarket owners to promote the sale of nationally advertised brands and the need to eliminate loss-leader selling.[57] Albers recommended the elimination of the numerous antagonisms that had existed between food manufacturers and retailers. With reduced tensions between these corporate entities, the full benefits of vertical integration were more possible. Food manufacturers increasingly organized their companies so that administrative management could coordinate the wholesale process, from the growth or purchase of raw goods to factory production and, finally, to marketing their products through distributors. The coordination of inputs and outputs was necessary for an efficient organization, but the grocery companies had made matters difficult with a variety of price discounts and loss-leader sales. Albers' recommendations meant that manufacturers' marketing and supermarket retailing could become more efficient and more economical for all business interests. The supermarket as a retailing tool furthered the corporatization of business within food retailing and also within manufacturing.

The supermarket was preparing to play a significant role in labor relations. Grocery companies, especially large chains like A&P, had problems with union organizers. With the rise of the union movement, many organizers attempted to organize clerks and butchers, but many grocery chains were highly resistant to inroads by unions. In 1934 organized labor attempted to make A&P comply by threatening to stop the delivery of goods to A&P warehouses in Cleveland. Later, the unions began to picket the company's stores and warehouses. Rather than comply, A&P's president, John Hartford, closed all A&P stores in Cleveland, at a loss of $300,000 a week in gross business. During the brief life of the National Recovery Administration (NRA) in the 1930s, executives in grocery companies cooperated in establishing and revising governmental codes that regulated the food industry. To implement the revised codes, NRA compliance directors and field adjusters often attempted to unionize store employees, and company executives complained vehemently to officials that such tactics were against the codes that they helped to write.[58] Although unable to avoid the growing union movement, grocery companies foresaw the supermarket's potential to counter labor union demands. Fewer clerks were needed to run a supermarket than were needed for an equivalent number of smaller stores to generate an equal volume of trade. The supermarket altered the nature of labor conflicts by reducing the size of the labor force.

The supermarket was evolving into an architectural design that had major consequences for the labor relations in the grocery trade. As design innovations made store operations more efficient, the velocity of trade increased, as did profits. But to employees and the union people who picketed it, the supermarket was increasingly becoming a business opportunity for an elite business class. The typical shopkeeper who owned an independent grocery store was not able to afford the capital investment of a supermarket. New people entering the grocery trade earned wages that would never enable them to open a store of their own. The supermarket was a corporate design with a big price tag and it was having an impact on labor relations.

THE EVOLUTION

The chain store movement led to the near demise of the individual storekeeper and the rise of grocery retailing as a corporate business. As independent retailers joined affiliated independents, the corporate model of grocery retailing became the dominant form of business. That transition led to forms of economic control that were to transform trade relations and store design. Increasingly, the corporate organization within and between food manufacturing and food retailing depended on managing the economic inputs and outputs of food goods. As their organizations performed similarly, efficiency increased, but to transform organizational efficiency into the limits of space, store design was a critical step to secure profits. Corporate chains such as A&P, Kroger, and Safeway provided store designs that were efficient mechanisms for trade, and in response affiliated independents were formed to bring corporate chain advantages to the independents. Bulk buying allowed affiliated independents to reduce their overhead costs just as corporate chains had done, but systematic store design through the micro adjustments of food departments and displays enabled non-affiliated as well as affiliated independents to focus their stores on more efficient, higher volume sales.

The rise of mass retail distribution was pushed by technical advancements, population growth, and the automobile. The small grocery store was no longer an efficient mechanism for handling the potential volume of trade, and the supermarket was the solution. Before World War II, the pioneering efforts of supermarket owners were transforming how all grocery companies and the remaining independents would conduct business in the future. Although the depression in the 1930s and World War II slowed growth, the supermarket was essential to the metamorphosis of grocery retailing into a new corporate system. The full potential of the supermarket was yet to come.

Chapter 5

THE SUPERMARKET BOOM

The evolution to the supermarket had set the stage for a new era in grocery retailing. Whether independent or part of a chain, business people in the grocery trade realized that a large store capable of high-volume trade was the economic model for the immediate future. Although the economic depression of the 1930s prevented overall profit growth in the retail grocery business, grocers converting to the supermarket demonstrated its economic power by showing profits and capturing trade. Yet, this new type of store was in only an early stage of development. The supermarket was not yet a refined, engineered design for maximizing profits. It was a synthesis of the principle of high volume retail distribution and the need for efficiency brought on by an economic depression. The nation began to recover gradually from the great depression, but World War II led to one last stage of development before the supermarket could flourish in all regions of the United States.

THE WORLD WAR II ERA

World War II was a time of economic stasis and transformation in the grocery store. Even as the United States approached entry into the war, supermarkets were expanding, and grocers were converting to a high-volume level of trade by increasing store size. When the war came, economic growth virtually stopped. Supermarket construction and the refurbishing of old stores ceased as the nation converted to a wartime economy. Government regulations and programs assured that building materials were used primarily to supply the armed forces. But building expansion was less necessary during the war, because a great number of Americans were fighting overseas. This change alone had a dramatic effect on supermarket management.

Women provided the labor force during the war, and their influence was felt in the grocery store. Before World War II, almost all grocery clerks were men. Like in other businesses, grocers had no choice but to hire women as workers if they were to remain in business. Although chain stores and independents lost a trained labor force, they received a temporary reprieve by hiring women in entry-level positions. During the war, grocers were temporarily able to reduce labor overhead costs by paying women lower wages than experienced male employees who entered military service. This economic advantage, however, extended only to large independents and chain stores. Many mom and pop stores were unable to compensate for labor shortages, especially when pop went to war. In the first three years of the war, over 81,000 grocery stores closed, the majority of them family owned.[1] World War II created not only a new labor pool but also helped to quicken the destruction of the traditional family-operated grocery store.

Grocery store owners had to adapt to the new retail market that was shaped by the war. In 1942, the government mandated food rationing so that overseas troops would be adequately supplied. At the same time, the wholesale and retail price structure of all goods was frozen.[2] The U.S. government issued ration books that limited the amount of food goods that a customer could buy. Government controls limiting the volume of trade meant that grocery management had to develop innovative means to capture retail business in a constrained market.

Food promotional schemes became a way to capture the attention of customers. Stores issued booklets that emphasized good eating habits, good nutrition, and the importance of not wasting food.[3] Not all food goods were treated equally in advertising and booklet promotions. Meat, butter, sugar, eggs, and condensed milk were highly controlled during the war. These foods were sent overseas, and condensed milk was also used as baby formula. Although rationed, vegetables were more available than these goods, and grocers actively promoted produce. At the same time, grocers needed promotions that would attract repeat customers. Many stores encouraged customers to bring their own grocery bags as a way to save paper for the war effort, a tactic that simultaneously reduced overhead costs for stores. Grocery stores, especially supermarkets, promoted campaigns that were in the spirit of the war effort but were also profitable.

One of the greatest limitations facing grocers was the rationing of gasoline. As supermarkets became larger and more prevalent, grocers built fewer stores, and chain store management eliminated many older, small stores. Increasingly, stores were more distant from one another than they had been. This problem was greater for supermarkets with parking lots than for small, neighborhood stores, because the large volume supermarket depended on shoppers being able to drive to their store. To counteract this problem, some supermarket managers conducted ad campaigns that urged shoppers to car pool for their shopping trips, and they went so far as to create a clearinghouse at their stores for customers seeking car pools. Although car pooling was promoted as a courtesy for customers, this service was a means for management to gain a market advantage during an era of limited expansion.

Grocery stores faced labor shortages, food restrictions, and gasoline rationing, but grocers learned to use innovative sales techniques to respond to these shortcomings. Self-service, frozen foods, and non-food items were a few ways grocers circumvented the market constraints mandated by the war effort.

Self-service had been introduced into supermarkets during the 1930s, but grocery management had not totally completed the conversion to self-service. Packaged goods, such as canned goods and boxed cereals, were easily converted to self-service, because such items were not labor intensive. Clerks had only to stock the shelves with these pre-packaged goods. On the other hand, meat, produce, and dairy products were perishable and were not as easily converted to packaging. Inadequate refrigeration units and packaging materials had prevented grocery management from developing ways to pre-pack perishable food for self-service. Grocery management needed to implement self-service to make up for the wartime labor shortage.

Self-service in the meat department was a significant way to decrease labor costs and increase sales. Grocery managers had realized that converting to self-service reduced the amount of labor needed to prepare and sell a food product because customers provided the service labor themselves. The main barrier was the design of refrigeration compartments used to display meat. Although glass meat counters were used in the 1920s, these cases were ultimately inefficient in a supermarket. Customers looked in the case, made a selection, and waited their turn to be served. The butcher took the customer's selection, made any necessary cuts, wrapped the meat, weighed it, and wrote a price on the package. The meat counter was the last refuge of clerk service, because no open, self-service meat case had been developed. In the late 1930s, A&P engineers were the pioneers that developed the first self-service meat counter. The result was that meat sales increased by about 30 percent without increasing labor costs. A&P had taken the lead in developing the refrigerated case, and some supermarkets converted their glass front cases to open cases so that customers could handle their own purchases.[4] Although meat departments were rarely completely self-service during World War II, innovative store managers who introduced some form of self-service at the meat counter reduced their overhead. At the same time, grocery management realized that there was a connection between the volume of meat sold and other purchases in the store. They found that for every dollar spent on meat purchases customers spent four more dollars for other items in the store, and as meat purchases increased, other purchases increased as well.[5]

By necessity, frozen foods became more prevalent during wartime because canned goods were shipped overseas and tin was needed for production of war goods. Before World War II, fruits and vegetables were often displayed

5.1 Clerk Service Meat Counter, Falley's Grocery Store, Topeka, Kansas, 1941 (Courtesy of the Kansas State Historical Society)

without cooling, but the frozen food industry was just emerging. Although founded in 1923 to manufacture frozen foods, the Birds Eye Company did not begin to penetrate the supermarket trade until the late 1930s. A major problem was the design and production of frozen food cabinets. Even when cabinets became available, many grocery retailers were reluctant to buy them for fear that frozen vegetables and fruits would prove too expensive. Prepared frozen foods, such as brick soups, creamed chicken, and roast turkey with dressing, were available as early as 1939. Such food items meant reduced labor in the kitchen for consumers, and some supermarkets did introduce self-service frozen food cabinets. During World War II, fruits and vegetables were the mainstay of frozen foods. Initially it was the corporate chains such as Jewel Food Stores in Chicago and King Kullen in New York that expanded into frozen foods. Refrigerated cabinets were in short supply, and initially grocers used the coffin type, with closed tops like ice cream cabinets. In 1943, the Penn Fruit Company grocery chain not only equipped all its stores with self-service units but also removed the covers from the cabinets. Customers responded by buying more food items in open, self-service cabinets.[6] Yet, the growth of frozen foods was limited because equipment manufacturers had to devote their energies and resources to wartime production and could not meet the demand for cabinets.

Whereas self-service and frozen foods helped supermarket management to sustain an advantage over competitors, their expansion into non-food products was substantial and significant. Because supermarkets had to fill empty shelves, health and beauty aids and general household goods replaced many food products, filling shelves made empty by rationing.[7] Before the war, some supermarkets had experimented with a concession system in which store space was leased to a concessionaire who sold non-food items. Store management soon realized that they could use their wholesale network to buy health and beauty aids, and they sold these goods themselves. The critical issue for supermarket managers was to sustain a dollar volume of sales per square foot of retail space whether or not food was sold. Non-food goods enabled supermarket management to expand their diversity of goods which were able to attract customers. By entering the non-food goods trade permanently, supermarket management created economic stability and diversity as well as strengthening the supermarket as a one-stop shopping place.

THE POSTWAR BOOM

By the end of World War II, the supermarket was a retail system that had been forged by the expansion of mass retail distribution and economic hard times. Grocery managers had learned that the supermarket could significantly out-perform the small traditional grocery store. Yet the conversion to the supermarket was limited because the depression had slowed the suburbanization of America and car ownership. World War II had followed, and although Americans were employed, on the battlefront or the home front, they were unable to spend their disposable income due to rationing and the wartime economy. Victory and the war's end began a new age of American prosperity.

This postwar economy was an era of full employment and high disposable income for goods and services. World War II had a devastating effect on most developed countries, but the United States emerged largely unscathed because the mainland was never attacked. With its factories in place, the United States quickly became the world's leading export nation. With such a flow of dollars into the nation's economy, the American people wanted to buy goods that they had been forced to postpone for years. At the same time, the population boom was in full swing as war babies became young consumers. The increase in births and increased disposable income led the American family to want consumer goods to fit its needs. Most families wanted to own a new home and to buy an automobile, and these demands shaped the predominant American landscape of the future, suburbia.[8] Once the postwar economy was unleashed, the suburban movement flourished and the supermarket flourished with it.

Remaining local neighborhood stores were unable to respond to the postwar rise of supermarkets in suburbia. Retail grocery expansion became a race to the suburbs, a race that only big-time competitors were able to win. Large affiliated and non-affiliated independents and corporate chains had the necessary capital or financial leverage to invest in store expansion. In comparison, most owners of small neighborhood grocery stores had neither the investment capital nor the real estate expertise to enter the era of suburban grocery retailing. At the same time, the neighborhoods around the mom and pop stores began to change. More affluent families moved to the suburbs, and the families who moved into their vacated homes often had smaller incomes. The competitive gap between all independent local grocers and chain grocers became greater as corporate managers for the chains moved into the suburbs with new supermarkets.

The postwar growth of supermarkets was tremendous. In 1946, the supermarket accounted for only 3 percent of the total number of grocery stores in the United States, and its sales were 28 percent of total volume sales in the nation. By 1954, the supermarket still represented only 5.1 percent of all grocery stores, but its sales represented 48 percent of total sales volume. The total number of retail grocery stores had not increased significantly, but the supermarket's sales volume had increased by 71 percent.[9] There were several reasons for this dramatic increase in sales. First, although there was a small increase in the number of supermarkets, many small stores were eliminated. Between 1946 and 1954, the major corporate chains reduced their total number of stores by over 31 percent.[10] Corporate management had clearly adopted the strategy of abandoning small stores located in the inner city and expanding in suburbia with supermarkets, and at the same time supermarkets were growing larger.

New household appliances in the suburban home helped the supermarket make the transition from a successful experiment to a dominant design for retailing. American families moved to suburbia not only to own a home but also to have more space, and they were encouraged to fill their new, larger homes with household goods. In the decade following the war, the typical home increasingly included a refrigerator, an electric mixer, a washing machine, and a vacuum cleaner. In the 1960s, dishwashers and clothes dryers became more common.[11] It was the suburban households that could afford these items the most, and these appliances needed to be supplied by retail services. But the most important household item to the grocery trade was the refrigerator. The sale of refrigerators in the United States increased by 82 percent from 1946 to 1955. In the same time period, grocery management increased the number of items carried in their stores by 57 percent.[12] As suburban households increased both their ability to store food and the amount of disposable income available for food and non-food items, the supermarket inevitably grew to meet the suburban demand.

Many new supermarkets were located in suburban shopping centers. Commercial real estate projects followed suburban development after the war just as the taxpayer strip had followed suburban expansion at the turn of the twentieth century. These centers were located on a town's old commercial approach strip or on a new arterial street designated for commercial use in new suburban areas. In the 1920s, developers built the nation's first shopping center complexes, which typically included a grocery store. By the late 1930s, they often used a corporate chain supermarket as an anchor store in their shopping centers.[13] The postwar layout patterns for shopping centers typically repeated earlier linear layouts used on taxpayer strips and early shopping centers. Developers often built L-shaped centers on corner lots to maximize store front exposure to passing traffic. U-shaped centers were less common and were usually located on sites in the middle of the block. In all these layouts, supermarkets became anchor stores linked to other retail shops.[14] The shopping center reinforced one-stop shopping, because a customer could shop at a number of stores without having to travel. Just as important, shoppers became accustomed to shopping at the same place whether or not they visited other stores. The postwar shopping center was by design a Big Bear Supermarket turned wrong side out. Whereas Big Bear had leased floor space inside the building to other retail concessionaires in the 1930s, these retail goods were now outside the grocery store but within the same building complex. Shopping centers were retail magnets in which a supermarket had strong drawing power.

Grocery management had to decide whether or not they wanted to lease space in a shopping center or to own a store and site. Many corporate chains,

5.2 L-Shaped 1 Stop Shopping Center with a Supermarket as an Anchor Store, Washougal, Washington, 1950s (Courtesy of Richard Longstreth)

such as A&P, had preferred to lease rather than buy store space. In fact in the 1950s, A&P had a company policy of a maximum lease of five years. Shopping center developers wanted longer leases to secure the financial ability to pay the mortgages on their projects.[15] Grocery chains knew that a fast-growing suburbia was in flux, and many chains decided to lease space rather than to build their own supermarkets. Before the war, grocery management had used some statistical analysis to locate stores, but with the small stores of that period, the location of a single facility was not critical. With larger and fewer stores, grocery management had to be more careful in locating new stores. They often depended on shopping center developers to lead the way for capturing good sites and gaining loan approvals from financial institutions that insisted on sound investment and site analysis.[16] With continuous expansion, grocery management knew that today's good location was potentially tomorrow's obsolete site as new centers followed suburban growth. Using a lease in the shopping center made economic sense to many grocery chains. Management thought it was more important to follow the tide of suburban movement, rather than to invest capital in a store site that potentially had a short economic life.

Leasing space was often an unavoidable but difficult alternative for non-affiliated independents and affiliated-independent members. Not having the financial security of large corporate chains, these grocers had to finance their own stores on an individual basis. The capital requirements were just too high for most grocers. Supermarkets were significantly more expensive than the increasingly obsolete small grocery store. At the same time, these non-affiliated independents and affiliated-independent members were less able to compete with corporate chains for locating stores in the best shopping centers. Developers were willing to offer corporate chains, such as A&P and Safeway, lower rental rates than individual store owners, because the corporate chains were more able to attract customers. Local grocers could gain shopping center locations when they worked together with developers before a project was approved and built. In a few cases, developers found it profitable to include an independent grocer in a large shopping center by locating the store immediately beside a corporate grocery chain store. The developer's strategy was to maximize the center's drawing power without damaging the retail mix of stores.[17] Developers, however, tended to take a chance with affiliated and non-affiliated independents only when the shopping center completely dominated its own trade area.[18]

Shopping center development trends began to have an effect on supermarket operations. In the 1950s, three types of centers became distinguishable—neighborhood, community, and regional. The neighborhood type had a gross floor area of 40,000 square feet, and the community type averaged 150,000 square feet with the regional center averaging 400,000 square feet. The regional type was the last stage of development for shopping centers, but it set a limit on supermarkets. Its pulling power was based on comparative shopping and serving a population base of 100,000 or more. Although the supermarket was included in early regional centers, developers found that it was not a successful economic player, because supermarkets seldom pulled customers from distances farther than five to six minutes in driving time.[19] The neighborhood and community shopping centers became the realistic locations for supermarkets rather than the regional centers.

There was an inevitable economic hierarchy between store owners in these centers. A supermarket had to blend with other retail activities rather than dominate them if all the shopping center's stores were to be profitable. Given this principle, developers did not want a supermarket to have square footage out of proportion to the total available leasable space. Grocery chains were converting to larger stores, and by 1956, the average supermarket was 18,000 square feet. Increasingly, corporate chains were leasing space in community shopping centers in order to maximize volume sales through large super-markets. With developers preferring corporate chain store tenants, other grocers were often left with only the neighborhood center as a lease alternative. A neighborhood center supermarket was functional at 12,000 square feet, and non-affiliated and affiliated independents and voluntary chain members were more able to afford a facility this size than the larger stores found in community shopping centers.[20] Yet, a neighborhood supermarket was unable to sustain a volume of trade as large as a supermarket in a community shopping center. Corporate grocery chains were able to further their market domination over other grocers by leasing space in larger shopping centers, which had greater customer drawing power.

Grocery management decided to finance and build their own supermarkets when they were convinced that the surrounding market trade area was sufficiently stable. Under these circumstances, non-affiliated independents and affiliated-independent members who could afford a mortgage loan were able to benefit the most by becoming a landlord. Federal tax deductions on mortgage interest and building depreciation were significant in reducing overhead costs while building up loan equity. Undoubtedly, the ownership approach was attractive to grocers when shopping centers developed slowly in their communities. These conditions were most beneficial to non-affiliated independents and affiliated-independent members, but corporate chains did not ignore store ownership when they considered it a worthwhile alternative. Although the lease approach was used in towns, grocers often built their own freestanding supermarkets with parking lots in order to establish a high volume business. The need to build freestanding supermarkets in many American towns was as true for corporate chains as it was for independents and affiliated independents. In cities, shopping centers did not encapsule every supermarket and freestanding supermarkets were a common sight in the 1950s. Grocery management had to decide constantly whether it was more profitable to lease a building or to build their own facility.[21] Real estate investment worked best for grocery management when retail trade areas for their supermarkets remained fixed rather than changing with booming suburban expansion.

In a few cases, buying and leasing store space were combined together by grocery chains. The Alpha Beta Food Markets, Inc. chain used a sequential strategy with their "Buy, Build, Sell, and Lease Back" policy. The chain bought the land and built a store building to meet market needs. They then sold the property to large banks and insurance companies from whom they leased the property.[22] Equipment leasing was even done by some chains. The reasons for this sequential strategy were twofold. First, the chain was able to design a store to meet their exact needs to maximize profits. Grocery chains were not always able to satisfy their design demands when working with a shopping center developer. Second, corporate management was able to free up investment capital and to remain flexible with their store locations. By selling the store and leasing it, corporate management was able to secure new building loans with their freed-up capital. Thus, their capital was always revolving from one store to the next. Corporate management gained mobility, because if a store location proved to be less profitable than anticipated, they were able to discontinue their building lease and locate a new store elsewhere. Under these conditions, a grocery chain could move money and space at its discretion to maximize profits.

Affiliated-independent members had a distinct advantage over non-affiliated independents for new store development. Locally owned affiliated independents, such as I.G.A. and Red & White, did have a national image, although not as strong as corporate chains, such as A&P, Kroger, or Safeway. Non-affiliated independents were largely unknown to the public, and shopping center developers and bankers were hesitant to consider their plans for store expansion. In comparison, the affiliated independent store owners gained support from their grocery management. Most national headquarters of affiliated independents had established finance corporations that provided low-interest assistance loans to their members, and with this support, local banks became more willing to loan affiliated-independent members the necessary money to build new stores. An affiliated independent's corporate management, however, was only willing to finance feasible projects. This financial and analysis edge over independents enabled affiliated chain members not only to build new stores but also to occupy new ones as tenants in shopping centers.[23] Bankers and developers were willing to support affiliated independents more than non-affiliated independents, although neither of these grocers were as strong as corporate chains.

During the 1950s, there were significant economic undercurrents coming from the location and dominance of large supermarkets. There was a shift from the freestanding store to the shopping center store. From 1954 to 1955, the number of supermarkets located in shopping centers increased from 48 percent to a majority of 53 percent, and most of these stores were in large community shopping centers.[24] Corporate chains led this shift to large stores in large centers, but affiliated and non-affiliated independents were changing as well. Initially, affiliated-independent members made the shift from small stores to the superette, essentially a small dollar volume supermarket. But as the 1950s progressed, these grocers significantly reduced the number of small stores and gradually, the number of superettes. Affiliated-independent ownership of large supermarkets was increasing. From 1954 to 1956, affiliated-independent members and non-affiliated independents increased their supermarket ownership from 2 to 4 percent, and during this same period, these supermarkets finally became more dominant in volume sales than superettes and small stores.[25] The corporate chains had led the way to large supermarkets in large shopping centers, and affiliated independents were beginning to follow them.

POSTWAR DESIGN

After World War II, design innovation became an important means to boost the supermarket's volume of trade. Previously, the supermarket had been an economic success, but success was mainly based on the store being large rather than attractive or efficient. The war had prevented any significant building construction, and during the postwar boom, grocery management had many opportunities to experiment with the design of new supermarkets.

The most dramatic postwar supermarket design could be seen in the free-standing store. Before the war, architectural expression in supermarkets was advanced when grocery management hired architects who sometimes applied the styles of Art Deco and Streamline Moderne. Postwar architecture in America, however, was fully entrenched in the modern movement. Although brick was still used in building facades, steel and glass had become more prevalent in building design. Aesthetic overtones of the international style were evident in store facade designs emphasizing exposed structural steel elements and expansive glass areas. More modest storefronts used brick, but with glass added as a dominant facade element. In most of these designs, store owners used flat roofs and flat canopies. The need to articulate exterior facades became more critical for grocery management because each side of a building faced either a street or its own parking lot. The traditional taxpayer strip store required the owner to articulate only the front facade, but with the freestanding store, it was necessary for management to maintain a cosmetic front on every building facade that was exposed to the public's eye. Side facades received some modest aesthetic treatment, if only the continuation of a brick pattern or canopy. Perhaps the most important element that enabled the freestanding store to have a singular identity on the strip was the parking lot. Supermarkets were larger than most other retail businesses, and the parking lot's open space enabled passersby to view the supermarket. Modern design placed less emphasis on ornateness, and with a facade emphasis on structural elements, glass, and tower signs. The supermarket on a large parking lot was a major statement on the strip, designed to impress the automobile driver rather than the pedestrian.

Supermarkets in shopping centers were more constrained in design than freestanding stores. Although developers wanted supermarkets for their customer pulling power, they wanted these stores to fit visually within the overall design scheme of their shopping centers. Although the store was sometimes physically separated from other building sections of the center, the supermarket's facade design conformed to the overall architecture of the building complex.[26] The supermarket sustained its individual identity through its signage and the ability of shoppers to see grocery goods through a glass facade. Supermarkets in shopping centers were part of an integrated retail package, and developers had to present a visually unified image to sell the package.

Glass was a critical building material for promoting the supermarket. The traditional grocery store typically used glass windows to display food goods and small signs to announce prices and sales. Grocery management changed the window format in the postwar supermarket. The small, traditional store was oriented to the scale of the pedestrian, whereas the supermarket was proportional to the automobile. When passing customers read window signs in the supermarket, they were driving either on a major street or in the store's parking lot, not walking on a sidewalk. It became less necessary for grocery managers to display food products in their large supermarket windows, because customers who decided to stop and then to shop were still too distant to view window displays. They were either on the road or in the parking lot. The window frontage of supermarkets essentially became a billboard. Windows were constantly changing with butcher paper signs announcing special sales, but there was a constancy. A window storefront was increasingly used by grocery managers to sell the store's image. With well-lighted interiors seen through glass facades, customers were able to imagine that the supermarket was a modern cornucopia, which meant that the store was able to serve any desire for food goods that a customer might have. Glass became the lens through which to market the supermarket.

Store owners used building signs to identify the store immediately. Numerous supermarkets used a vertical sign that often appeared to be an integral part of the building's structure. In the 1930s and 1940s, many Art Deco–styled stores included a central tower, which store owners used both as a sign and as the main building entrance. As the supermarket was moved farther back from the street to provide parking, this small tower served as a dramatic sign to identify the supermarket on the strip. The use of such towers was most apparent with the freestanding store where the store owner was able to dictate the store's design. Developers were less willing for tower signs to be a part of a supermarket's design in a shopping center, because such signs were much larger than signs for other retail stores in the complex. Instead, they used tower signs to promote the whole shopping center.[27] The tower

5.3 The Modern Movement, Buri Buri Supermarket, 1950s (Courtesy of the *Progressive Grocer*)

sign was a more critical design element to promote the freestanding super-market than its counterpart in a shopping center.

Some store owners experimented with supermarket floor plans in the 1950s. B. Sumner Gruzen was one of the first American architects to consider seriously the design of supermarkets. In the 1930s, he initially emphasized rectilinear layouts with the systematic repetition of aisles.[28] But with postwar expansion, grocery management began to criticize the fact that supermarkets were too standardized and looked too much alike.[29] Gruzen agreed that the standardization had become a rut when he said: "How many housewives, if they were taken to a market blindfolded, and then had the blindfolds removed, would be able to name the market in which they were shopping? The average housewife would be unable to do so unless specific names identified the store!"[30] Lansing Shield, president of the Grand Union grocery chain, asked Gruzen to provide an innovative layout design for one of the company's new stores, and he did. His design solution was a wagon wheel approach in which the wheel spoke space was grocery gondolas and aisles. Wall displays and checkout stands were not radically different, only the interior floor area. Other architects proposed diagonal and herringbone aisle arrangements, but these layouts proved to be an inefficient use of space. Gruzen's wagon wheel approach was 20 percent less efficient than a conventional plan with a rec-tilinear grid layout. Grand Union corporate management was hoping that the benefits of Gruzen's design innovation would be greater than the costs of spatial inefficiency.[31] But as the 1950s progressed, floor plan layouts of food departments with gondolas and aisles remained essentially rectilinear layouts as in the past, and successful interior design experiments occurred elsewhere in the supermarket.

Many interior plans were shaped by economic reasons. Refrigerated meat counters had typically been placed at the rear of the store near backrooms for meat processing and other food storage. Produce was put in refrigerated, self-service counters, and a nearby backroom work space was needed for produce clerks to prepare fruits and vegetables for display. At the same time, many store owners found it profitable to confront customers immediately with their produce departments rather than having them at the back of the store. To resolve this dilemma, store engineers designed an L-shaped interior work-room space that ran along one side wall and the back wall. Some stores used both side walls and created a U-shaped configuration. Store engineers con-tinued to use the rear backroom in small grocery stores, less than 10,000 square feet, because the added workroom space for produce could be ad-equately included along the store's back wall. Store engineers found that larger square footage gave them more flexibility in laying out backroom space.[32] But grocery management did not always want flexibility in their floor plan layouts. The Winn-Dixie chain decided in the 1950s to have four different store sizes, with all their stores having the same basic plan. Store depth remained about 140 feet, but the width varied from 70 to 120 feet.[33] By

5.4 Tower Sign, Kwik-Chek Supermarket, 1950s (Courtesy of the Food Marketing Institute)

5.5 The Supermarket as Design Efficiency, Rusty's I.G.A., Lawrence, Kansas, 1950s (Courtesy of the Kansas Collection, University of Kansas Libraries)

standardizing their plans, the Winn-Dixie chain was able to control design costs, quite opposite to the Grand Union wagon wheel experiment. Although experimentation was tried, most store owners relied on interior plan changes that reduced overhead costs.

The interior atmosphere of supermarkets was significantly influenced by equipment systems. After World War II, equipment manufacturers focused their attention on the design of open-refrigeration cabinets, which were larger and more efficient than prewar systems. This equipment allowed store owners to further complete self-service, especially with meat and frozen foods. Although open refrigerated cabinets were introduced during the war, most store owners actually installed this equipment in the postwar years. They installed systematic lighting systems that allowed for incandescent lighting instead of traditional fixtures with light bulbs. A major step was air conditioning, and by 1956, 80 percent of all new supermarkets had music and air conditioning.[34] These equipment systems enhanced not only customer comfort and convenience but also the image that the supermarket was modern. The modernity achieved through these systems, however, was an extension of Taylorism, scientific management for production. Lighting displayed products more clearly to customers. Air conditioning encouraged shoppers to extend the time of their shopping trips by eliminating physical discomfort. Self-service counters helped to reduce labor needed to service customers. Equipment systems increased electrical energy costs, but store owners found that the economic benefits of these systems outweighed the costs.

Grocery management improved the design of display cabinets and shelves. In the 1930s, shelf cabinets called gondolas were usually made of wood, and during World War II, metal cabinets were not possible due to war production requirements for metal. Grocers even used the traditional laundry basket for displays in the 1940s. In the 1930s, open-top display tables were popular among grocers for showing canned goods, but most of these display tables were small because most grocery stores were limited in size.[35] After the war, grocery management changed display equipment to match the size and volume trade requirements of supermarkets. Gondolas were made of steel with adjustable shelves, but there were differences among store owners concerning the height of gondolas. Some managers thought that gondolas should be short to discourage pilferage and enable the customer to have a full view of the store. In time, however, store owners used gondolas above eye level, but within an arm's reach to maximize shelf space. End displays, positioned at the end of gondolas along major thoroughfare aisles, were often managed and designed by trained personnel from the grocery company's headquarters whose task was to promote certain food products.[36] Store managers increased the size of open-table displays to island cabinet displays for produce, which were increasingly popular among grocers. These islands allowed not only a larger volume of food goods but also wide aisles, which contributed to a more open floor plan in the produce section. Such openness was undoubtedly an attempt by managers to make their produce department more visually appealing to customers.[37] All display designs fulfilled two functions in supermarkets. First, management wanted equipment to be more productive, either by being larger or more efficient in design. Second, they wanted displays to be more appealing in order to entice customers to buy more food goods. Grocery management increasingly saw the cabinet displays as stationary machines on a factory floor used to produce an increased volume of retail sales.

Grocers introduced new elements for the interior design of supermarkets as a response to changes in the American way of life. In the 1950s, many supermarkets included kiddie corrals. With play equipment or a television set, baby boom children were occupied while the mother did her grocery shopping. As a matter of convenience and strategy, grocery management aimed to encourage housewives to shop more often and to focus their attention on buying groceries rather than tending their children. The color of the store's interior became more varied. In the past, supermarkets were stark white in order to stress order and cleanliness, but with stores increasing in floor space, the total white approach became not only monotonous but also harsh. Grocers wanted the supermarket to feel visually as a psychological extension of the home as well as to be functionally efficient. Bright and soft colors made the store interior more appealing to shoppers, and at the same time, grocery management was able to distinguish food departments by color, which was a means for shoppers to learn quickly how the store was organized. Color visually allowed grocery management to departmentalize their stores while making shoppers feel comfortable.[38] Behind the shopper's stage set, changes were also made. The coffee break had emerged as a demand by American labor as a reprieve from work. Organized labor began to have a penetrating effect on all aspects of American work. These factors led to the creation of the employee lounge.[39] However modest, the lounge was a spatial political statement that labor relations could not be ignored by management. At the same time, the lounge made labor relations visually concrete and unchanging, especially when the store manager had an office. Although without great fanfare, concepts introduced in store interiors reflected changes and responses to American culture and labor relations.

Many interior changes were mechanistic devices to reduce labor costs and to provide a higher volume of sales and faster service. Grocers introduced the price tag stamp as a means to reduce the time clerks spent writing food prices by hand on every food package. At the same time, grocery management introduced price tag molding, which illustrated the price of a product on the edge of a gondola shelf. Price tag molding was a device that not only made the customer instantly aware of prices but, according to grocers, also encouraged impulse buying. Manufacturers increased the size of the shopping cart. In the postwar period, Americans were able to afford more goods, and

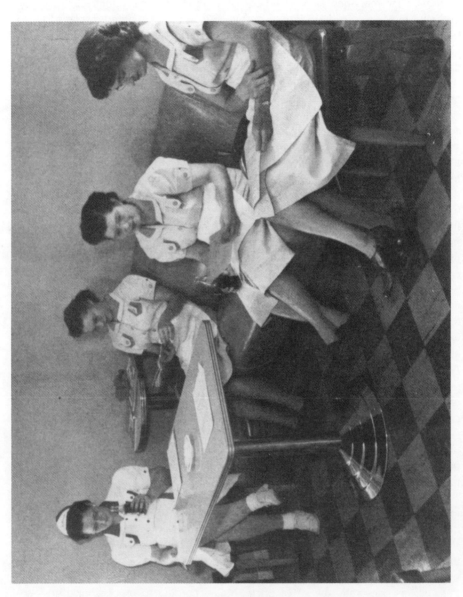

5.6 Introduction of the Employees' Lounge, 1950s (Courtesy of the *Progressive Grocer*)

a larger cart was an enticement to increase their food purchases. The checkout stand had been a traditional bottleneck for processing customers, and changes were made. Cash registers listed individual purchases on an itemized slip, and cashiers were able to avoid customer fraud and to account fully for purchases.[40] Cashiers were taught not to look at the register's keys but to focus only on looking at the price tag of the food product. This change in procedure significantly saved time at the cash register. To speed up the cashier's processing of sales, the round, turntable checkout counter was introduced.[41] But the cashier's role was not just to process customers. A more important role was to prevent customer dissatisfaction among shoppers caused by having to wait in long lines. If cashiers were inefficient, the supermarket lost customers to another store. Indirectly, cashiers contributed to volume sales by keeping customers satisfied. Whether it was a pricing device, an improved grocery cart, or a mechanized checkout stand, grocery management increasingly found it necessary to introduce efficiency devices for supermarkets as they increased in size.

A basic change in the interior appearance of the postwar supermarket was the types of products sold and the equipment used to display them. Most prominent were non-food items and prepackaged perishable food goods. The further advancement of self-service and product expansion in the supermarket was a major reason for interior adjustments to the store.

Grocery management initially introduced non-food goods as a means to counteract the shortage of many food goods during World War II, but they soon realized that this necessary move was an idea with a future. After the war, management significantly expanded floor space for non-food goods. Health goods, cosmetics, children's books, magazines, records, glassware, hardware, toys, hosiery, and even children's wear were introduced or expanded in supermarkets during the 1950s.[42] The gondola shelf system was adequate for displaying most of these products, but special display cases, such as for records and magazines, had to be added. But more than anything else, non-food items became distinguishable in the supermarket as entire aisles were devoted to these goods. Although in a systematic fashion, supermarket managers were partially recreating the general store atmosphere that had ceased to exist. This consolidation, however, had more to do with bringing the hardware store, the clothing store, and the local pharmacy shop into the grocery store. Increasingly, non-food goods changed the interior of supermarkets from just food to a variety of displayed items.

Grocery management made major adjustments to store interiors in the postwar era in response to self-service innovations made during the war years. Self-service had been increasingly emphasized in the grocery store since the early days of A&P economy stores, but after World War II, management aims were directed to "complete" self-service in all food departments. In 1946, there were only twenty-eight supermarkets with complete self-service in the meat department, but by 1953, 53 percent of all supermarkets in the United States offered total self-service for prepackaged meats. Management's reason was clear: do anything to reduce labor costs and to increase volume trade. Initially, customers did not approve of complete self-service meat counters, because they wanted personal service. Yet, management promoted self-service as a form of convenience to maximize profitability. Complete self-service was extended to the dairy department, and by 1953, over 90 percent of all supermarkets had complete self-service dairy departments with prepackaged cheese and cartoned milk. Fresh fruit and vegetables were even prepackaged for complete self-service in 44 percent of all supermarkets by 1953.[43] Produce departments never became totally dominated by prepackaging, but grocery produce clerks increasingly became background suppliers to counters rather than customer servers. Complete self-service was also expanded by the increased popularity of frozen foods. Grocery management built new supermarkets with projected figures for the linear feet of cabinet space for frozen foods, but store managers constantly found these projections to underestimate the demand for these goods. To implement complete self-service for meats, dairy goods, and frozen foods, grocery management needed improved refrigeration equipment, and this equipment changed the interior character of the supermarket.

Complete self-service for perishable foods helped to create an interior ambience of customers being served by machines rather than people. The growing linear feet of refrigeration units visually demonstrated that these pieces of equipment were increasingly essential to the supermarket. A consequence of making food cabinets more visible and accessible to shoppers was that butchers and produce clerks increasingly worked behind the scenes. The butchers' activity was seen less by the public, and although produce clerks had often readied produce before customers, they were increasingly given a workroom in the back of the store to prepare goods for display. As equipment was put out front for the shopper and labor was located away from the display area, the supermarket increasingly presented a public image of systematic efficiency without human labor and its problems.

Grocery management went to great lengths to demonstrate that the supermarket was community minded by creating festive and cultural stage plays. Beginning in the 1930s, store owners had created festive events for supermarkets, and after World War II these exhibitions became even more flamboyant. Grand openings and promotions often had a carnival atmosphere. Clowns, Indian dancing, and special promoters, such as Johnnie, the bellboy from Philip Morris cigarettes, were used to draw the customer's attention. Taxi service was even provided at a very low cost for shoppers with groceries, a surrogate form of public transportation. One supermarket manager went so far as to have a wedding held in the store as a promotional device. Free vacations, store anniversaries, and holiday promotions were all used not only to add gaiety to store advertising but also to demonstrate that customers could participate in a form of public celebration. Some supermarkets had art exhibits, and other stores helped the local community by serving as a branch

5.7 Frozen Foods and Self-Service Refrigeration Cabinets as New Supermarket Technologies, late 1940s (Courtesy of the *Progressive Grocer*)

of a public library system. Grocery management aided all sorts of public campaigns. Blood drives, United Way campaigns, high-school band car washes in the parking lot, and other events were used to draw present and future customers.[44]

Trading stamps became a major promotional device in the postwar boom. Department stores introduced trading stamps in 1891, but food chains did not fully offer stamps until 1953. Customers received an amount of stamps relative to their grocery purchases. After saving the stamps, they visited a redemption center to exchange their stamp booklets for a variety of products, such as household goods, toys, and recreation equipment. Some grocery stores used stamp companies, such as the Sperry & Hutchinson Company, which issues S&H Green Stamps, to provide stamps and to operate redemption centers. Grocery management had mixed feelings about trading stamps. Some store operators found that the sales benefits from stamps outweighed their costs while other store owners did not.[45] Grocery managers who were eager to gain an edge over their competitors adopted trading stamps immediately. However, a few chains and independents ceased their involvement, whereas others waited to become involved. A&P only began using trading stamps in 1961 because corporate management held the belief that offering the lowest sales price was a better marketing device than using trading stamps.[46] Grocery management continued to have mixed feelings about the benefits versus the costs of using trading stamps to promote food sales.

The supermarket had become a more efficient machine through technical innovations and physical design. Increasingly, grocery management focused on maximizing the volume of sales in their stores, but the increased number of items began to complicate economic efficiency. In 1946, an average supermarket carried 3,000 different items, and this number had increased to 5,800 by 1959.[47] Inevitably, supermarkets grew in square footage to accommodate this increased volume, and grocery management had to be concerned about multiplying their mistakes from a small store into a supermarket that was five times as large. Micro design concerns, such as end displays for aisles, became more critical as aisles multiplied in number. As a total shopping store, managers realized that not every item could attain high turnover, but improper display and over-allocation of shelf space to low-turnover products led to reduced profits. At the other end of the scale, store location was even more significant than in the pre–World War II era. When compared to a small store, a large supermarket was a great expenditure, and it had to be more secure and provide long-term profits from a single spatial source.[48] Grocery management saw supermarket design as the design of economic productivity, and this machine was only as good as the management and labor who ran it.

CONFLICTS OVER SPACE IN THE POSTWAR ERA

Conflicts over supermarkets were of two types. First, chain wars were continued in suburbia, and second, the rise of unionized labor after World

War II created new confrontations for grocery management. Both of these conflicts had implications for the spatial character of all grocery stores.

The domination of corporate chains continued in the postwar era, but these organizations had more trouble in sustaining their advantages than in the past. The federal government began to take an active role against corporate chains by filing anti-trust suits against them. In a twelve-year battle against A&P, the federal government attempted to dismember the company into its regional divisions, but it failed. However, A&P's Atlantic Commission Company (ACCO) was ordered dissolved by the federal courts. ACCO was A&P's wholesale produce company which acted as both buyer and seller. As a result, A&P "was forbidden to purchase any food products for the outside trade [other grocers], or to act as agent or broker in any area where it was selling at retail."[49] Most of the complaints surrounding ACCO was A&P's ability to control prices through wholesaling. For all the publicity surrounding the A&P anti-trust case, very little damage was done to the company's structure, although A&P became very conservative in its wholesale practices in order to avoid further legal entanglements.[50] The A&P case brought public attention in the 1940s and 1950s to the fact that large corporate chains were a major force in the retail grocery trade. However, the A&P case reflected old battles from the 1930s when the Robinson-Patman Act was enacted by the U.S. Congress to control corporate chains. In the 1950s, new corporate dynamics set the stage for an entirely new legal battlefront, anti-merger cases.

Chain merger was a strategy used by many corporate chains to sustain their power base in the grocery trade. After World War II, American suburbia grew quickly, and all grocers had a share of the building expansion pie. In the late 1940s and early 1950s, grocery management was constantly trying to fill the demand for new stores, but by the late 1950s, suburbia was saturated with supermarkets. Although new locations were pioneered, corporate management realized that economic growth could not be sustained if they were constrained to their current store sites. To expand their store locations, many corporate chains purchased other grocery chains. Corporate management realized that there were fewer problems in acquiring existing locations than in pioneering new stores. The control over space was regional as well as urban. By acquiring smaller chains, a large corporate chain was able to spread the risk of failure over a wide geographical area. If one region was to suffer economic hardships and loss of buying power, it was easier for a corporate chain to sustain such a loss if it had stores in other regions. Chain management had to decide what to do with the inventory of stores that they purchased from another chain. Inevitably, they closed unprofitable stores and sold the building property. Profitable stores were remodeled to meet their company requirements. The merger movement quickened the pace of eliminating older, smaller stores, which were located in the inner city. Simultaneously, the addition of profitable locations expanded the total volume of sales of the buying chain. With chain mergers, trade areas tended not to become oversaturated with supermarkets, but as a result suburbanites had fewer grocery chains from which to shop.[51] Merger was a means for larger corporate chains to sustain their competitive advantage over affiliated and non-affiliated independents and small chains through the control of store locations.

Chain mergers gave the purchasing grocery chain greater access to capital. Because of their size and diversified store locations, larger corporate chains were better able to borrow more easily and cheaply from lending institutions. Such funds were used to upgrade stores as well as to build new facilities or to equip leased space. Corporate management often favored the lease approach, because new supermarkets increasingly required expensive equipment, such as refrigerated cabinets for self-service, and huge inventories for stocking food products. Given these large costs, management in corporate chains became less inclined to invest heavily in real estate.[52] Although the lease approach allowed many corporate chains to expand, chain acquisition was the critical step that enabled a chain to gain the financial leverage for store expansion. The managements of corporate chains realized that their leverage over money led to their leverage over space and vice versa.

The chain merger movement was definitely on the rise during the 1950s. In 1949, six companies acquired another company, and 72 stores were involved. But in 1958, thirty-eight companies had acquired seventy-eight other companies for a total of 421 stores changing hands. From 1949 to 1958, eighty-three companies had acquired 315 other grocery chains, and 2,238 stores were sold that cumulatively had done $1.9 billion in sales at the time of purchase.[53] Corporate chains, however, differed in their use of this merger strategy. A&P avoided the method altogether, whereas Safeway only used it in limited circumstances. The merger was mainly used by medium-sized corporate chains that wanted to increase their economic power. The National Tea Company, Winn-Dixie Stores, Inc., the Kroger Company, and the Grand Union Company were major players in the merger game. These four companies combined purchased fifty-five companies with 1,049 stores that had $775 million in sales.[54] In sum, these four corporate chains accounted for 51 percent of all mergers between 1949 and 1958. The greatest reaper of medium-sized chains was National Tea of Chicago. In St. Louis, Missouri, the company acquired C.F. Smith Stores Company; Northwest Piggly Wiggly Company; G.T. Smith's Market Basket, Inc.; Dale Supermarkets; and 28 Food Center Stores. National Tea bought 28 Capital Stores of Baton Rouge, Louisiana; Ashton's Supermarket of Gulfport, Mississippi; H.A. Smith Markets of Memphis, Tennessee; and Montag's Supermarket Chain, also of Memphis. Later, National Tea acquired the Maker's Food Chain of Michigan and stores from Illinois Valley Stores; Devan's Food Stores in Mobile, Alabama; Logan's Supermarkets of Nashville; and Council Oak Stores in Minnesota and Iowa. From 1949 to 1958 National Tea acquired 24 chains and 485 stores. Winn-Dixie Stores of Jacksonville, Florida, incorporated in 1952, was a merger of 335 stores that was formed by the predecessor chains of Winn & Lovett and Dixie Home Stores as well as Table Supply Stores, Steiden Stores, Margaret

Ann, and Kwik-Chek. Later, Winn-Dixie acquired stores from Jitney Jungle Stores of Alabama; Edins Food Stores of Columbia, South Carolina; Ketner-Milner Stores of North Carolina; and H.G. Hill stores in New Orleans. In 1958, Winn-Dixie had acquired eleven grocery chains and 306 stores. Many corporate chains, both large and small, used the merger strategy, but it was a filtering up process. Small-sized chains bought independents, but these chains were sometimes bought by medium-sized chains. The large chains were then buying the medium-sized chains.[55] Gradually but surely, the merger movement was concentrating the control of space and money into fewer and more powerful chains.

Anti-merger cases against corporate chains began to appear in the 1950s. The Federal Trade Commission (FTC) took action against both National Tea and Kroger companies in anti-merger cases, but a key case was decided in 1966 by the U.S. Supreme Court. Vons Grocery Company, the third largest chain in Los Angeles, was challenged for its acquisition of Shopping Bag Stores, the sixth largest chain in that city. The Supreme Court "firmly stated that mergers of substantial competitors must be blocked in markets that, while highly competitive, are nevertheless tending toward oligopoly."[56] The Federal Trade Commission issued strong policy statements against mergers. In 1967, the FTC issued an enforcement policy that it would investigate any acquisitions by chains with annual sales exceeding $500 million unless the acquired retailer was very small. But corporate chains had heeded earlier investigative threats of the FTC, because after 1964, the merger movement had drastically declined.[57] The federal government eventually limited the merger movement, but corporate chains used the merger in the 1950s as a means to gain control over their competitors.

Although the merger approach was used for expansion, many corporate chains also sold equity securities to procure funds for store expansion. They sold both preferred and common stock to acquire funds. In the mid-1950s, one store operator sold $250,000 of preferred stock to store customers over the counter at $10 per share with a minimum purchase of five shares.[58] Selling stock was a common means for grocery management to finance expansion, because they knew that it was less expensive to reimburse shareholders than it was to pay a bank loan. Moreover, grocery management was able to lower annual returns to stockholders if the company was facing financial difficulties. Successful grocery chains that were family owned were less likely to issue stock. A&P only introduced public ownership of its stock in 1958 after the death of George Hartford, the last family member in A&P's executive management.[59] The issuance of stock, either by a major chain or an independent, was a clear indication of the increasingly large-scale character of the grocery store. To maximize economic opportunities, grocery management had to operate as a corporation.

Economic expansionism also included new product lines, but increasing the number of new items in the supermarket created problems. Corporate chains and affiliated independents continued to add their private brands in their stores. Management used them as a backup device when they were unable to gain a favorable contract agreement from food manufacturers for national brands. Although this strategy had existed ever since grocery chains had began manufacturing their own food lines, the economic stakes had become bigger with postwar growth. The most heated political conflict between businesses occurred when grocery management expanded the number of non-food items in the supermarket. Drugstore retailers deeply resented what they saw as an invasion of their business trade by grocery management. At first drug retailers conducted an economic boycott of manufacturers and suppliers who supplied supermarkets with the same health and beauty aids that were carried in their drugstores. But drug retailers realized that boycotts had only short-range political benefits with the long-range economic cost of constraining their market potential by selling a wide variety of product lines. As a result, they turned to state legislatures for help. In many states, drug retailers were successful in lobbying for laws that required certain drug products to be sold by a registered pharmacist. Although such laws did limit what non-food items supermarkets could sell, many health and beauty aids did not require a pharmacist's approval.[60] As a result, supermarkets expanded their market potential by treading into the economic space of another business chain. Whether it was private brands or non-food goods, grocery management saw the need not only to create their own economic defenses but also to expand with an economic offense, and they were willing to sustain the inevitable political conflicts in order to succeed.

Organized labor provided a new political battlefront for grocery management. Unions emerged as a political force after World War II, but their origins were before the war. The Retail Clerks International Association (RCIA) was founded in 1898, and the Amalgamated Meat Cutters and Butcher Workmen of North America was an affiliate to the American Federation of Labor in 1897.[61] Neither union had any substantial influence in the grocery trade until the emergence of chain stores. As independent grocery stores and butcher shops went out of business, more clerks and butchers were working under the same roof in combination stores and eventually supermarkets. The chain store and supermarket movements clearly began to consolidate labor under corporate management in large retail stores. Yet few chains or affiliated independents had unionized labor during the 1930s. Between 1932 and 1935 not more than thirty grocery companies were in some form of union, and members of these unions were mainly warehouse workers and truckers for larger chains.[62] Unions did make inroads oddly enough by supporting anti-chain legislation. In return for their political support for this campaign, the Meat Cutters achieved a national agreement with Safeway in 1935 that opened the door for unionization of nonunion stores owned by the company.[63] Whereas unions had formed the basic foundation to combat grocery management before World War II, the postwar era of growth in the U.S. provided the labor power to make them effective.

The 1950s were a decade of growing tension between organized labor and grocery management. In 1933, the Retail Clerks International Association had only 5,000 members, but in 1953 the RCIA had increased in membership to 246,000. In 1955, 60 percent of all RCIA members were grocery clerks.[64] The Amalgamated Meat Cutters grew not only by increasing union membership but also by lesser unions merging into its organization.[65] But union workers were under threat. As grocery management introduced complete self-service in their stores, they reduced the size of their labor force, especially in the meat department. Moreover, they reduced overhead costs by using part-time employees. Over 45 percent of a supermarket's overhead was due to labor wages, and grocery management saw reducing their full-time employees as a way to cut costs. In 1950, approximately 70 percent of grocery store employees were full time with 30 percent of the work force being part time. By 1960, approximately 55 percent were full-time workers compared to 45 percent part-time employees.[66] Having organized both full-time and part-time employees, unions were successful in raising wages during the 1950s. Moreover, union management negotiated for restrictive labor practices in order to control what workers were responsible for performing. Cashiers, baggers, service clerks, butchers, meat wrappers, and other workers were designated with specific job descriptions.[67] Grocery management faced rising wages and less flexibility with reallocating employees, and as a result, managers furthered their attempts to have complete self-service and to use other tactics for reducing overhead costs. Increasingly, grocery and union management were battling over who, what, when, where, and how labor was used in the supermarket space.

The battle over supermarket space even occurred between unions. Conflicts between the RCIA and the Meat Cutters arose, because both unions operated in the same store. There was no initial division of supermarket space. Both unions negotiated with grocery management for wall-to-wall agreements. These contracts put all supermarket workers, clerks, and butchers under one union, the Meat Cutters or the RCIA. Eventually, differences between these unions were resolved when they divided the store's space by work function.[68] There were spatial disputes between the RCIA and the Teamsters. Local RCIA unions instigated clerk's work clauses with grocery management to delimit work areas between clerks and truck drivers. In some stores, drivers operated as stock clerks by making regular stops and setting up displays. The RCIA saw this work as a tactic by the Teamsters to penetrate the store's work space. This move was favorable to grocery management, because they were able to reduce their clerk work force, but clerk's work clauses prevented such tactics.[69] In all these disputes, unions battled to protect their members' share of the supermarket work space.

Union conflicts with grocery management included not only the super-market's interior but also the external production of new store space. After having been elected by employees of a grocery chain to represent them, local RCIA unions often began their contract negotiations with an accretion clause. Such a clause secured unionization for any new stores that the chain opened in the union's area, and shop rules were automatically implemented.[70] As grocery management used new supermarkets to increase profits, the union movement increasingly ensured that their workers followed those profits and shared them.

Unions realized the value of time in arbitrating new contracts with grocery management. The supermarket was by design a high turnover machine that constantly needed to be refueled. Restocking shelves as well as selling per-ishable goods, which have a limited shelf life, had to be done continuously. With low profit margins and high turnover, time was a critical element to grocery management. A clerk or butcher strike destroyed the fast pace that the supermarket required to sustain its profitability. In comparison, clerk strikes in department stores caused less upheaval, because these businesses had significantly both higher profit margins and lower product turnover than the supermarket. A strike shutdown was a significant daily cost to grocery man-agement with the supermarket's high overhead costs and low profit margins. As a result, grocery management was eager either to avoid a strike or to negotiate terms quickly. Although supermarket managers sometimes used non-union labor to prevent a total shutdown, they realized that store operators depended on the skills of their permanent employees to sustain profitability. Some local unions also realized that a simultaneous shutdown of stores for all grocery chains was dangerous, because they did not want the community to rise against their efforts. As a strategy, the RCIA's Local 665 in St. Louis staggered their contracts on an annual basis with Kroger and A&P. With the Kroger contract in one year and the A&P contract in the next, Local 665 sustained labor demands without public resentment.[71] Unions understood that time was a political weapon that could operate for or against them, and they strategically tried to use time to pressure grocery management without intimidating the public.

Organized labor knew historically that the temporary use of space was important in forming new unions or in conducting contract negotiations. A strike became a play with a scene set when picket lines were formed. In trying to push their cause in non-unionized chains, union organizers pushed their efforts by picketing the chain's stores. In reaction to such a move in 1966, Maurice Warshaw, President of Warshaw Giant Foods, stated: "There is no labor dispute between Warshaw Markets and its employees! Our employees are not on strike! The pickets are not our employees, but are Union business agents and other people hired by the Union."[72] Such tactics were used by unions in the 1950s to give the union a visual presence not only to grocery management but also, and more critically, to the grocery clerks and butchers that they wished to recruit. Forming picket lines, whether to unionize a chain or to negotiate a new contract, became increasingly difficult for union leaders, because their stage space was limited. Grocery management typically prevented picket lines from forming on the private property of their supermarkets. Picketers were able to create a picket line on the public right-of-way or on public sidewalks in front of a freestanding store and still remain fairly visible. But with the increasing number of supermarkets in large shopping centers, union leaders faced problems. Shopping centers were built on private property, and as the RCIA discovered, union picketers were unable to form picket lines without being jailed for trespassing.[73] Unions realized that their ideas required space for protesting, and they struggled to attain a political stage at supermarkets for workers to picket against grocery management.

The union's political influence on grocery retailing, however, was uneven. Corporate chains were becoming largely unionized, whereas affiliated and non-affiliated independents were not. Local unions were placing emphasis on their organizing efforts with corporate chains, because these chains had more centralized management and store ownership than the affiliated and non-affiliated independents. When A&P and Kroger built new stores in an urban area, an accretion clause in the union contract automatically unionized these stores. Working with large corporate chains was advantageous to union management, because they were able to influence the greatest number of their members with the fewest number of contracts.

Union leaders could negotiate contracts very efficiently with corporate chains that owned hundreds of stores, but they did not replicate this feat with affiliated independents. Unions were unable to negotiate with I.G.A., Red & White, or any other affiliated independent's corporate management. Affiliated-independent members owned their own stores, and any one member had significantly fewer stores than any large corporate chain. The same conditions existed for non-affiliated independents. As a result, local union leaders had to develop more contracts with more store owners than with corporate chains. With the resources they had, union leadership thus used most of their resources developing contracts with corporate chains and inevitably spent their remaining time negotiating with affiliated and non-affiliated independents. This union strategy resulted not only in higher wages for employees but also in higher overhead costs in corporate chains than in other stores. With the wholesaling advantages but without the union labor costs experienced by corporate chains, affiliated independents were able to achieve a competitive advantage against their traditional foes. They passed their reduced overhead costs on to the consumer and reaped profits through either increased sales or a better profit margin than the corporate chains.[74] Although unions gained a foothold in the supermarket, they had fewer union members in affiliated independent stores than in corporate chain stores.

The political conflicts over supermarket space changed significantly in the postwar era when compared to prewar times. In the 1930s, corporate chains

5.8 Retail Clerks Picketing Shop-Rite Stores on a Public Sidewalk Versus Store Property, 1960s (Courtesy of the State Historical Society of Wisconsin)

fought for their existence against anti-chain legislation supported by other grocery retailers and wholesalers. In the 1950s, the courts and other chains, such as drug retailers, became active against them. But the most potent threat was organized labor, which grew immensely in the 1950s, gaining support from grocery clerks and butchers. The political battleground shifted mainly from corporate chains versus independents to grocery management versus unions.

DYNAMICS OF THE POSTWAR BOOM

The postwar growth of American suburbia was the key to the supermarket boom. With the United States dominating the world economy, the nation's prosperity was soon converted to meeting consumer demands. In the 1930s, grocery management changed the direction of store design from the small store to the supermarket. Although new store construction virtually ceased during the war years, this period allowed for a number of refinements, such as complete self-service, refrigerated cabinet design, and the addition of non-food goods. By the end of World War II, grocery management was building vastly improved supermarkets. The suburban movement provided the ideal conditions for the supermarket to flourish.

The organizational dynamics of this expansionist era changed the grocery store. Supermarkets became the dominant economic means of conducting business. In 1948, supermarkets were responsible for 28 percent of total grocery sales; by 1963, this statistic had risen to 69 percent. The small store was being squeezed out of the market place, and the squeeze was uneven. Corporate chains initially expanded into shopping centers via the supermarket, and affiliated independents quickly followed. The 1920s was the decade of the corporate chain, but in the postwar era the affiliated independents became competitive. In 1948, corporate chains and affiliated independents each captured roughly 35 percent of total grocery sales, whereas non-affiliated independents earned 30 percent. In 1963, the market share of corporate chains grew to 37 percent, and affiliated independents increased to 44 percent in total sales. In contrast, non-affiliated independents fell significantly to 19 percent.[75] These trends demonstrated that large grocery companies were more able than pure independents to take advantage of the supermarket as a way to expand economically.

Overhead costs significantly influenced growth trends in the retail grocery business. John Hartford's basic philosophy for A&P in the 1920s was to minimize the margin, the percentage difference in price between selling a food item to a consumer and buying that item from a food manufacturer or wholesaler. A&P prospered on this philosophy, which resulted in low prices but high volume sales. Margins, however, began to increase in the 1950s. In 1950, the average margin on grocery department sales for all stores was 14.6 percent, and by 1960, the figure was 19.8 percent.[76] Margin increases were caused by new kinds of overhead costs. Air conditioning, mechanical equipment, finer building materials, and large building lots were new expenses that increased a store's overhead costs. Corporate chains and affiliated independents were more able to keep lower margin increases than non-affiliated independents, because these companies had bulk buying advantages and a management staff to study cost problems. Thus, the total sales share of non-affiliated independent grocers fell in the 1950s. The economic growth of affiliated independents over corporate chains, however, was largely due to affiliated independents being able to avoid unionization more easily than corporate chains could. Because corporate chains had highly centralized management, union negotiators were able to form unions more easily with them than with affiliated independents, which were highly decentralized in store ownership. Controlling overhead costs was an essential ingredient for determining who profited from the expansion into American suburbia.

The supermarket's economic power became evident in the American landscape. More grocery stores were becoming supermarkets rather than superettes or small stores. The total number of stores in the United States continued to decline, but the square footage of store space continued to rise in order to match the nation's growing population. Increasingly, this square footage was put into the supermarket. As Americans measured progress by new development projects in their communities, the supermarket was increasingly part of the scene.

By the end of the 1950s, the American psyche had been transformed by the supermarket. Increasingly, Americans said: "I need to go to the supermarket," instead of: "I need to go to the grocery store." With all the internal struggles in the retail grocery business, the supermarket was the unchallenged design to market food goods in the postwar era. Yet, more growth and new conflicts were in the supermarket's future.

Chapter 6

THE GROCERY STORE PARADE

The retail food industry entered the 1960s with great expectations. Grocery management had developed successful techniques and methods for their supermarkets during the suburban expansion of the 1950s. The nation's economy was prosperous in the 1960s, and the American public wanted more diverse goods and services than the conventional supermarket offered. In the 1970s, Americans faced economic recessions and wanted their food costs to be lower than before. To accommodate these trends, chains and independents developed a wide variety of store types to meet the diversity of customer demands, and this development resulted in market segmentation of food retailing. Yet, the supermarket continued to be a dominant store format which provided the standard against which grocery management developed new store types. At the same time, organized labor became a more potent force that grocery management could not ignore. From store design to chain reorganization, corporate management still found ways to combat unionism.

STORE LOCATING TRENDS

As suburban expansion occurred, methods for locating new supermarkets became important. Locating a store in the postwar boom was relatively easy. The suburban residential market initially expanded faster than new stores to serve the suburbanites could be built. By the end of the 1950s, supermarket owners had filled the retail store shortage. Increasingly, grocery chains and independents no longer assumed that a new suburban store would increase profits. When a supermarket became larger, a store's market area had to increase in size to sustain sales volume per square foot. Store owners that competed for the same market area with new, larger stores expected lower volumes of sales with higher building costs.

Some store owners were pragmatic in selecting locations. The Kroger Company relied heavily on the concept of similarity of experience. Corporate management simply chose locations that were similar to other Kroger store sites that had proven to be profitable.[1] Another grocery chain had an adventurous form of pragmatism. George Jenkins, founder and owner of the Publix chain in Florida, and his associate, George Blanton, used a helicopter to seek out superior locations. A company employee said: "They have a knack for going in an area and getting a feeling of whether this [area] is a growth situation. Part of the knack was to observe from the helicopter the housing patterns near a site, and the roads and highways leading to it."[2] These pragmatic approaches were based on past successes and aggressive acquisition of sites that fitted the chain's site location criteria.

Systematic models began to emerge as analytic techniques to forecast new site locations. Population trends, income patterns, transportation networks, city planning requirements, and store saturation were issues that company management investigated. These issues were matched with the type and size of store that a company wanted to build. Management obviously wanted to build a supermarket in a large, high income area with a good transportation network. At the same time, they wanted not only approval from city planners but also no competition from other supermarkets.[3] To meet all of these aims was ideal, not real. But in an era of prosperity and building growth, the key criterion for many grocery chains was supermarket saturation. To calculate this saturation, company management multiplied the number of consumers in an area by the average food expenditures per customer in the area. This result, which predicted total food sales, was then divided by the total square footage of retail grocery space within the area. The resulting index gave the amount of food dollar expenditures per square foot in the trade area. When investigating many trade areas, corporate management chose the area with the highest index of supermarket saturation. At the same time, the food sales per square foot had to be profitable.[4] To make such calculations, analysts used mathematical techniques to identify market areas and to forecast population and food expenditures.[5] These locational techniques enabled grocery management to assess store location opportunities in a unified manner rather than through ad hoc expansion.

Even as supermarkets were expanding into new areas, corporate management had to decide which stores needed to be closed. Many of the methods used to predict new store locations were used to analyze old stores. As suburban expansion occurred, management analyzed many inner-city stores, because higher income groups had moved to the suburbs. At the same time, trade area boundaries changed when new grocery stores entered an area. Reanalyzing older store locations enabled management to estimate the continued economic viability of a location. Store owners also had sales records of their individual stores, and they were able to compare a store's index of saturation with trends in store profits. Comparing sales trends with the index of saturation enabled them to decide how well a store was being managed under the economic constraints of its trade area.[6] These analytic techniques enabled grocery chain management to establish priorities as to which stores should be closed and which ones should remain in operation.

As corporate chains and affiliated independents increasingly located their stores in the suburbs, store owners in inner-city areas had to modify their stores in order to survive economically. Many independent grocers bought or leased stores previously owned by corporate chains. These store owners often stocked specialized food products to serve ethnic groups. Quite often, they remodeled their stores to upgrade the store's image to attract customers. But these supermarket owners had less floor area, less parking space, and lower sales volume than their suburban counterparts. Non-affiliated independents were particularly hard pressed economically because these spatial and profit limitations allowed less margin for error, especially at the single store level. As the supermarket moved to the suburbs, independent grocers often moved in to fill the market gap left by the exodus of larger grocery companies.[7]

Although analytic techniques helped to locate new stores and eliminate old ones, these methods were not sufficient. Store saturation in trade areas became an increasing problem. Newer, larger supermarkets constantly made inroads into the trade areas of smaller stores. At the same time, there was only so much room in suburbia for large supermarkets. Grocery chains learned the necessity of working with shopping center developers to gain access to good locations. At the same time, these chains went on their own to develop sites. But with increasing competition for store locations and trade area saturation, grocery chains faced problems in store expansion.

The 1960s brought an end to the unlimited store expansion into suburbia, and the growth trend was still toward larger but fewer supermarkets into the 1980s.[8] With capital investment going into fewer supermarkets, store location became more critical, because supermarket over-saturation in a trade area was more costly if management made a bad location decision. Chain management changed how those locational decisions were made. The chain merger movement, which began in the 1950s and continued into the 1960s, was curtailed. In 1966, the U.S. Supreme Court decided against the chain merger of Vons and Stop & Shop in Los Angeles. This court decision curtailed merger activity among the major corporate chains, and grocery chains were less able to depend on mergers as a primary strategy to capture store locations.[9] As company mergers were allowed, grocery chains used this corporate device to increase their trade volume. Analytic techniques were also used to minimize losses and maximize gains in store locations. In the end, chain management used analytic methods and mergers for locating supermarkets to maximize the flow of profits at a given time and place.

NEW ARCHITECTURAL PACKAGING

Grocery store owners realized that architectural design was a stage set to draw the attention of customers within their trade areas. The United States was prosperous in the 1960s, and Americans made shopping purchases that they could not afford in earlier times. In addition to good grocery prices, they wanted a pleasant place to shop and chains and independents responded by changing the design of their supermarkets.

In the early 1960s, many grocery chains and independents abandoned the appearance of the efficiently designed box for more dramatic shapes and storefronts. Although rectilinear plans were typically used, roof shapes and store fronts were modified. Some new stores were built with flat roofs, but many chains and independents used single clear span arches, continuous arches, single gables, and continuous gables. Store architects extended these roof shapes to create decorative canopies for the front facade. For flat-roof stores, canopies were attached, and store architects used these canopy designs to create a stage setting. In Dallas, Texas, the Minyard chain built a store front with stone, and the canopy had angular arches that were reminiscent of Frank Lloyd Wright's Taliesin West.[10] The Frenchs Food Market in Oak Ridge, Tennessee, is reminiscent of Eero Saarinen's T.W.A. Terminal at John F. Kennedy Airport in New York City. All of these design changes reflected popular trends in architecture, and store owners adapted these building designs to enhance their ability to capture customers who wanted a pleasant place to shop.

Building facades were not always modern in design. A few chains and independents opted for traditional motifs. A&P was the most noted chain to adapt traditional design by using a colonial motif for most of its stores. A&P stores were typified by a pitched roof, a cupola, red brick, and traditional lettering. A few other chains and independents used American colonial as a design approach, but A&P was such a large chain that no other company matched A&P's traditional image.[11] The use of traditional design was a psychological contradiction in some respects. Americans had grown to accept the modern movement in architecture as a symbol of a progressive nation. Traditional design had been rejected by most American designers, but many people felt that traditional design had a warmth that modern design lacked. Customers accepted the traditional approach, and the image of supermarket as a stark machine of volume sales production was beginning to change.

Architectural styles became more traditional during the 1960s and early 1970s. In the 1950s, the supermarket was epitomized by the efficient factory, but this new era emphasized a historical image. Supermarkets were designed in a variety of historical motifs. The American colonial approach became more apparent, but store architects introduced other forms of cultural imagery. Supermarket facades were designed as Swiss chalets and American

6.1 Dramatic Modernism, Frenchs Food Market, Oak Ridge, Tennessee, 1960s (Courtesy of the *Progressive Grocer*)

barns. In Overland Park, Kansas, The French Market was modeled after the old Paris food market, Les Halles. The Pantry Supermarket in Arcadia, California, was designed in a traditional Spanish style, and Crawford's Supermarket in Glendale, California, was designed in a turn-of-the-century New Orleans style reminiscent of the French Quarter.[12] The make believe character of these supermarkets was similar to the Disney Corporation using the Castle Neuschwanstein as the entrance to Disneyland. The supermarket's facade was a symbol designed to persuade the customers to shop in one store versus another. The use of historic motifs enabled store owners to promote the hope of entertainment as well as good prices for potential customers.

Some grocery chains and affiliated independents attempted to relate the design of their supermarkets to the surrounding areas by using a design method called the blending technique. A supermarket's architectural style was coordinated with the design of nearby residences. Many store owners used natural materials such as wood and rough-hewn stones to give new supermarkets an earthy, more permanent look. Shake shingles and stone walls for front facades gave the supermarket a subdued feeling. A Straub's supermarket in an upper-income area of St. Louis was totally camouflaged as a residence. Rather than introducing major grade changes to the building site, architects kept a site's natural contours as much as possible. Parking lots were landscaped with shrubbery and trees. Designers sometimes provided entrance gates with discreet signage to announce that the customer had arrived at the local grocery store.[13] The blending approach was often used to fit the supermarket into a locale rather than making it stand out as was done on commercial strips in the 1950s.

These blending techniques often reinforced the perception that aesthetics equaled status, an idea with widespread currency among the upper classes who lived nearby. A few store owners had faced the problem of attempting to build supermarkets in wealthy neighborhoods where homes were traditional in design. Residents often demanded that local zoning boards require the incoming supermarket to be traditional in style. In the 1960s, the grocery industry began to emphasize consumer dynamics. Researchers found that store owners had to orient their store products to the consumer class in the trade area. For low-income customers, grocery management had to emphasize certain food products, but in addition to product selections, upper-income groups wanted quality surroundings during their shopping trips.[14] Blending techniques helped to fulfill property demands of the upper classes who realized that blended architectural designs for commercial buildings would minimize reductions in their residential property values. Design blending was often an economic trade-off between store owners who wanted to build a supermarket and local residents who wanted to prevent their neighborhood property from being financially degraded by nearby commercial activity.

6.2 The Supermarket as a Cultural Theme, Sipes' Supermarket, Tulsa, Oklahoma, 1960s (Courtesy of the *Progressive Grocer*)

6.3 The Blending Technique, Straub's Supermarket, St. Louis, Missouri, 1960s (Courtesy of the *Progressive Grocer*)

RECONSIDERING INTERIORS

Just as the exterior facades of supermarkets changed in the 1960s, so did their interiors. Grocery chains focused on three areas of change—interior design, departmentalization, and volume controls.

Store architects redesigned interiors in an attempt to find innovative plan solutions. A small number of designers continued to experiment with floor layouts in the 1960s and 1970s, just as they had in the 1950s. Supermarkets were designed in hexagonal, octagonal, circular, and triangular shapes, and these building forms led to different aisle arrangements. The Canal Villere Supermarket in a suburb of New Orleans, Louisiana, was designed with radial aisles that pointed toward the checkout stands. In Alderwood Manor, Washington, the owners of a Shop N Save Market used an X-plan arrangement of aisles.[15] But these geometric experiments were more novelties than they were productive solutions. None of these designs was able to improve on rectilinear plans in terms of maximum efficiency of selling space. Certified Professional Supermarket Designers placed their emphasis on the rectilinear plan as a formula to minimize wasted space.[16] Although a few experiments with plan layouts were done, store owners reaped few economic benefits for their efforts.

Such experiments in plan design occurred not only when new stores were designed but also when old ones were remodeled. Many of the supermarkets built in the 1950s needed to be remodeled, because physical wear, dated equipment, and passe designs reduced store sales. Although exterior facades were reworked, architects often had to make major interior overhauls to upgrade a supermarket.[17] Remodeling attempted to reformat the 1950s supermarket from an efficient food sales machine to a modern entertainment center.

The major internal revision of the supermarket was the installation of food departments. The various types of food products were stacked in departments that were uniquely designed to vary the store's aesthetic atmosphere. The collective effect of these food departments was reminiscent of an earlier age. Meat and produce departments were designed to have the aura of the old butcher shop and green grocer, even though self-service had replaced the green grocer. Delicatessens, bakeries, health boutiques, and flower shops were added to supermarkets in the 1960s and 1970s. The thematic thrust of the exterior facade was carried through to the interior design of old and new store departments.[18] Spanish, American colonial, New Orleans French Quarter, and other styles helped store architects to design the departmental scene sets when they used the historic design approach. Even when store exteriors were subdued with the blending approach, the supermarket's interior was actively divided into departments to sustain the customer's shopping attention. Departmental design enabled store owners to focus customers' attention on selected products in a given place while stimulating them to consider other food purchases when the departmental atmosphere changed. Rather than treating customers as a processed object in a factory, store owners began to design environmental stimuli to elicit a desired buying response from customers.

Store art became more prevalent in the 1960s. Mosaic murals were sometimes used as public art at entranceways to give the supermarket a sense of community. In the mid-1960s the owner of Lakeside Foods in Lake Forest, Illinois, spent $12,000 for a wall painting and relief with a nautical theme at the rear of his store behind the meat counter. Some stores used reliefs of food plants and animals to depict food-related images. Other store owners used decor to implement a store's particular theme. Department architecture was emphasized. Store architects often designed separate facades and free standing structures for bakeries, delicatessens, flower shops, and other departments.[19] This individualized interior architecture enhanced not only the store's theme through multiple interpretations but also the aura of old-fashioned shopping. Temporary displays continued to be used as an art form as in earlier times. Store managers arranged food produce, canned goods, balloons, and other devices to create promotional displays. Halloween, Thanksgiving, Christmas, Valentine's Day, and the Fourth of July were seasonal holidays that enabled store managers to push certain products, and displays within and separate from various food departments were constructed to promote sales.[20] Grocery management realized that a store's aesthetic appeal had to be both fixed and changing to attract prosperous customers in order to maximize sales.

Store designers experimented with new materials and equipment in the supermarket. Some stores were installed with carpeting for the entire retail area of the store. In commenting about carpeting in a Publix Market in Florida a customer said: "It's relaxing and you don't have the feeling that you want to rush through your shopping." Another customer felt: "It proves what we've known all along. Lauderdale has real class." Finally, a Publix corporate manager concluded about customer behavior: "Remember, she's buying food and the appearance of the store."[21] Carpeting was used as a means first to attract prosperous consumers and then to prolong the length of their shopping trip.

New lighting techniques were introduced. Designers used polarized lighting, mercury lights, and spot lighting to soften illumination in the supermarket. Before the 1960s, store owners installed uniform high-illumination systems to give a modern look of efficiency, but later managers realized that this approach did not work well with departmentalization. To set apart one department from another, they changed lighting levels for each just as a stage director might change the lighting from one scene set to the next. Individual lighting fixtures and indirect lighting at given locations helped to individualize a store's departments. At the same time, managers wanted glare on food packaging to be less so that customers found food items to be more attractive.

Lighting became a medium in which store managers could strategically focus emphasis on product lines in order to maximize sales. At the same time, lower lighting levels resulted in energy savings, and mechanical systems either recirculated heat from light fixtures or discharged heat from the store depending on the season of the year.[22] Store owners used new lighting techniques to implement the departmental approach and to reduce overhead costs.

REFINING THE MACHINE

Although many interior refinements had aesthetic appeal, some design changes were still made to increase efficiency. These modifications were primarily increased space, shelf design, central meat processing, and checkout stand systems.

Supermarkets continued to grow in square footage. During the 1930s grocery chains and independents had learned the hard lesson that a large store will outperform a small store in terms of volume sales and profit. The lesson still applied. New food products, non-food items, and increased variety in packaged portions also led store owners to increase store size. From 1946 to 1966, the number of items sold in a supermarket more than doubled, whereas the ratio of number of food items to store square footage remained generally stable.[23] This growth was due to management's desire to sustain the advantages of volume trading while maximizing customer appeal through product diversity.

There were definite efficiencies to building larger supermarkets. If total square footage remains constant, a grocery chain of ten stores that were each 25,000 square feet in size was more efficient in warehousing than a chain of 25 stores which were 10,000 square feet in size. When building new stores, grocery management certainly found it to be more economical to build ten stores versus twenty-five. There were fewer real estate and zoning transactions. During construction of a larger store, management could have lower per unit equipment costs, because they bought more items at a given time. In this circumstance, the first chain was able to make fewer warehouse deliveries than the second one. With fewer stores, accounting systems were somewhat simplified. A few manufacturers were willing to make direct deliveries to a large supermarket, but they were unwilling to offer this service to a smaller store. This added service reduced further any delivery costs that might occur. When store owners built larger stores, they had more flexibility in choosing layout plans. By building larger stores, grocery management was somewhat forced to departmentalize their retail goods so that customers could guide themselves in a self-service system. This departmentalization became a marketing asset as store owners learned to diversify their display techniques to encourage customer buying. A larger supermarket furthered the idea of one-stop shopping in the minds of shoppers. The grocery trade had become the largest retail business in the United States, and people began to depend on the supermarket having virtually any item they wanted. By 1971, the supermarket represented only 18 percent of all grocery stores, but it produced 75 percent of total retail grocery sales volume.[24] Larger supermarkets enabled grocery management to reduce some overhead costs and increase marketing flexibility.

Increased display and storage space enabled store owners to predict more accurately their labor needs. Studies showed that larger stores produced more sales volume per employee than smaller ones. For a small store, a manager, a cashier, a clerk and a butcher might be necessary but this configuration might not be the most efficient number of employees relative to floor space. In a large supermarket, management was better able to predict how many clerks were needed to cover stocking and servicing a store's square footage. If 7.5 clerks were needed, management was able to mix efficiently full-time and part-time employees to service store space. At the same time, store managers were able to gather their clerks as a team to fulfill some emergency need, where the manager of a small store could not.

There were a few inefficiencies when grocery management increased store size. As they built larger supermarkets, grocery management learned that sales volume per square foot began to fall. A&P's economy store in the 1920s as well as King Kullen and Big Bear supermarkets in the 1930s were based on maximizing sales per square foot, because volume turnover throughout the store maximized spatial efficiency and lowered wholesale costs. The reduced efficiency of new supermarkets was the result of product item diversity. The new stores maximized customer product choice, whereas the owners of these earlier stores minimized wholesale costs by buying fewer product lines but selling them at a high volume. But supermarket owners were increasingly willing to shift to maximizing product choice, because the American people in a stable economy were willing to sacrifice the lowest price for product diversity.

Grocery management was also concerned about the micro-scale of shelf design. Before the 1960s, space allocation for shelf design had been largely a hit and miss matter. But with research developed in the 1960s, store owners adapted new shelving techniques. They learned to block their merchandise on gondolas. Shelf space was now divided vertically as well as the obvious way of putting goods horizontally on a shelf. A customer now faced a vertical rectangle of a certain line of goods, and this clear, visual arrangement enabled customers to shop more quickly and leave more time for impulse buying. Store owners found that continuous, horizontal shelf arrangements along long gondola aisles looked efficient, but the design produced lower volume sales than this new arrangement. They installed special display slots to interrupt the visual monotony of continuous shelf arrangements within an aisle. This change enabled store managers to create focused arrangements within aisles. Food departments were now divided not only between one another but also internally. Store owners found that special, temporary displays at the ends of aisles created more sales volume than permanent ones. As a result, they increasingly used end display for special promotions. Store managers also realized that grouping products increased sales. By placing syrups and molasses by pancake mixes as an integrated approach, store owners increased the sale of each item, because many customers bought both items simultaneously. All of these shelf design techniques were attempts to simplify visual messages and to create visual stimuli over both time and space. This increased diversity in design enabled management to focus the shopper's attention more efficiently, and the result was an increase in sales volume.[25]

Micro-scale shelf design concerns were related to the interior design of backroom storage areas. Store managers attempted to minimize the ratio of storage space to retail selling space, because a square foot of floor space in storage meant one less square foot to sell food goods. Store managers began to pay greater attention to turnover per product. By knowing turnover rates, they were better able to restock shelves on a timely basis. Knowing shelf timetables better enabled store management to take goods from the warehouse straight to the shelves. Storage space became limited to high volume goods where the transportation cost of many service trips was more expensive than the loss of retail selling space. At the same time, broken stock in the back room was practically eliminated.[26] Improved inventory controls enabled store managers to increase the percentage of interior space assigned to retailing versus storage.

Centralized meat processing was an innovation that not only increased interior retail space but also significantly reduced labor costs. Store management invested a great amount of capital in back rooms for meat preparation. When butcher shops were combined with the grocery store in the 1920s and 1930s, store management initially assumed that the butchers' shop work would remain in the supermarket. But they began to realize that machines increased the work efficiency of meat cutters to the point that they had more equipment and meat cutters than were necessary in every store. By building a central meat operation, grocery management significantly cut their labor costs. The bonus for store space was twofold. When new supermarkets were built, management eliminated the space and equipment needs for meat processing in the design of these stores.[27] They either reduced a store's total square footage or, more likely, devoted a greater percentage of space to retail sales. In old stores, the back room space was initially used for storage, but with interior remodeling, store managers converted the vacated meat processing space into retail space. Centralized meat processing increased the spatial flexibility of store interiors to increase sales, and it also eliminated jobs.

The Uniform Pricing Code was introduced in the 1970s, and it had a significant impact on the efficient use of interior space. A computer code was placed on each packaged label, and at the checkout stand, the checker moved the product over a scanning device that read which item was sold and its price.[28] Eventually, grocery management tied this checkout information to store inventories. Far more accurate than the manual inventories by clerks, the Uniform Pricing Code enabled management to make exact estimates as to when and how much of a store item was needed. Replacing items on the shelf became more efficient. At the same time, store management was able to make more timely deliveries from a central warehouse, and this advance enabled them to calculate more exactly their need for back room stock of store items. As a result, store managers were able to reduce further the amount of floor space that needed to be devoted to storage.

After 1960, the supermarket became an attraction as well as a retail machine. Grocery management increasingly realized that customers responded to their stores as a packaged good just as they did with food items. Architectural design, both exterior and interior, became a marketing technique for grocery management to capture customers away from other stores with less enticing designs. At the same time, store managers remained vigilant about finding new techniques to improve spatial efficiency within their stores. They found that larger stores, shelf design and displays, centralized meat processing, and the Uniform Pricing Code enabled them to increase efficiency of sales within a given space. The supermarket increasingly became a refined corporate space for maximizing profits.

THE PARADE OF CHALLENGERS

The supermarket was the dominant retail mechanism for grocery retailing in the 1960s, but internal weaknesses and external influences began to emerge. By using the supermarket as a singular approach, grocery management enabled other entrepreneurs to exploit new approaches to grocery retailing. At the same time, the public began to criticize food prices and food quality. External to grocery retailing, the energy crisis of the 1970s caused increased overhead costs, and the desire of the American public to eat out more often reduced grocery sales volume. Grocery management had treated the supermarket as an invincible retail mechanism, but their faith began to be confronted by a parade of alternative retail stores, criticisms, and life-style changes.

A large supermarket had the asset of sales volume, but its liabilities became location and time. With supermarkets increasingly dominating trade and eliminating small establishments, the density of grocery stores decreased. There were fewer stores, and their locations were increasingly spread out. Shoppers were driving farther to do one-stop shopping. In the eyes of aggressive entrepreneurs, the supermarket did not have the advantage of timely shopping. People were able to do one-stop shopping in a supermarket, but customers who bought only a few items did not enjoy the long drive and a long line at the checkout stand. Grocery management had traditionally limited shopping time. Late store hours, even twenty-four-hour service, was common in supermarkets on the West Coast before World War II, but most Americans were accustomed to the supermarket closing at 8:00 P.M. and being closed on Sunday through the 1960s. Although the supermarket was a retail powerhouse, business interests realized that its spatial and time gaps could be exploited.

The convenience store emerged as the solution to counter the space-time limitations of the supermarket. The convenience store had its origins in 1927 when Joe C. Thompson of the Southland Corporation in Dallas, Texas, opened stores with a limited set of food goods for shoppers who came by car. Ice and gasoline service were also combined with these stores. But the impact of these early stores was small, because few Americans owned automobiles. The growth of the convenience store became evident after World War II when automobile ownership began to increase significantly. At the same time, the suburbanization of America and the supermarket's displacement of small grocery stores created opportunities for convenience store owners to identify spatial gaps for their market niche. They managed the time gap with longer store hours. The importance of time is epitomized by the Southland Corporation when it renamed its outlets 7-Eleven stores. Opened from 7 A.M. to 11 P.M., these stores, and others like them, were able to capture early morning and late evening shoppers that supermarkets had not served.[29] Customers began to shop at convenience stores during the same hours that supermarkets were open, because they preferred to shop at a nearby location when they needed only a few items. As the supermarket continued to force small grocery stores out of the large volume, one-stop shopping market, the opportunities increased for convenience store owners to exploit quick, limited item sales on the customer's terms. One industry critic noted:

What the American Consumer was looking for was a food store that stayed open seven days a week 'til all hours of the night; one that was a mile or less from home; one where you didn't have to wait endlessly in line to get checked out; one where you wouldn't feel self-conscious arriving in hair curlers, or in a bathing suit, or barefoot, or sweaty in a baseball uniform. Today's convenience store has answered that need.[30]

Some companies attempted to meet the customer's desire for convenience and management's need to control labor costs through automated grocery shopping in the 1960s. The entire store was a series of vending machines without a clerk. The customer could buy milk, bread, butter, eggs, juices, coffee, soft drinks, canned goods, candy, sandwiches, party foods, and cigarettes. Labor costs were reduced to restocking the vending machines, and to take advantage of reducing labor costs, automated stores were open twenty-four hours a day.[31] The automated store was able to maximize the time gap created by supermarket management who set limited store hours. Yet, the automated convenience store was a short-lived phenomena. Even in a convenience store, customers wanted service. Automated stores reduced the customer from someone who was served to an economic unit determined

6.4 7-Eleven Convenience Store, Dallas, Texas, 1960s (Courtesy of the Southland Corporation)

by the amount of coins in a machine. At the same time, these stores did not carry goods as diverse as the typical convenience store. In the end, the automated store was too inflexible and too alienating for customers.

The interior design of the convenience store under corporate management harkened back to a previous era. At first, these stores were similar to mom and pop stores, which were not highly systematic in their arrangements. Corporate management, however, emulated the A&P economy stores of the 1920s. In the 1960s, convenience stores ranged from less than one thousand to four thousand square feet with parking for five to fifteen cars. The typical store had a rectilinear floor plan with the length of the store facing the parking area. Inside, management typically arranged gondolas in rows, which paralleled the length of the store, to minimize aisle space. Unlike the mom and pop stores, which attempted to offer a full line of food goods, convenience store chains selectively limited their goods that customers tended to buy on impulse. Cigarettes, beer, soft drinks, candy, ice cream, ice, bread, some canned goods, and toiletries were sold. Fruits, vegetables, and meats were sometimes sold, but many convenience store chains eliminated these items for products with a higher shelf turnover.[32] The convenience store, like A&P's economy store, emphasized self-service, high turnover of a limited assortment of food items, and a convenient location. Also like the A&P economy stores, the Southland Corporation organized its 7-Eleven stores with interior shelf systems and layouts that were essentially the same in all stores. Although the supermarket was a superior approach to volume sales, corporate management of convenience stores found past lessons in small store design to be profitable.

The growth of the convenience store occurred first in the Southwest and then in the South. Just as corporate grocery chains emerged in the East because companies like A&P and Kroger were based there, the convenience chain was strong in the Southwest because the 7-Eleven chain was founded in Texas. During the suburban growth period between 1945 and 1960, 7-Eleven was the only corporate chain that had the financial resources to consider large-scale expansion. By 1960, the Southland Corporation had grown to five hundred stores and had captured one-third of all convenience store sales. In 1960, 66 percent of all convenience stores in the United States were located in Arkansas, Louisiana, Oklahoma, and Texas. The convenience store eventually blossomed into a national phenomena, and many chains that began in the 1960s became strong corporations by the 1970s. By 1970, convenience store owners had captured 3 percent of total U.S. grocery sales.[33] Although the supermarket was an efficient machine within the constraints of its purpose and design, it was unable to dominate its market in the areas of time, space, and convenience. Corporate convenience store chains systematically exploited the space and time weaknesses of the supermarket.

During the 1960s, the public began to criticize the supermarket for its food quality. As mass marketing grew after World War II, manufacturers increased their usage of food additives to enhance food tastes and to preserve food items. At the same time, farmers used more chemical fertilizers to increase food production. Grocery chains had always advertised that their stores offered high-quality products, but consumer groups began to challenge these claims. Critics exposed the fact that many cereals were puffed with air but with few nutrients. Manufacturers increasingly used food coloring and flavor imitations to make foods, such as meats, more attractive to customers. Candy companies substituted synthetics for chocolate in their candy bars. By the 1970s, Americans consumed 6.7 pounds of food additives per year in their diets, and public officials were not fully aware of the health consequences.[34] Grocery chains were more than bystanders to these criticisms. Having their own private food brands prepared by food manufacturers, management for major grocery chains and affiliated independents played an indirect but active role in food additives being introduced in the supermarket. Food additives prolonged the shelf life of foods and increased product attractiveness. Both of these benefits in large-scale manufacturing and retailing were amenable to the supermarket owners' need to sustain a high level of volume sales while minimizing product losses. The American public became aware of these inconsistencies, and consumer groups and governmental officials investigated the food preparation methods of manufacturers.

The public also attacked grocery chains for their food prices in the 1960s. Customers spent more for food items because of store overhead costs, promotion techniques, and area price manipulations. As they eliminated small store competitors, supermarket owners competed more against one another. They tended to be equally efficient, and store design became one way of distinguishing one store from the next. These architectural improvements, as well as air conditioning and other mechanical improvements, increased overhead costs. The public increasingly realized that the stage set designs of supermarkets were not free. The public had responded favorably to these improvements, but they began to object to other overhead costs. Store advertising was not only costly but also deceiving. Loss leaders were highly advertised, but customers often had difficulty finding the items on store shelves. Through store layout and shelf placements, some store owners enticed customers to buy more profitable items. Grocery management attracted shoppers with games offering prizes and trading stamps, and consumer critics noted that such tactics increased the costs of food items as much as 4 percent of sales.[35] There were pricing tactics that were less obvious to consumers. Large corporate chains, such as A&P, Safeway, and National Tea, practiced price zoning. Where sales volume was low and competition was keen, corporate management reduced the prices of certain food items. In trade areas where competition was weak, these chains charged higher prices. Such variable pricing became a hidden cost to consumers living in a trade area dominated by a corporate chain.[36] Critics and consumers increasingly criticized how supermarkets were designed, promoted, and located to maximize profits.

Both store owners and manufacturers manipulated food products. Some store managers set varying prices for cheese portions cut from the same wheel and labeled them as different types of cheese. The traditional problem of fixing scales continued as customers were overcharged for meats and produce. Consumer critics saw food packaging as a problem, because the cost of the package became a greater percentage of the sale price than the food item. Some manufacturers manipulated the product's size to hide costs. In the 1970s, the Nestlé Company increased the size of its candy bars 15 percent while increasing their price by 50 percent. With such changes, customers were unable to compare the volume of a product with its price.[37] Grocery management realized that the physical manipulation of food products was as important for profits as the design and location of the supermarket that housed these goods.

The quality and pricing of food goods led consumers and retailers to support retail alternatives other than the dominating supermarket. Many shoppers who wanted quality goods formed co-ops or sought out farmers' markets and health food stores. As a result, they often found that they were able to cut food costs. Most people wanted to spend less money for their food bills, and entrepreneurs responded by opening warehouse markets. Supermarket owners were unable to sustain a captured audience who believed in the prices and quality of their food items.

Aggressive consumers organized co-ops during the late 1960s and 1970s to counter what they thought were exploitative supermarket prices and low quality food goods. This new wave of cooperatives had its roots in the civil rights, student, and anti-war movements that created greater political awareness and a desire for participatory democracy among young people.[38] Co-ops operated either as retail stores or pre-order centers in which members' orders were made, organized, and delivered on a set schedule. Anyone was allowed to join, and each member had a vote on the co-op's policies. Being non-profit, members were able not only to save money but also to be selective about food products. In California, members of the Berkeley Co-op used political tactics in operating their store. They placed warning signs on shelves for foods high in sodium to inform customers with health problems. When a food manufacturer was the wrongdoer in a labor dispute or charged with anti-environmental practices, co-op management posted signs in their store to inform other members. The Berkeley Co-op avoided end displays to promote impulse buying, and they refused to install colored lights to improve the appearance of meats and other products. Co-op stores were functionally designed without promotional interiors, such as the nautical or New Orleans French Quarter themes sometimes seen in a supermarket. Instead, co-ops were reminiscent of mom and pop grocery stores. Members sensibly arranged food items in aisles, and they did not strategically place highly profitable items at eye level on shelves to maximize sales as was done in supermarkets. Honesty in presenting food products extended to relationships between members. Co-ops became informal community centers where members chatted with one another while they shopped. The overall atmosphere of co-ops was one of people fulfilling basic needs rather than being manipulated toward maximizing food purchases.[39] Co-ops offered an alternative to consumers who saw the supermarket as an exploitive retail space for profits.

Although initially successful, co-ops eventually declined in number. Urban cooperatives had the greatest problems, because these groups were founded by many community activists who were not originally from the immediate community. The decline in active community organizations affected these cooperatives, because the U.S. government terminated funding programs for neighborhood development. Suburban cooperatives were more stable than their urban counterparts, but there were problems. Membership was normally between thirty and fifty people, but with a high annual turnover in membership, suburbanites had difficulty maintaining primary group relationships to run the co-op. Yet, it was this small group involvement that many members sought. At the same time, they found the economic benefits in participating in a cooperative were small.[40] Cooperatives were a community reaction to supermarket practices, but many co-ops failed due to inadequate organizing, inadequate funding for urban groups, and a lack of economic benefits for suburbanites.

Consumers in some cities saw the public market as a means to find quality food items that they found missing in supermarkets, but there were political obstacles. Many public markets or farmers' markets had disappeared. With mass distribution systems, corporate management of chains had devastated public market trade, first with the economy store and then the supermarket. City officials had allowed public markets to fall into disrepair, and developers replaced these buildings with more profitable enterprises. Yet, with the political upheavals in the 1960s and the public desire to regain a sense of community, people endeavored to save old markets. Plans were drawn to demolish the Indianapolis City Market and replace it with an office complex, but public supporters fought in the courts to save the market, and the legal conflict was so intense that the case reached the U.S. Supreme Court in 1968. Public market advocates won the case, and the city took an active role in restoring the market by providing competent management.[41] Other markets were lost to urban redevelopment. In the 1970s, Boston's Haymarket was reduced from a daily market comprised of 24 city blocks to a single block that was opened only once a week.[42] Consumer advocates supporting the preservation of public markets faced opposition from business interests and public officials, and there were both successes and failures in saving these markets.

Political conflicts over public markets led to challenges over a city's cultural identity and to class confrontations. Other than Baltimore, no city was so highly identified by its public markets as Seattle. The Pike Place Market had fallen into disrepair by the 1950s, and developers began to put pressure on public officials to redevelop the area. The business establishment formed the Central Association and wanted to demolish old market buildings and to replace them with office buildings and a multi-story parking lot. The mayor and the Central Association supported a redevelopment plan, and the city of Seattle applied for an urban renewal grant in 1964 from the Department of Housing and Urban Development. Concerned citizens organized Friends of the Market, and they fought back politically and legally for ten years to save Pike Place. One of their major weapons was getting the market complex placed on the National Register of Historic Places. This strategy gave legitimacy to saving Pike Place. With a plethora of plans and a public referendum in 1971, seven acres of the Pike Place Market were saved, and the buildings were restored.[43] There were numerous other battles to save public markets as a consumer alternative, and the movement to save them was epitomized by Laure Olin, an architect, who recalled the conflicts over the Pike Place Market:

Here the issue finally came down to one of social thought, not architecture. It was urban souls who believed in diversity and felt that the haves must face up to their brothers, the have-nots: that whatever was wrong with downtown Seattle, it was not the public market and its denizens, but rather the grim vision and lives of the more affluent who neither lived in or liked the city.[44]

Consumers gained the economic savings and quality of life they sought in public markets. Consumers were found to save thirty-four cents on the dollar for the same produce goods if they shopped in farmers' markets rather than supermarkets. A shopper could find a produce item cheaper in a farmers' market 91 percent of the time when compared to the supermarket. In California, researchers compared consumer preferences between farmers' markets and supermarkets. Preferring farmers' markets, shoppers found them to be cleaner, friendlier, more personal, faster, less expensive, more natural, more sociable, and happier than supermarkets.[45] As the ecology movement gained momentum in the United States, a few consumers became more concerned about being economic, responsible shoppers as well as recapturing a sense of public life, and many shoppers chose the public market as an alternative. But the public market was not easily replicated, and it was a local institution without the systematic advantages of mass distribution for a wide variety of food goods. Some shoppers used the public market for produce, fish, and meats, but the supermarket was totally oriented to one-stop shopping for both food and non-food items. The public market was a partial economic solution for cities that valued them, but the effect of such markets was negligible compared to the public's demand for supermarkets.

Some consumers wanted quality foods without regard for price, and small specialty shops fulfilled this demand. Gourmet shops and health food stores became more prominent in the 1960s as the American public had more disposable income. Some small supermarkets, called superettes, were devoted to high-income consumers. These stores sold exotic fruits, the finest lines of canned goods, and other foods that were not typically available in any supermarket. But these superettes were so limited in their food lines and price ranges that these stores were able only to meet the partial needs of high-income groups. At the other extreme, ethnic grocery stores in large cities often served low-income groups, because store owners realized that supermarkets were unwilling to stock a variety and volume of ethnic foods to serve their communities. In Chicago during the 1970s, 80 percent of the grocery stores in Spanish neighborhoods did not compete with supermarkets.[46] Specialty stores met particular customer needs, but these stores captured a very small portion of food sales when compared to the supermarket.

In contrast to the desire for quality goods, many American consumers wanted a grocery store alternative that offered lower prices. The inflationary pressures of the nation's economy in the 1960s put increasing pressure on a household's budget. National food surpluses practically disappeared. Aided by the political ferment of the times, resentful shoppers boycotted chains for charging high prices, and these chains experienced lower profits and sales volume. Amid these pressures, the discount store became an attractive alternative for store owners.

The discount movement began in the early 1960s and was flourishing by the end of the decade. Some chains and affiliated independents foresaw the demand for discount stores, and they experimented by building freestanding discount food stores under names not associated with their other stores. When inflation and shopper boycotts occurred, corporate chains openly expanded with discount stores. Rather than building structures, some older stores were repainted along with minor repairs and converted into discount stores. By re-imaging their stores and lowering prices, operators were able to capture sales in a saturated market that was dominated by supermarkets owned by large chains and major affiliated independents. But lowering food prices also required store owners to make significant changes in store operations. By reducing all prices as much as 5 percent, store owners were able to increase the volume of sales, but to be profitable, cutbacks were necessary. They eliminated trading stamps, games, and other gimmicks, and they reduced the total number of food items by 15 to 20 percent. The elimination of promotion techniques was an immediate reduction of overhead costs. Reducing food items was strategic, because food items with fast turnover increased the amount of sales per square foot. Initially, owners shortened store hours to cut labor costs, but in time, they lengthened store hours to compete more directly with the conventional supermarket.[47] The discount movement was a return to the economic premises of supermarkets in the early postwar era, which emphasized sales volume and holding down overhead costs.

During the 1970s, many store operators opened warehouse supermarkets that deemphasized quality design and atmosphere. Owners reduced food prices even lower than the initial discount stores, and there were interior and operational consequences. Food items were stacked high on metal shelves rather than on gondolas, and many products, such as canned goods, remained in their carton with the top portion of the cardboard box cut away. This crude form of shelf display, however, was economically efficient when warehouse store owners used cash registers that were installed with price scanners. With the Uniform Pricing Code marked on food items, store clerks were required only to put the carton of goods on the shelf, not to mark the price of each item. Meat and produce displays were simply arranged without decorative devices to emphasize these areas as specialized food departments. Checkout stands were somewhat modified. Store owners eliminated sacking clerks, and to sustain a fast flow of processing shoppers, a pivotal board was installed on the stand. As one customer was packing groceries, the pivotal board acted as a divider for the checker who was checking out groceries for another shopper. The metal shelves, food goods in cartons, the simplified designs of food departments, and the checkout stand gave a bleakness to the warehouse supermarket. There were no architectural themes and design articulations used in these stores as had appeared with supermarkets in the 1960s.[48] Store displays were straightforward, and as a result, the visual absence of a concern for aesthetics gave customers the message that warehouse markets were saving them money.

The new warehouse approach harkened back to the beginning days of the supermarket. The King Kullen and Big Bear supermarkets of the depression era succeeded on the principle of offering low prices by lowering overhead costs, and the spatial outcome resulted in a bare bones architectural setting. Some warehouse supermarket owners also combined their store with an adjacent discount department store, although usually separated by interior partitions.[49] This combination method had been used in the Big Bear supermarkets with great success. Like the early supermarkets, store owners converted old buildings into warehouse stores, but there were two differences. The 1930s supermarkets were installed in buildings used formerly for industry and other commercial uses. The warehouse supermarket of the 1970s was often a building that was previously a typical supermarket. In the 1930s, supermarket owners were able to choose almost any site to compete with small stores, but their counterparts in the 1970s had to be aware of trade area saturation because they competed with other large stores. Given the economic recession of the 1970s, the 1930s depression era techniques for supermarket design and operations made economic sense to many chains and independents who operated warehouse markets.

Although supermarket owners faced challenges from retail competitors in the grocery trade, they also increasingly had to confront the public's desire to eat out in the 1960s and the 1970s. American households were prospering from the nation's strong economy in the 1960s. With more disposable income, families chose to eat out rather than to eat at home. At the same time, women were increasingly entering the labor force, and the woman's traditional role of preparing meals at home lessened. Women ate lunches at work, and they

6.5 Edwards Food Warehouse, Newton, Massachusetts, 1981 (Photograph by Chester Liebs, copyright, from *Main Street to Miracle Mile*, Boston: Little Brown)

wanted less work at home. Children and teenagers frequented fast food franchises more often, because their parents gave them allowances, which were more possible to give in an era of prosperity. As households took more trips to eat out, they made fewer shopping trips to the supermarket.[50] Store owners had typically considered other retail grocers to be their competitors, but increasingly all owners in the grocery business had to recognize competition from everywhere prepared food was sold.

The growing parade of retail alternatives in the 1960s challenged the supermarket as the single formula for grocery retailing. Convenience stores were the most accessible in location and time. Co-ops, gourmet shops, and public markets offered high-quality products. Discount stores and warehouse markets offered the lowest prices. Restaurants and fast food establishments increasingly offered potential shoppers an alternative to grocery shopping and home meals. In each of these circumstances, the supermarket was outperformed by the competition. Although no longer able to monopolize the retail sector, store owners responded with changes in the supermarket.

MEETING NEW CHALLENGES

Chains, alongside affiliated and non-affiliated independents, could not sustain the conventional supermarket as an unchanging formula for maximizing profits. Shopping hours, quality of food, prices, and competition from eating out were problems that owners began to address.

Corporate chains and independents eliminated the time barrier. Traditionally, most supermarkets had closed in the early hours of the evening. In the 1950s, stores were typically open until 8:00 P.M. in the winter and 9:00 P.M. in the summer. Store hours changed in the 1960s to 11:00 P.M. in response to the convenience store's economic threat. Owners extended store hours to midnight in the 1970s, and by the 1980s, many supermarkets were open every day of the week, twenty-four hours per day. Owners eliminated not only the possibility of losing potential sales but also the shoppers' psychology that the convenience store was their only alternative. Although there were increased labor costs involved in sustaining a minimal crew of clerks in the late hours, there were economic efficiencies. Supermarket managers had typically kept their stores lit all night to lower theft rates, and they found it more economical to operate air conditioning and heating systems continuously rather than starting and shutting down these systems. As a result, late night and early morning sales helped to pay for energy costs that store owners had previously treated as an unrecoverable loss during a down-time period. Supermarket managers were able to use their labor force more strategically by extending store hours. Clerks stocked shelves during the late hours, which meant they need not interrupt customer shopping during the day. This time shift in store operations then enabled store clerks to devote more time to personal service with customers, an attribute that many shoppers wanted.[51]

Although unable to overcome the locational advantages of the convenience store, supermarket owners maximized their ability to increase sales by eliminating the barrier of traditional store hours.

Supermarket owners began to put greater emphasis on the quality of their food goods. Health food products, organically grown fruits and vegetables, leaner cuts of meat, greater varieties of fish, canned goods with less oil and salt, and other specialized items enabled grocers to compete more effectively against farmers' markets, co-ops, and health food stores. Managers in upper-income areas devoted entire aisles to foreign foods and gourmet delicacies, and they expanded their wine selection to increase the variety and quality of vintages for customers.[52] Although self-service was still used as a strategy to reduce labor needs, managers asked their clerks to devote more time to personal service so that shoppers would feel that both goods and service were of good quality. Supermarket owners were unable to duplicate the store atmosphere and food items offered by the gourmet and specialty stores, but they were able to prevent economic erosion by retaining upper-income shoppers. Although retailers of quality foods were never a serious threat to the supermarket, chains and independents were unwilling to surrender the quality food market in their stores for fear of reduced sales volumes.

In contrast to the quality food shops, the discount store and warehouse market did pose a serious threat to the conventional supermarket. Chains often chose to follow the trend, converting some of their stores to the discount format. This strategy enabled them to broaden their market mix by having some stores that offered the lowest prices, whereas others provided a greater variety of goods and more services. Other limitations and alternatives also forced owners of conventional supermarkets to emulate discount and warehouse stores.

Overhead costs had to be reduced to lower prices, and changing store architecture was a viable solution. Supermarkets in the 1970s and 1980s were not as flamboyant as in the 1960s. Although their buildings were well-detailed, store owners deleted architectural motifs and themes that had captured shoppers' attention. Building facades were modified to meet a new economic problem, the energy crisis. In the early 1970s, energy costs soared as the United States began to depend substantially on foreign oil. The immediate solution to this problem was the elimination of glass facades, which were not energy efficient. Store architects faced the challenge of designing front facades that could be appealing even without window sections. Roof structures and arcades provided visual interest to a supermarket without adding energy costs. A wall graphic displaying the name of the store often became a design feature that dominated the front facade as a form of ornament, and the sign's energy cost was negligible. Store interiors were modified with more energy efficient lighting, and some manufacturers improved the energy consumption levels of refrigerated display units. The affluence of the 1960s began to fade in the 1970s, and supermarket architecture reflected these changes by cutting costs.

A major weapon chains used to counter the discount and warehouse markets was the introduction of generic brand grocery products. Initially introduced in France in 1976, the Jewel Company was the first grocery company to introduce generic brands in the United States. Most firms took a wait-and-see attitude, but in 1978 the movement began to take hold when the Dillons chain in Kansas and Missouri began offering generic brands for both food and non-food products. By 1980, 14,600 supermarkets in the United States were marketing generic brand products. Large families and more educated people tended to want these products.[53] Certainly saving on food costs was a consideration, but many shoppers felt that the differences in quality for private and national brands in supermarkets were not worth the added costs. Store managers provided special aisles for generic goods and even decorated them with black and white crepe paper, the symbolic colors for generic items. Although these goods allowed corporate chains and affiliated independents to improve the balance of trade between them and warehouse supermarkets, the generic movement disappeared as better economic times came to pass.

Chains as well as affiliated and non-affiliated independents could no longer ignore the eating-out challenge, and they responded with their own fast food alternatives. Delicatessen departments and bakeries were introduced in the 1960s to offer prepared take-out foods. Some supermarket managers experimented with a cafe in which food and drinks were purchased from the deli departments. But their attempts to create a fast food section failed, because store managers lacked the market analysis and food product refinements that fast food franchises such as McDonalds and Long John Silvers had developed. However, store owners were able to capture the market segment for a food product line in whih they excelled, produce. The American public's concern for health and diet was initially addressed by restaurants specializing in salad bars. With the produce at hand, store managers began to convert a portion of their produce departments into salad bars, and shoppers were able to design their meals at the counter and take them home. Supermarket owners, however, achieved only modest successes against the eating-out challenge. As they could afford it, American households increasingly wished to escape the drudgery of preparing meals in the kitchen, especially in one person households and households where both spouses worked. The increasing work demands placed on middle-income household members began to influence household eating habits, which supermarket owners were unable to overcome.

Supermarket owners' responses to outside challenges continued to be measured by the size of their stores. In 1978, the average size of a new supermarket was 32,500 square feet, whereas the average size for closed stores was 12,800 square feet. The trend continued into the 1980s with new supermarkets averaging 40,000 square feet and some stores being built with over 70,000 square feet.[54] To compete against their challengers, grocery chains had to provide a wider variety of goods and services, and this variety required them to increase floor space. Eventually known as superstores, these supermarkets were designed for one-stop shopping and service. This strategy was a middle-of-the-road approach. Store owners offered low- and high-cost goods, longer shopping hours, and take-out foods for shoppers. Still, they were unable to outperform other retailers who specialized in specific sectors of the food retailing industry. Nevertheless, chains and all independents with superstores were able to optimize a combination of services that approached the advantages offered by convenience stores, public markets, co-ops, specialty food stores, warehouse supermarkets, and eating-out establishments.

Supermarket owners in the 1980s, however, faced two significant innovative challenges that were external to the retail food industry, both oriented toward mega-scale retailing. First, the hypermarket design maximized the diversity of retail goods and services. Second, the warehouse club store maximized sales of selected grocery goods and other retail items. Both store types were significantly larger in building and economic scale than the conventional supermarket and its resulting prototypes.

The hypermarket, which first developed in France, emerged as the ultimate retail store. The French company, Carrefour, began when a food wholesaler and a non-food retailer joined to operate their first supermarket in 1960. They were influenced by discount stores, such as K-Mart, which were growing on the outskirts of many American towns. Carrefour opened its first discount store in 1963, but unlike American retailers, they combined the supermarket and the shopping mall into one facility, the hypermarket. Carrefour's hypermarkets included not only a supermarket but also a cafeteria, a garden center, a furniture center, an auto center, and several boutiques. In the 1970s, Carrefour dominated the hypermarket trade in France and led in the international expansion of hypermarkets. The first hypermarket in North America was built in Montreal, Canada, in 1973, but the Oshawa Group, which owned this store, was unable to make the hypermarket a successful approach to retailing. The hypermarket finally made its mark in the United States during the 1980s. In 1984, the Bigg's Company built the first European-style hypermarket in the Cincinnati suburb of Batavia. By 1989, there were eighteen hypermarkets in the United States, and the average size was 175,000 square feet with some stores being larger than 200,000 square feet.[55] The hypermarket is historically based on the U.S. discount store's economic principles of ample parking, one-stop shopping, and discount pricing. French grocery companies expanded on these retailing principles, which then reverberated back to the United States.

The economic formula for the hypermarket was to combine three retail functions—the supermarket, the discount store, and the shopping mall. Each of these retail formats was based on one-stop shopping, and the hypermarket

6.6 Wal-Mart Hypermarket, Topeka, Kansas, 1991 (Author's Collection)

consolidated these three formats into a stronger, single magnet for shopping. The physical scale of hypermarkets has been epitomized by the human functions within it. Retail clerks speed about on roller skates to move from one part of the store to another. As many as fifty checkout stands serve as assembly line exits to serve shoppers. During a shopping break, people can have a hamburger and a soft drink at a McDonalds or visit a beauty parlor for a hair set. The ultimate aim behind the hypermarket is to offer the shopper as many retail goods or services as economically and physically feasible in one store.

The hypermarket approach, however, has its critics. Conceptually, it is equivalent to the comprehensive factory. When Henry Ford built his River Rouge factory, he combined the transport of raw materials, manufacturing mills for steel and glass, and car assembly plants. River Rouge was a combined factory that maximized the principle of production in one place. As Spiro Kostof, an architectural historian, noted: "At its height a huge industrial empire supported the operation of this sprawling behemoth, for Ford did not like to be dependent upon anyone. . . . Yet Ford would learn . . . that grand designs do not always yield correspondingly grand results."[56] Corporate discount chains, such as Wal-Mart and K-Mart, built hypermarkets with many of the economic principles that Ford had in mind when he built the River Rouge factory. Walter F. Loeb, a retailing analyst, said about hypermarkets: "These bigger stores probably will cannibalize businesses of other food and general merchandise stores."[57] The hypermarket is the annihilation of architectural and economic diversity, because building types and their settings are eliminated by placing them under one roof and location.

The future of the hypermarket, like Henry Ford's River Rouge factory, is limited. River Rouge was dependent on all of its elements to be constantly in working order, but worker strikes in some parts of the factory, material shortages, and any other form of shutdown made River Rouge work at less than full capacity. Although a hypermarket's huge size enables store managers to optimize the number of clerks needed to service its square footage, there is the problem of sustaining volume sales. Debra Levin, a financial analyst, notes: "We do not expect any wide proliferation of this format. Hypermarkets basically need volumes of $100 million annual revenues to break even. This format depends on traffic from a radius of 20-30 miles . . . it tends to be a more difficult place to shop because of travel time and store size . . . with a great emphasis on everyday low pricing by many of the retailers throughout the country, it is tougher for these [hypermarket] outlets to differentiate themselves on a price basis."[58] Whereas the hypermarkets enable powerful discount chains to concentrate their marketing efforts, price competition and the large capital investment into one store are its liabilities. The hypermarket is a huge fixed capital space that is unable to respond quickly to the changing landscape that retail investors constantly create and then dismantle.

The wholesale club format emphasizes economic inputs rather than comprehensive services as in the hypermarket. Robert Price, owner of Price Club Stores, opened the first warehouse club store in 1976, and the store format grew exponentially in the 1980s as discount chains, such as Wal-Mart and K-Mart, adapted the club approach. The reason for this economic growth was the ability of these chains to control their clientele and to bypass whole-saling functions. To capture a stable clientele, discount chains target customers who buy in bulk. Businesses, groups, and individuals are pre-screened in order to minimize bad check losses. Customers now pay an annual mem-bership fee, which enables the store owners not only to secure an upfront profit but also to discourage shoppers who cannot afford the fee. Membership patterns are consistent nationally with 70 to 75 percent retail customers and 25 to 30 percent wholesale customers. Yet, 60 to 65 percent sales volume is from wholesale customers.[59] Unlike the conventional retail store, the whole-sale club store not only reached retail business and customers but also re-placed wholesale distributors. With shoppers buying in bulk, most wholesale club chains avoid a central distribution center, and they have manufacturers deliver their goods directly to the store. Targeting customer clientele as well as combining wholesale and retail functions were key control inputs that made the wholesale club a profitable format.

The wholesale club places a strong emphasis on inventory turnover. The key lesson from the chain stores of the 1920s and the initial supermarkets of the 1930s was that volume sales are maximized by sales per square foot. To accomplish this end, store owners limited product lines to those items that had the greatest turnover. Unlike large chain supermarkets, which sell as many as 30,000 items, warehouse clubs typically carry only 3,000 to 4,000 items. With some product lines, store managers use an in-and-out strategy for turnover. Some products are only allowed to be on the shelf for six to twelve weeks at a time. Seasonal foods and products such as jewelry and compact disks are given limited shelf time, because store managers realize that some products have an initial high turnover that slows down below desired profit levels.[60] Given the low prices of warehouse clubs, every store item must have a sufficient turnover to produce a profit and to maintain its position on the shelf.

The warehouse club format emphasizes tight control of overhead expenses. Corporate discount chain managers locate their stores in sub-prime locations to avoid high land costs, and although the typical store averages over 100,000 square feet in size, architectural amenities are bare boned in order to hold down building expenses. Labor costs are minimized. Fifty percent of the employees are part time, and there is little or no unionization in warehouse clubs. By being open 75 hours per week as compared to 125 hours per week in a chain supermarket, store management is able to eliminate practically any overtime labor costs. In addition to reducing the on-site overhead costs, warehouse club store managers do not use advertisements.[61] Combined, these cost controls are possible, because corporate management has proven that shoppers are attracted by low prices more than by architectural design, store location, customer service, and advertising.

Wholesale clubs have been highly successful for a few major chains. Sales grew from $900 million in 1983 to $21.5 billion in 1990 for all wholesale clubs. But the economic benefits were concentrated into a few hands. By 1990, four chains, Sam's Wholesale Club (of Wal-Mart), Price, Costco, and Pace (of K-Mart), had captured 86 percent of total U.S. sales in the wholesale club market. These chains quickly developed into a national oligopoly, and although some U.S. regions have yet to be fully developed with wholesale clubs, future competition is limited. Warehouse clubs require high initial investment and economies of scale that only large chains have. Moreover, established chains have saturated most metropolitan areas with one wholesale club, and they have the knowledge and resources to capture the remaining market areas. Unlike the development of the supermarket, corporate retail chains quickly dominated the wholesale club format, leaving little opportunity for independents to enter competition. Although comprising only 3 percent of U.S. food sales, the warehouse club format still demonstrated how corporate chains can capture market shares by using their large-scale operations.[62]

The conventional supermarket was no longer a spatial mechanism that monopolized retail growth in food merchandising. In 1980, the conventional supermarket captured 55 percent of all supermarket trade. Other market shares were 12 percent for superstores, 3 percent for warehouse supermarkets, and 5 percent for convenience stores. In just ten years these distributions changed significantly. By 1989 superstores had 20 percent of total retail trade, whereas warehouse stores and convenience stores had each increased to 11 percent of the total market sales. Although less important, food-drug combination stores and wholesale club stores were gaining an increasing share of retail sales, and the hypermarket was a potential threat. In contrast, the conventional supermarket dropped to 30 percent of total trade.[63] Although other forms of retail stores shared market sales, superstores, warehouse markets, and convenience stores were the main causes of reduced sales in the supermarket.

Grocery management in the United States was changing the format of the supermarket, but the corporate structure of food retailing was changing as well. The owners of conventional supermarkets, superstores, food-drug combination stores, warehouse supermarkets, super warehouse stores, and convenience stores were often the same firms. Although varying from one firm to another, corporate chains such as A&P, Kroger, Safeway, and affiliated independents used a mixed strategy of store types to balance their sales volume. This approach reduced the possibility of a company losing its share of market trade by limiting itself to one store format. Grocery management had learned the importance of being adaptable. By continuing its economy stores rather than converting quickly to the supermarket in the 1930s, the all-powerful A&P almost met with economic collapse. Grocery management knew that the volume and design of space was critical to economic success, but they realized that no one design was immune to economic obsolescence. Multiple changes in the retail food trade led corporations to implement multiple spatial solutions to compete. The changing spatial character of retail grocery trade was economic, and grocery management's decisions for the redesign of space were also political.

NEW STRUGGLES

The business struggles in the retail grocery business from the 1960s through the 1980s were both old battles and new ones. Grocery management continued to find technical ways to reduce labor costs through store design. Unions still strove to improve pay and working conditions for their members. Chains continued to wage corporate battles. Mergers through chain buyouts still occurred within the retail industry. But corporate chains now found themselves subject to leveraged buyouts, financial wars with corporations external to the grocery trade. The modern era of conflict between grocery management and store workers in the grocery store remained continuous and changing.

Grocery management realized that design experimentation in the supermarket gave them opportunities to reduce labor costs. Beginning in the 1960s, a significant change to reduce labor costs was centralized meat processing. By placing meat cutting work in a central facility rather than in every store, grocery management was able to reduce its meat cutter labor force. Eliminating employees literally meant eliminating work space in the supermarket. In planning for new stores and remodeling old ones, designers typically converted the work area into retail shopping space for self-service customers. The Unified Pricing Code along with price scanners significantly reduced labor costs. Grocery companies often trained check-stand cashiers to be skilled workers, and grocery management in chains had traditionally given awards to cashiers for their proficiency. But grocery management saw that the Uniform Pricing Code gave them significant controls over assessing store inventories and eliminated errors at the check stand. Cashiers using price scanners were 52 percent faster than those using conventional cash registers. Skilled cashiers who knew how to operate cash registers and had math skills were no longer needed. Clerks at a lower wage scale were able to operate price scanners, and as a result, store managers reduced their labor costs with price scanners. Union management did not favor the substitution of price scanning for item pricing with a skilled cashier, but they were unable to prevent grocery management from converting to this computer pricing system.[64] There have been experiments with customers using automated self-scan stands with a built-in security system that will not accept any item that has not been scanned. The cashier staff is reduced to checkers who ring up receipts and accept payment. Both corporate chains and affiliated independents have tried this automated system, but the results have been mixed.[65] Although experimentation was not always successful, grocery management was still able to reduce labor costs through design refinements in their supermarkets.

Store workers were constantly under economic pressure from grocery management, but unionism made its national presence felt through growth in membership. From 1966 to 1978, the Retail Clerks International Association grew from 552,000 to 736,000 in membership. The Meat Cutters Union was less successful; its membership increased from 500,000 in 1968 to 529,000 in 1972, and then dropped back down to 500,000 in 1978.[66] Central meat processing undoubtedly played a role in the reduction in union membership for the meat cutters. Yet, overall growth in the union movement was directly affected by urbanization. The population growth of American urban areas meant that more grocery stores were located in cities rather than in small towns. In rural America, union organizations faced the formidable task of organizing a critical mass of retail clerks and meat cutters who wished to form a union. Moreover, small town America sustained its independent character and less-than-accepting attitude toward unionism. The postwar migration to cities provided unions a larger concentration of workers from which to recruit.

Union growth was sometimes uneven, because there were regional differences that affected labor. Union activity in food retailing is traditionally higher in the West, Midwest, and East than in the Southwest and South. Moreover these southern regions were less urban than many other areas in the United States. As a result, supermarket workers received lower wages in the Southwest and South. But urbanization and the Sunbelt growth created better circumstances for unions to organize workers when chain concentration began in these regions. At the same time, unions grew in membership when major national chains, such as Safeway, had accretion clauses in union contracts. These clauses ensured that any new store would automatically be unionized. With population growth in the Sunbelt, major national chains inevitably built new stores, and unionism became more prevalent than before in the Southwest and South. Although still less unionized than other areas of the United States, urban growth led to greater union activity in the southern regions.

Unionism was becoming nationally stabilized in the retail food business while achieving a mixture of labor victories and losses. In 1979, the Retail Clerks and Meat Cutters Unions merged to create the United Food and Commercial Workers Union (UFCW), the largest national labor organization of the American Federation of Labor and Congress of Industrial Organizations (AFL-CIO). This merger was emblematic of the increasing concentration of workers in urban areas and the increasing domination of fewer chains over local retail trade. Corporate labor was more clearly facing corporate chains, and organized labor had an effect. Between 1972 and 1984, the retail food unions gained victories in 57 percent of the National Labor Relation Board elections for unionization. From 1970 to 1980, food store wages increased an average of 8.4 percent which was a higher rate than the non-agricultural economy.[67] But in the 1980s, the earnings of grocery workers declined from 85 percent of the non-agricultural economic sector in 1983 to 65 percent in 1989. This drop in income was due to grocery management placing a greater dependence on part-time workers. In 1983, 41 percent of all supermarket employees worked full time, and by 1989 it had dropped to 36 percent. Part-time employees earned less income than full-time workers, and with part-time work becoming more prevalent, the overall salary average for super-market employees decreased. With these working conditions of part-time work, store employees became more willing to support unionization to better their incomes. By 1990, half of the chains and 12 percent of the independents were unionized.[68] Unlike the national trend of declining unionization, union-ism in food retailing was sustained in elections, but union management was not able to prevent the fall in average wages that grocery management gained by converting full-time jobs to part-time positions in the supermarket.

The stability of local market conditions also became a key ingredient for the success of organized labor. When a few corporate chains dominated the grocery trade in a metropolitan area, grocery management in those chains faced little competition, and they were able to stabilize high food prices and profits. Grocery chains were creating local oligopolies, but the domination of three or four chains meant that union management was able to concentrate its organizing efforts and contract negotiations to capture a share of the chains' profits. In some metropolitan areas, no single chain or small group of grocery chains captured a large share of the local economic market. Under these circumstances, price competition between store operators was significant, and grocery chain management was less willing to grant salary concessions to unions.[69] At the same time, local union management was hampered in con-centrating its negotiation efforts when many union contracts had to be exe-cuted for a large number of competitors. In some cases, local unions even faced difficulty in locating absentee store owners, which made unionizing efforts even more difficult. Although oligopolies created an economic hegen-omy over local market conditions, union management often struggled to sustain worker benefits under competitive conditions when corporate chains did not economically dominate a metropolitan region.

Corporate chain and union relations were also shaped unevenly by tran-sitional economic conditions in metropolitan areas. Some chains made poor store expansion strategies, felt that profit margins were too constrained by high labor costs, thought that market expansion and profits were better in another city, or decided on these concerns in some combination. If a major chain exited a metropolitan area, the oligopoly of a few chains was weakened, and in many cases affiliated and non-affiliated independents filled the market gap. The chains no longer dominated the local economic market, and price competition between stores increased. Being more unionized than indepen-dents, corporate chains had more difficulty in sustaining profits due to higher labor costs. Quite often, there was a snowball effect. As the oligopoly of a few corporate chains weakened, all major chains, such as A&P, Kroger, and Safeway, tended to leave a metropolitan area. Price competition increased further, and just as important, local unions faced monumental problems sustaining worker benefits or continuing union contracts. Unions faced a deterioration of political power as corporate chains became less powerful in a metropolitan area. Yet, the reverse conditions happened when a few corporate chains entered metropolitan areas and began to dominate market trade. These uneven transitions were beneficial or costly to grocery store workers, depending on the direction of the economic transition in a metropolitan area.

Many grocery store workers ultimately faced difficult economic conditions. Some regions of the country, such as the West Coast and portions of the East Coast, have stable chain and union relations. But even in these regions, corporate chains have left metropolitan regions. Grocery clerks and meat cutters in some metropolitan areas, such as Pittsburgh, Dallas, and Kansas City, have seen corporate chains enter their cities, create oligopolies, and then leave. Even under stable conditions within the grocery trade, national economics have played havoc with union management attempting to achieve benefits for their workers. As a result of these economic instabilities, many local unions typically found themselves reacting to their political circumstances rather than being able to be proactive.

The local economic instability that grocery store workers faced was partially due to inefficiencies and corporate takeovers in the retail food industry. Both large and small chains were affected by outside investors who saw the opportunity to exploit a corporate grocery chain's economic weaknesses. Chain takeovers were both internal to and external to the retail food business.

The first major chain to become susceptible to a corporate takeover in the 1980s was the industry's most famous company, A&P. No grocery chain historically epitomized big business in the grocery trade more than A&P, but the company had made serious mistakes since the deaths of John and George Hartford in the 1950s. Stockholders initially received good financial returns from their stock shares, but A&P's management made numerous strategic errors in maintaining the corporation's economic prominence. Too many marketing decisions were made in A&P's New York corporate headquarters rather than allowing regional managers to respond to their area needs. Moreover, A&P was not aggressive in building suburban stores, and their supermarkets lacked the location and size for complete shopping that other chains exploited. A&P eventually suffered losses, and their profit margins were minimal at best. In 1962, A&P was still the dominant corporate grocery chain with 33 percent of sales among the top ten chains, but in 1973, Safeway surpassed A&P in total volume sales and became the nation's leading grocery chain.[70] While other major corporate chains were expanding and producing strong profit margins in the 1960s and 1970s, A&P was experiencing an economic decline.

A&P was also highly susceptible to being taken over by outside investors, because the company's pension fund was a prominent asset. A&P's Pension Plan Trust in the 1980s was worth approximately $400 million. Corporate management felt that the Trust was overfunded, because such cash assets were highly attractive to corporate raiders. A&P's corporate management did make stated provisions in the trust plan that prevented corporate raiders from capturing the Pension Plan's surplus funds, but A&P's continuous decline in business and the presence of the Pension Plan's funds made the company attractive to outside investors. By eventually gaining a controlling percentage of company stock, corporate raiders can often divest such funds for their own use. Erivan Haub, a major West German food retailer, gained a majority of A&P's stock in 1981, and soon afterward began to dismantle the Pension Plan and its surplus fund provision for A&P employees, both management and workers. A class action suit was filed against A&P by former employees, and they received a court settlement of $50 million in 1985. Other court cases ensued. Yet, Haub's ability to capture the Pension Plan Trust enabled him to underwrite his A&P stock investments. Although portions of the Pension Plan remained in place, A&P's corporate management was able to divert $275 million in employee pension funds for other investment purposes.[71] A&P's historic policy of using its profits to reward its employees through a retirement plan was devastated. In the end, corporate management raided the employees' Pension Fund Trust for its own profitable ends at the expense of A&P's employees.

Although less dramatic in scale, a small chain was susceptible to a takeover when local market conditions became unstable. The Milgram chain in the Kansas City area was founded in 1913, and the chain grew and prospered. Just as A&P had done, however, Milgram's management made some poor strategic decisions. They built stores that were smaller in size than their competitors. Fewer store managers and clerks were required to run thirty stores that were 10,000 square feet in size than to operate ten stores that had 30,000 square feet. Even with an amount of total square footage equal to their competitors, Milgram's operating expenses for their stores were higher. The company's poor decisions for store expansion were compounded when major corporate chains decided to leave the Kansas City area. In the early 1970s, 60 percent of the local market was dominated by a few major chains, and this oligopoly stabilized food prices. In 1976, the Kroger Company left the Kansas City area. A&P and Kroger decided that labor costs were too high. Moreover, they needed to expand and upgrade existing stores, but the costs were too great. A&P moved out in 1982, but its stores were eventually taken over by a large local wholesaler who converted the stores to be independently owned by affiliated independents. Soon afterward, Safeway vacated the Kansas City area.[72] There were no big chains left to sustain an oligopoly. The changing conditions of designed space and oligopoly led to unstable economic conditions for a local corporate chain.

This local economic instability led not only to the fall of the Milgram stores but also to the loss of wages and jobs for grocery workers. With new supermarkets being mostly non-union, Milgram was the only large local chain with union labor. Milgram faced severe economic difficulties. Its store sizes were inefficiently small. Without an oligopoly of a few big chains, price competition in the Kansas City became inevitable, and with Milgram's labor costs being higher than its competitors, Milgram not only had to lower food prices but also to accept lower profit margins and eventually financial losses. All of these economic conditions forced Milgram's management to sell their chain in 1984 to Wetterau, a St. Louis grocery wholesaler company. Wetterau then dismantled the Milgram chain: "all of its thirty-six stores were either closed outright or closed temporarily while new ownership was installed and the union workforce was pushed out."[73] The decline of an oligopoly led not only to the fall of the Milgram chain but also to the decline of unionism in the metropolitan area.

The leveraged buyout of Safeway was a major takeover conducted by investors external to the retail food industry. Corporate takeovers, such as with A&P and Milgram, were accomplished by companies within the food industry. Safeway, on the other hand, was purchased by leveraged buyout investors who borrowed heavily to buy a majority of Safeway's public stock and then made the company private. Taking control of management, they sold portions of the company's assets and used its cash flow to pay for their stockholding debts. Herbert and Robert Haft began to buy Safeway stock in the open market in 1985, and they offered to buy the company at $64 a share. Safeway management feared that this buyout would result in the dismantling of the company. To avoid this outcome, Safeway officials sold their chain in 1986 to Kohlburg Kravis Roberts and Company, KKR, which gained 73 percent of Safeway's common stock at the price of $3,105,000,000. At the time, Safeway was the largest corporate food chain in the United States, and its buyout demonstrated that the retail food industry was easily subservient to the economic power of financial investors.

Corporate profits were substantial in the Safeway leveraged buyout. Shareholders gained an 82 percent rise in their stocks at the time of the buyout as compared to stock prices three months earlier, and warrants to their stockholdings awarded them almost 6 percent ownership in the company. Safeway's corporate executives made $28 million in the sale, and they were able to buy 10 percent of the new Safeway Company at $2 per share, which later increased to more than $12 per share. The Hafts made $100 million by selling their shares to KKR, and as a consolation prize, they were given the option to buy 20 percent in new company shares. Soon afterward, the Hafts sold their option to KKR for $59 million. KKR charged Safeway $60 million in fees to put the company sale together, and the firm acquired a 20 percent share of eventual profits from any sale of Safeway. Investment banks received $65 million, and law and accounting firms received $25 million in the sale. Investors' profits in the leveraged buyout of Safeway were extensive.

Financiers' profits came at the expense of Safeway's work force. Corporate management sold 1,100 of its 2,235 stores, and the labor force to support these stores was eliminated as well. More than 300 staffers from the company's corporate headquarters were released. The major job cutbacks, however, were store managers, grocery clerks, meat cutters, and other support employees. Moreover, the reduction in Safeway's labor force was uneven, because corporate management decided to remain in some regions but pulled out altogether in some cities. In Dallas, Texas, the entire area division was terminated, and almost 9,000 Safeway employees, who had an average of seventeen years of service, were fired. Local grocery competitors bought over half of Safeway's stores, but they were unwilling to hire unionized workers. Former Safeway employees who found work at other grocery stores received new salaries that were half of their previous hourly rates. Just as important, their new store employers typically demanded that they work part-time, and without full-time employment status, these ex-Safeway employees lost their medical benefits. Safeway management also made life difficult for their former employees whether or not they found new employment. Severance paychecks from Safeway's headquarters were late coming. Former employees were often unable to pay household bills and outstanding loans, and they often had their automobiles and homes reclaimed by loan agencies. Life became so desperate for some former employees that they had heart attacks, attempted suicide, or succeeded in killing themselves.[74] Safeway's leveraged buyout laid waste not only to jobs and work places of grocery workers but also to their social well-being and homes.

The same leveraged buyout tactics used on Safeway were applied in 1988 to the Kroger Company, the nation's largest chain. Kroger's attraction to investors was that its parts were worth more than its whole. The chain included 1,300 supermarkets, 935 convenience stores, and 38 manufacturing units, and these assets were easy for investors to divide and then to sell at a profit to other competitors. Yet, Kroger's fixed capital assets were not as attractive as Safeway's. Ninety percent of Kroger's stores were leased, whereas Safeway owned its real estate. Although its lease arrangements made Kroger less attractive to outside investors, they knew that these lease arrangements could be sold to competitors who wanted new store locations.[75] Seeing the potential of these assets, Herbert and Robert Haft once again began to execute a leveraged buyout, but this time, they were out-maneuvered by Kroger's corporate management. Under the leadership of Joseph Pilcher, Kroger officials devised a plan that offered "shareholders a hefty dividend and employees a significant ownership stake in what remains a public company."[76] Unlike Safeway, Kroger's corporate management chose to prevent a leveraged buy-out.

Even without a takeover, the threat of a leveraged buyout caused gains and losses within the Kroger Company. In addition to stockholders' dividends, the company's recapitalization resulted in corporate executives receiving $17 million in benefits and corporate consultants being paid $25 million in advising fees. To finance its recapitalized debts, Kroger's corporate management had to make cutbacks. Over three hundred staff people at its headquarters were released. With the sale of one hundred stores and other operations, Kroger officials fired more than four thousand employees. Terminated Kroger employees, however, were compensated with severance pay and medical benefits that were far greater than ex-Safeway employees received. But these cutbacks in the work force were insufficient to cover the costs of the leveraged buyout war. To lower overhead costs in order to pay for outstanding company loans, store employees' salaries were cut 9 percent.[77] Although Kroger employees did not suffer economically as much as Safeway's work force, there was a repeated pattern. A leveraged buyout, whether threatened or realized, resulted in financial investors and corporate executives reaping capital benefits, whereas the company work force suffered job losses and pay cuts to finance these capital gains.

During the 1980s, some retail clerks became frustrated with corporate chains that treated the supermarket mainly as a financial investment rather than a productive place to work. Retail clerks made critical comments about their work loads and their ability to be productive.

One A&P cashier complained about her work load:

I was hassled till I almost fell off my feet. They drove us dizzy with check-outs at all kinds of crazy prices. . . . I was so weak from bagging, bagging, checking, checking. And what was it for? It was to wipe out my own job! . . . We were worked to a rag just so they could make a little bit more on us before they locked us out of the jobs we needed to eat. God, I tell you, there I was checking out my own damned life.[78]

Speaking about job training and management, union members of Local 1357 of the United Food and Commercial Workers in Philadelphia said:

You get a one-day orientation and then you're at it. You have to understand. There's turnover and shift changes and switching around of clerks, and what the hell, you can't figure out what's going on. One guy tells you one thing, another guy tells you something else. It's a wonder anything gets done right when people have to sort of figure it out as they go along.[79]

Wendell Young, a union organizer who had worked for Food Fair and Penn Fruit, noted the dilemmas of spatial efficiency as related to worker conditions:

Even when the market chains invest in major overhauls, they leave out the most important elements. One chain had a whole network of shabby stores. They poured money into redecorating, but they really didn't change the terribly inefficient way the company operated . . . supermarket space is some of the most expensive floor space in the merchandising field. Yet, the inefficiency is such because of poor employee morale and poor management that literally millions of dollars are lost weekly to loss of productivity and service.[80]

In response to such conditions and the need to save jobs, A&P workers in Philadelphia established a worker cooperative. When Erivan Haub took control of A&P in 1981, he proceeded not only to gain control of the Pension Plan Trust but also to close numerous A&P stores, which he deemed insufficiently profitable. In reaction, Philadelphia A&P clerks worked through their local UFCW unions to save their stores. As head of one UFCW local, Wendell Young, recommended to union members that they buy out all of A&P's thirty-two Philadelphia stores. Young and other union leaders had to address union workers' fears. A&P management was initially taken aback that workers were willing to invest in stores that A&P had been unable to achieve desired profit margins. In 1982, both parties came to an agreement. A&P reopened twenty stores under a new labor agreement of higher wages. Employees were now able to participate in a special trust fund that permitted employees to share in market profitability through incentive bonuses. One percent of gross sales went into the employee trust fund and was owned by the employees. A critical provision in the final agreement was that workers had the option to take over stores that A&P decided to phase out. To organize for these buyouts, grocery workers pledged their savings to the O&O Corporation, Owned and Operated. The O&O Corporation was the management group that administered these worker-cooperative stores. Unlike other grocery chains, the O&O Markets are owned and operated by their workers.[81] Union leadership demonstrated that the management-worker division was not inevitable in the grocery business.

With all its innovation, the worker-owned O&O Markets remained a rare response to the financial manipulations of large grocery chains. Many retail clerks and meat cutters lost their jobs or feared unemployment. They were less knowledgeable and less economically liquid than major investors such as Erivan Haub, the Haft brothers, and Kohlburg Kravis Roberts and Company. At the same time, financially stable corporate chains and affiliated independents had no interest in helping to create worker cooperatives. As a result, investment in supermarkets remained under the domination of corporate chains and affiliated independents.

The business struggles from 1960 to the present were uneven in their outcomes. On the one hand, grocery management found new ways to configure store space that allowed grocery chains and independents to minimize labor costs. On the other hand, union membership grew, and union leadership was able to gain higher wages and better benefits for grocery store employees and, in rare cases, it helped to establish worker-owned stores. Corporate grocery chain management increasingly faced an equivalent organizational framework from organized labor as retail clerks and meat cutters consolidated their unions into the United Food and Commercial Workers Union. But the union movement was unable to counter all of the grocery chains' economic strategies. When corporate chains moved out of metropolitan areas, the oligopolies of a few chains collapsed, and local unions were not always able to sustain unionism when local affiliated and non-affiliated independents hired non-union employees. Mergers and leveraged buyouts often eliminated not only local oligopolies but also stores and their work force. Corporate management redesigned the grocery store to reduce its labor force requirements, and corporate takeovers often annihilated the workplace altogether. Management (of corporate chains and of all independents) was constantly dismantling the supermarket's design and location only to reconstruct it for more profitable ends at the expense of unionized labor.

THE MODERN PARADE

The retail grocery industry entered the 1960s with hopes for a bright future, and the supermarket was the flagship for that future. Location and architectural design were initial spatial concerns of grocery management. In an age of economic prosperity, they realized that design efficiency was no longer enough. Supermarkets had to be visually appealing to attract customers to locations that maximized sales. But in a prosperous age and a changing society, the conventional supermarket was no longer able to monopolize retail grocery trade. Today there is a parade of various store types, both larger and smaller than the conventional supermarket. The expanding market economy of the retail food industry could not be confined by a single design configuration of the grocery store space.

The grocery store parade of the modern era was a series of innovations and confrontations that intensified economic competition in the retail food industry. The emphases on architectural aesthetics and store location enabled store owners to attract customers and persuade them to extend their shopping trips. Supermarkets became larger in size to handle a more diverse set of products, and different store types—from the convenience store to the warehouse market—provided shoppers with more alternatives to meet their needs. Grocery management used these devices to expand their economic markets or to capture others. All of these innovations were profit motivated, but the search for profits brought on demands by labor to share them. The other half of the parade was grocery management's attempts to control costs, mainly labor. Efficiency in store design, mechanical devices such as price scanners, the formation and dismantling of oligopolies, and leveraged buyouts were all corporate tactics to minimize labor costs or to eliminate organized labor.

Capital formation and its dissolution in the grocery store were physically designed and administratively manipulated by grocery management to sustain their economic power over an increasingly organized labor force of grocery workers.

Chapter 7

THE EVOLUTION OF THE GROCERY STORE SPACE

The history of the grocery store is a history of economic competition over space. Entrepreneurs create new store designs at new locations to capture profits at the expense of competitors whose stores do not have such design changes. Economic and technological conditions in a historic era shaped store design, and as these conditions changed so did the American grocery store. But change was uneven. When the marketing approach to food retailing was stable, design changes were largely incremental. In contrast, innovations such as the supermarket led to significant changes in food retailing. Whether design changes were large or small, a guiding business principle was to use architectural design as a means to make a grocery store more profitable and competitive.

THE GROCERY STORE AS A GROWTH MACHINE

The evolution of the grocery store space is historically inseparable from its growth as a retail industry. From its early small business stage to the modern era of corporate capitalism, conflicts over spatial design have been both averted and caused by the growth of American cities and territory.

During the era dominated by public markets, economic expansionism was primarily a matter of providing space to meet market demands. In cities, public markets initially filled a vacuum for townspeople who were unable to provide all their food necessities. Public markets in streets created no excessive spatial demands, because commercial private property on the surrounding blocks provided other goods and services. But when cities began to grow, city officials needed street space to serve the growing demands of traffic. The loss of spatial flexibility that came with the move to the city block meant that the public markets had to compete economically with other businesses when land costs became part of their overhead. When markets were on the street, a new building addition along Market Street or in an open intersection proved to be a small problem for city officials. Market Street was the expansion site for food retailing as a growth machine. In contrast, public markets on the block were physically contained on a lot, and building structures on lots were often expensive. Street markets were typically one-story structures with simple spans, but to duplicate such floor space on the block, city officials were forced to invest not only in more expensive structures but also in land. As mass distribution and suburbanization progressed in American cities, the public market was unable to move with this growth, because such markets depended on their position as a central receiving and distribution point for food goods. As a high fixed capital investment with inflexible spatial requirements, the public market became an inefficient machine for economic growth.

Over time, city grocery stores fared much better economically than public markets, because these stores had spatial flexibility. Starting first as general stores and evolving into businesses strictly devoted to grocery goods, city grocery stores were small and decentralized. Cities expanded outwardly with residential neighborhoods, and storekeepers were able to move with growth by leasing or buying a small building. Their food items were more expensive than in public markets, but small grocery stores were more accessible to nearby residents. Although the public market became physically larger and had more stall merchants and employees, this labor force was ultimately limited by the spatial-economic limits of the public market space. In contrast, new grocery stores appeared as quickly as the city expanded, and new store owners and clerk jobs closely followed this growth. The small grocery store was the economic cell for market growth in American cities. Public markets experienced economic and political conflicts between stall merchants, street vendors, and farmers, because the public market space was confined and not easily enlarged. These conflicts between entrepreneurs, however, became less intense as food retailing grew with the abundant growth of small stores. At the same time, neighborhood conflicts were less intense, because small storekeepers had sufficient trade area in expanding residential areas. City grocery stores also minimized labor disputes, because the number of employees in each store was quite small. Thus, as cities grew, the small grocery store was a physical manifestation of the economic fact that small business owners were becoming more dominant in food retailing.

The country store was a growth machine both in the nation's frontier and its hinterlands. Much like its city counterparts, the country store flourished when it dominated local trade. Moreover, country storekeepers followed the nation's frontier just as city grocery stores followed residential growth. But unlike city food retailing, the country store played a critical role in the territorial expansion of capitalism. Such stores were the business frontiers of the United States. The railroads and the telegraph were critical in making money the dominant currency in the hinterland, and the country store was the financial distribution point. The country storekeeper was not only a grocer but also a banker, a real estate agent, and an entrepreneur in general. As crude as it was in its spatial design, the country store provided a space where capitalism in the United States frontier and hinterlands could advance.

The historic economic evolution in the grocery trade was the transition from simple free enterprise to corporate capitalism. In the early history of the United States, stall merchants in public markets, storekeepers of small city grocery stores, and country store owners were in charge of their own businesses. But with the rise of mass marketing, the individual business owner had to fight for economic survival. When the grocery chain system emerged, small food retailers were unable to compete with the rising financial advantages of corporate bulk buying. Small merchants operated with small inventories, which were often supplied by local and regional sources, and they were systematically confronted by corporate store formats. A&P's economy stores were often no larger than their small competitors, but these corporate stores were built on a foundation of mass retail distribution. The design of these stores reflected an efficient space systematically designed for economic reproduction. The corporate approach to food retailing introduced economic and spatial systems of competition to the market place. Small grocery retailers were hard pressed to compete successfully and to survive economically against these corporate stores.

The ability of corporate chains to reshape the economic rules of grocery competition led to a series of actions by retail grocers. Some grocers in public markets and stores gave up their businesses and worked for other stores. Other grocers organized as affiliated independents and continued to compete with corporate chains. A few non-affiliated independents were innovative and survived on their own. Economic competition increasingly occurred between grocery companies rather than between individual grocers.

The redesign of the grocery store by business innovators met with mixed success in the development of food retailing. The systematic design of the corporate economy store led to highly efficient store operations at the micro scale. Store items on the shelf had to pay their way by sustaining a volume of sales per square foot versus a net profit per food item. Store operators learned to organize floor plans, design food displays, and make shelf placements of goods that would maximize a customer's purchases. Yet, macro scale changes in architectural design led to economic upheavals. Innovative store owners used more building space to create the combination store and then the supermarket for mass retailing, and this spatial change made obsolete efficient economy stores that corporate chains and affiliated independents had refined. The supermarket was a technological innovation that awakened all grocery retailers from their comfortable attempts at refining the design of small stores. Moreover, the supermarket reshaped traditional distribution networks. Grocery companies were forced to realize that central warehouse facilities were less important as the supermarket increasingly received food directly from food manufacturers. Although the early supermarket was unrefined, the supermarket as a type became the industry's primary design paradigm, because the supermarket was better able to facilitate one-stop shopping and a high volume of sales as compared to the small store.

The evolution of grocery store design also changed the employment conditions for store employees as a labor force. Grocery management used store design to minimize labor costs. Quite simply, if a store's design could reduce the number of employees required to operate it, management was eager to implement that design. Initially, stall merchants in public markets, owners of small grocery stores, and country store owners treated the design of their retail space as a means to operate comfortably within their own individual work patterns. With the rise of corporate chains, and later affiliated independents, store owners were made constantly aware of the number of employees needed to operate the physical space of their stores. The economy store was the prelude to future labor relations. Grocery companies, such as A&P and Piggly Wiggly, minimized the number of retail clerks needed in their stores by reorienting floor plans and shelf space so that customers served themselves. But a small store could not optimize the ratio between retail floor space and the number of clerks needed to operate that space. A minimum number of employees is needed to operate any store, regardless of size. The supermarket allowed store owners to refine the ratio of employees needed to a store's square footage. As supermarkets became larger, these ratios were applicable not only to the store as a whole but also to food departments. Meat cutters, produce clerks, shelf clerks, and cashiers were all systematically analyzed by grocery management to determine how many workers were needed to support a supermarket's departmentalized space. Such analyses enabled store owners to conclude that one and a half clerks might be needed in a given department. As a result, part-time employees became an essential part of management's calculus to fulfill a half-time position based on ratio analysis. As the grocery store space was made larger, these labor to retail space ratios became better predictors of the needed size of the store's labor force. Grocery companies increasingly saw store design as a means to minimize labor needs.

The changing spatial structure in the grocery store led store workers to protect themselves by unionizing. As the grocery store became more economically designed through self-service and the use of ratios of employees to square footage, employees had to protect their jobs. The union movement helped to define employee work loads as well as benefits. Yet, workers often experienced difficulties defending their work space, because in the end, the store space was private property. Store employees were often unable to strike on store property, and instead were forced to parade on public sidewalks, which were often separated from the store by a parking lot. Moreover, union leadership was unable to protect all employee jobs. Central meat processing eliminated meat cutter space and jobs at the supermarket. The redesign of the cashier's space with price scanners eliminated the need for skilled labor, and store owners were able to convert high-paying skilled positions into low-paying unskilled jobs. With all these limitations, employees often became a vital force on the grocery store space. Worker strikes were able to slow down significantly the high sales volume on which efficient supermarkets depended. Low profit margins meant grocery companies could not sustain their retail system, which was based on the speed of high volume trade. Money, space, and time were integrally related in the conflicts between grocery companies and organized labor.

Conflicts between and within grocery companies were minimized as long as grocery management was able to sustain profits in historic eras of economic growth. American cities played a key role in this growth. Population growth and suburbanization helped to create expanding markets for store owners to exploit. Grocery management was willing to compensate its employees as long as economic growth continued. Initially there were few problems because small grocery store owners had few employees. But with the coming of the supermarket and corporate structures for mass retailing, economic competition and the concentration of employees into fewer but larger stores intensified class conflicts between and within grocery companies. Suburbanization after World War II helped to alleviate some of these conflicts, because grocery companies were able to expand their economic markets and sustain lower profit margins. Nevertheless, during this era the American union movement moved into food retailing. Grocery management maintained a fine balance between continued economic growth, increasing competition, and unionism.

The retail food business could not expand indefinitely. New supermarkets had more square footage than older ones, and store design became more efficient in terms of increasing customer demands and minimizing labor needs. But increasingly there were spatial limits to building new stores. As more supermarkets were built, trade areas between them became smaller, and economic competition increased. The only way for a grocery company to expand its store sites was to eliminate the competition. Price wars were one tactic, but a major tool used by grocery companies to sustain expanding markets was the merger. By buying a grocery chain or a group of independent stores, corporate chains were able to increase their company's growth potential. When buying another company, grocery management sold the unprofitable stores and expanded into the successful store sites previously occupied by the selling company. Thus, mergers enabled the buying grocery companies to be more dominant in cities where they were already doing business and to compete in new cities. Although they could not avoid labor demands entirely, grocery companies did use mergers to increase profits and to meet union demands for higher wages.

As supermarkets grew larger and the number of mergers increased, a small number of corporate chains came to dominate a city. Such oligopolies stabilized not only food prices but also union relationships. With no price wars, grocery management found it feasible to work with unions. Yet new competitors or internal mismanagement eventually led to company losses. As a result, local oligopolies often fell apart as corporate chains sold their metropolitan area stores. Fierce competition between the remaining grocery companies made it difficult for any company to remain profitable if they used union labor while their competitors did not. The resulting physical landscape was unstable. Grocery management sold many supermarkets to businesses that converted these stores into other enterprises. In some cases, stores remained vacant, casualties of price competition. The inability of grocery companies to stabilize business led to constant upheavals where supermarkets, often viewed by residents as local institutions, were built only to be uprooted later.

Market segmentation played a role in the destabilization of the grocery store space. Before World War II, there was little diversity in grocery shopping. Public markets were largely gone, and the supermarket was eliminating many small store owners. But with postwar economic prosperity and suburbanization, the American public became more diverse in its shopping demands. Grocery companies were able to expand their market growth by diversifying in food retailing. These companies no longer depended solely on the conventional supermarket. Convenience stores, discount stores, specialty food shops, super stores, warehouse markets, hypermarkets, and wholesale clubs became market means that enabled companies to maximize sales over space. From the convenience store that served a neighborhood to a hypermarket that served a regional area, grocery companies developed a diversity of store formats and designs that enabled them to cover multiple shopper demands. The conventional supermarket was no longer able to serve all needs and to maximize profits. But in this diversification, organized labor did not always follow. Grocery companies served as umbrella corporations for new lines of stores under a different name, and they did not readily extend labor contracts in supermarkets to their convenience stores or other store types. Market segmentation led not only to a variety of store designs and formats but also to an avoidance of organized labor.

THE ROLE OF ARCHITECTURAL DESIGN

Architectural design has played a key role in the evolution of the grocery store space. Larger space leads to a greater volume of trade, but design enables store owners to be efficient in their production of profits. Design is essential at both the macro and micro scale. Departmentalization enabled grocery companies to create systematic divisions that increased sales within and between these departments. Floor plan designs have continuously helped store owners guide and direct shoppers so that they will maximize purchases. At the same time, the design of shelf space and the choice of food items has enabled grocery management to maximize food sales per square foot. All of these design manipulations are intrinsically related to labor. Through systematic design, grocery management has directed the public to become not only efficient shoppers but also cost-reducing workers. Architectural design was historically critical in the development of self-service. By making the shopper a worker, store owners were able to reduce their labor costs. At the same time, they diluted the potential impact of organized labor, because fewer grocery employees resulted in a smaller army of workers who might rebel against company profits and policies. Architectural design has simultaneously provided for increased profit making and the control of labor relations.

From the mercantile era to the present-day corporate era, grocery management has used similar approaches to architectural design to gain economic power and to eliminate competitors. In the nineteenth century, the dominant building formats for grocery retailing were the public market, the small city grocery store, and the country store. Corporate chains economically attacked the public market and its host of stall merchants with the advantages of mass distribution. Their initial design solution was a systematically designed small store. Eventually, the economy store was replaced by a supermarket. The supermarket was unable to capture all trade, and competitors developed the convenience store. In retrospect, the supermarkets of today are equivalent to public markets in the past, and the convenience store is similar to the mom and pop grocery store of yesteryear. Even the country store is being replicated today. Casey's General Stores is a corporate chain of rural convenience stores that are spread throughout the Midwest in small towns and crossroads.[1] Public markets offered a diversity of food items, whereas nineteenth century city grocery stores and country stores sold a limited assortment of goods to nearby residents. These spatial patterns are being repeated today, but there is one crucial difference. We are in an era of corporate capitalism rather than simple free enterprise. Yet, it is ironic that today's modern supermarkets attempt to capture the aura of historic public markets through store design. Grocery store competitors have historically used a design format to destroy another store type and then adapted the conquered design format for their own ends.

Perhaps less noted, architectural design has enabled business interests to value the grocery store space for its historical and aesthetic value. Many public markets were major architectural edifices, and local citizens have saved many of these buildings through their historic preservation efforts. In a few cases, restored public markets have helped to spur downtown revitalization. The Indianapolis City Market was rehabilitated in 1976, and it was so successful in revitalizing the downtown area that business interests wanted to change the market's traditional functions to a fast food court. Business interests transformed the public interest intentions of historic preservation into demands for commercial gentrification that began to threaten the market itself.[2] This exploitation of historic structures, however, is the exception. Most buildings for grocery retailing have rarely included such aesthetic qualities. Many small stores and supermarkets were historically located either in low-cost buildings for lease or in functional buildings designed to minimize construction costs. Architects developed a few exotic store designs in this century, but public attempts to save such structures are minimal. The aesthetic qualities historically built into the grocery store space have been used for economic ends, but the public tends not to value the aesthetic value of these building structures.

Store owners also profited from food sales that were increased by the aesthetic appeal of their stores. For most of the twentieth century, grocery management saw architectural design mainly as a device to increase efficiency. Grocery companies did realize that store fronts and window displays could attract customers, but management did not emphasize fully aesthetic appeal in supermarkets until the 1960s. When store competitors became essentially equal in efficiency during an era of prosperity, they realized, just as with their food items, the package is as important as the product to attract customers. Architectural packaging using a variety of themes enabled store owners to shape an identity to attract shoppers. At the same time, architects designed supermarkets to blend with their surrounding neighborhoods. This blending technique allowed store architecture to stabilize surrounding real estate values rather than lowering them.

Efficiency, however, has historically played a more important role in store design than aesthetics. Elegant public markets, well-designed economy stores, or supermarkets with design themes were unable to survive the economic onslaught of competitors who offered lower prices and greater customer convenience. Public markets and country stores were replaced by economy stores, which were made obsolete by the conventional supermarket; it was then challenged severely by warehouse markets and other store types. In all these cases, aesthetic appeal in a store was typically sacrificed to lower overhead costs, which then resulted in lower, more competitive prices. Yet, when a store format becomes dominant and competitors have equal access to it, store aesthetic appeal often reemerges as an economic factor, such as the dramatic modernism and blending techniques used for stores in the 1960s. Although design efficiency dominates the use of architectural design, the profitable use of aesthetics is never eliminated.

Architectural design in the grocery store space has proven to be more than a shallow, subjective business technique. Throughout U.S. history, grocers have found that design, whether for efficiency or for aesthetics, resulted in higher sales volume and profits. Architectural design became the historic sculpting of fixed capital investments in the grocery store space. At the same time, the resulting drive by store owners to sustain their profits unavoidably had a political-economic impact. Mass distribution played a great role in the rise of corporate power in the United States, but ultimately, this mass distribution of food goods had to be located, arranged, and marketed in the grocery store space for this system to be implemented successfully.

Although perhaps not the major force in sustaining of food retailing, design has played a key role. Architectural design is intrinsically related to the business history of the grocery store space.

IDEALS VERSUS REALITIES

The future of the grocery store space is filled with hopes and desires as well as with skepticism and reality. Throughout U.S. history, retailers and shoppers have experienced a multitude of feelings and concerns about what a grocery store should be.

A futurist view must include technical possibilities. Stores have become diverse, and this trend will likely continue. Derivative store formats of the conventional supermarket are larger than in the past, and convenience stores represent a dispersion of small grocery establishments. Such size diversity is likely to continue, and market segmentation plays an integral part. Upper- and lower-class neighborhoods, urban versus suburban locations, and ethnic mix all play a part in determining the size and character of the grocery store space and what is sold. Yet, there are possible trends beyond these historic patterns. Isaac Asimov, the science-fiction writer, speculated that shoppers will shop at computerized convenience stores. Shoppers will call the store by using their computers and send their grocery lists to the store. Such stores will gather and pack the requested groceries, which are made ready for shoppers when they arrive to pay for their food items. Asimov's shoppers will be able to buy prepared gourmet meals, and drug prescriptions will be incorporated into food products. Vegetables will be grown in the supermarket's backroom in three days and put on the shelf just as with freshly baked bread. The supermarket will become so highly mechanized that little physical labor will be needed to service the store.[3] Grocery retailer consultants are already experimenting with the idea of the smart store. Through computer technology, customers will reduce or simplify their shopping trips. Instead of using a grocery cart to find staple products, such as canned goods and paper goods, a shopper may simply order them from home by scanning the Uniform Pricing Code off an empty package, coupon, ad, or catalog. The store then delivers these goods within the hour, or at a convenient time for the shopper. At the supermarket, the shopper may use a smart card to select items at food idea centers. These purchases are automatically charged to the smart card, and the order is picked and packed. The shopper then picks up the order at a drive-through location or prearranges for home delivery.[4] These speculations about the grocery store space are futuristic, but it is possible to imagine the total elimination of grocery retailing. In the TV show, "Star Trek: The Next Generation," crew members tell a computer to produce the meal that they wish to order. In a matter of moments, the computer creates the meal. Under these circumstances, there is no need for a retail store, much less a mass distribution system. Just as in the historic past, technical innovations provide new conceptualizations of space and shopping that make obsolete more conventional and traditional practices.

With all these future possibilities, there is still the argument for traditional ways of living. Christopher Alexander, an architectural theorist, notes: "There is one timeless way of building. It is a process through which the order of a building or a town grows out directly from the inner nature of the people, and the animals, and plants, and matter which are in it."[5]

The traditional ways in which a community are organized physically include the grocery store space. Alexander comments further:

the major shopping needs, in any community, are taken care of by the market of many shops.... Give every neighborhood at least one corner grocery, somewhere near its heart. Place these corner groceries every 200 to 800 yards, according to the density, so that each one serves about 1,000 people. Place them on corners, where large numbers of people are going past. And combine them with houses, so that the people who run them can live over them or next to them.... Prevent franchises and pass laws which prevent the emergence of those much larger groceries which swallow up the corner groceries—individually owned shops.[6]

This traditional way of building that Alexander suggests is bound to the community rather than the world of business. Historically, Alexander creates the rationale for a community place that is much like the image one finds in a painting by Pieter Bruegel. People are actively involved in play, socializing, and work in a community space that they actively help to create. Alexander wants the grocery store to be a common ground. This perspective of the grocery store space is about the quality of life rather than economic efficiency. Retailers have implemented most technical achievements in retail grocery store design in order to lower food costs. But Alexander's view argues that this economic assumption in the creation of place has gone too far. Store formats, such as warehouse markets and wholesale clubs, often have minimal aesthetic qualities that enrich the lives of the American public. At the same time, supermarket design, including aesthetic appeal, is geared to maximize a shopper's purchases. The design of the grocery store space is oriented to the community to maximize sales, and this outcome has minimized community social space, with economic space put in its place.

The historic legacy of the grocery store space is creative destruction. Christopher Alexander's vision of a timeless way of building stressing durable, sensitive environments largely represents a contradiction to the past. Grocery store entrepreneurs created specific store designs to maximize profits only to replace them in a business world of competition that demanded new designs to sustain profits. But the historic path of creative destruction was uneven. Not all attempted architectural ideas worked, and some ideas were only minor design adjustments. Nevertheless, effective architectural designs had consequences. Employees objected to designs that eliminated jobs. Many store owners were unable to survive economically when competitors introduced design innovations. Creative destruction included innovations, incremental improvements, and labor conflicts. Thus, the history of the American grocery store is an evolutionary history of progress and struggle in the American landscape.

NOTES

CHAPTER 1

1. John W. Reps, *The Making of Urban America* (Princeton: Princeton University Press, 1965), 141. See Carl Bridenbaugh, *Cities in the Wilderness* (New York: Ronald Press, 1938), 27–28; and John L. Wann and Edwin W. Cake, *Farmers' Product Markets in the United States: Part 1, History and Description* (Washington, D.C.: U. S. Department of Agriculture, 1948), 4.

2. Thomas F. DeVoe, *The Market Book: A History of the Public Markets of New York City* (New York: Augustus M. Kelley Publishers, 1970), 15, 37.

3. James N. Primm, *The Lion of the Valley* (Boulder, Colo.: Pruett Publishing Company, 1981), 15–18.

4. DeVoe, *The Market Book*, 28–29.

5. Reps, *The Making of Urban America*, 36–38; John McAndrew, *The Open-Air Churches of Sixteenth-Century Mexico* (Cambridge: Harvard University Press, 1965), 94, 96. Arcades surrounding plazas in Mexican cities were specified by Spain's Royal Ordinances of 1573: "The whole plaza and the four main streets diverging from it shall have arcades for these are a great convenience for those who resort there for trade." Although no arcades were built, it is very likely that the food market was part of the trade on the plaza, and within food stalls, these principles were loosely applied in the Texas colonial settlements.

6. John W. Reps, *Cities of the American West* (Princeton: Princeton University Press, 1979), 117.

7. DeVoe, *The Market Book*, 58–60, 73–74.

8. Reps, *The Making of Urban America*, 137–38.

9. DeVoe, *The Market Book*, 54; Arthur E. Peterson and George W. Williams, *New York City as an Eighteenth Century Municipality* (Port Washington, N.Y.: Ira J. Friedman, Inc., 1967), 61-63.

10. DeVoe, *The Market Book*, 54, 123.

11. Ibid., 182–83, 347.

12. John Thomas Scharf, *History of Saint Louis City and County* (Philadelphia: L. H. Everts, 1883), 748.

13. Reps, *The Making of Urban America*, 215–65.

14. DeVoe, *The Market Book*, 321.

15. Ibid., 382, 552, 555–56; Carol P. Miller, "Markets and Market Houses," in David D. Van Tassel and John J. Grabowski, eds., *The Encyclopedia of Cleveland History* (Bloomington: Indiana University Press, 1987), 659.

16. Mary L. Christovich et al., *New Orleans Architecture: The American Sector* (Gretna, La.: Pelican Publishing Company, 1972), 43.

17. DeVoe, *The Market Book*, 486; Kenneth H. Dunshee, *As You Pass By* (New York: Hastings House, 1952), 47.

18. DeVoe, *The Market Book*, 410.

19. Reps, *The Making of Urban America*, 177, 201, 279, 283. There is the remote possibility that the location of market houses on the square was influenced by the bastide plan, which was used for fortress towns in some parts of France, Great Britain, and Spain. The probability is greatest for Charleston, South Carolina, because the town grew out of its fortress installations. See Reps, ibid., 2–3.

20. Kenneth H. Dunshee, *As You Pass By* (New York: Hastings House, 1952), 224.

21. Walter M. Whitehall, *Boston: A Topographical History* (Cambridge: Harvard University Press, 1968), 41, 69.

22. Ibid., 96.

23. George B. Tatum, *Penn's Great Town* (Philadelphia: University of Pennsylvania Press, 1961), 25–26.

24. Reps, *The Making of Urban America*, 20. A plan of Wilhelmostad, Netherlands, in 1647 shows the location of a market house in the street.

25. Mary Cable, *Lost New Orleans: The American Sector* (New York: American Legacy Press, 1972), 33; Harold M. Mayer and Richard C. Wade, *Chicago: Growth of a Metropolis* (Chicago: University of Chicago Press, 1969), 18; Reps, *The Making of Urban America*, 215, 226, 265, 273; Richard C. Wade, *The Urban Frontier* (Chicago: University of Chicago Press, 1959), 318.

26. Maury Klein and Harvey A. Kantor, *Prisoners of Progress: American Industrial Cities, 1850–1920* (New York: Macmillan, 1976), 124.

27. Morris L. Sweet, "History of Municipal Markets," *Journal of Housing* 18 (6, 1961): 238; Robert F. Looney, *Old Philadelphia in Early Photographs, 1839–1914* (New York: Dover Publication, 1976), 73. It was not a foregone conclusion that market houses were immediately removed for the installation of streetcar tracks. On Philadelphia's Market Street in 1859, both market houses and a rail system existed together in the street.

28. Edward K. Spann, *The New Metropolis: New York City, 1840–1857* (New York: Columbia University Press, 1981), 47.

29. DeVoe, *The Market Book*, 321.

30. Ibid., 555–56. New York City's Tompkins Market was built in 1860, and its upper floors were used for military drill rooms and armories. Also see Nathan Silver, *Lost New York* (New York: Houghton Mifflin, 1967), 95. The Richmond Market in Baltimore was built in 1873, and its public building section was quite large and undoubtedly was used for a great variety of community purposes. See Marion E. Warren and Mame Warren, *Baltimore: When She Was What She Used to Be* (Baltimore: Johns Hopkins University Press, 1983), 49.

31. James M. Goode, *Capital Losses: A Cultural History of Washington's Destroyed Buildings* (Washington, D.C.: Smithsonian Institution Press, 1979), 263.

32. Ibid., 266; Warren and Warren, *Baltimore*, 46.

33. Goode, *Capital Losses*, 265–66. Structural advances were sometimes insufficiently designed in market buildings. The Belair and Lafayette Markets in Baltimore were built with iron columns on granite sockets. In 1871, both structures were destabilized by high winds that lifted off the roofs. The structural design had accounted only for vertical pressure. See John Thomas Scharf, *History of Baltimore City and County* (Philadelphia: L. H. Everts, 1881), 207–8.

34. Goode, *Capital Losses*, 262–64.

35. Scharf, *History of Saint Louis and County*, 750.

36. James D. Van Trump, *Life and Architecture in Pittsburgh* (Pittsburgh: Pittsburgh History and Landmark Foundation, 1983), 38.

37. Goode, *Capital Losses*, 262–65; and Scharf, *History of Saint Louis and County*, 750. Frederick S. Lightfoot, *Nineteenth Century New York in Rare Photographic Views* (New York: Dover, 1981), 123.

38. Van Trump, *Life and Architecture in Pittsburgh*, 39.

39. Wilhelm Goethe, *Italian Journeys* (London: George Bell and Sons, 1885), 40.

40. DeVoe, *The Market Book*, 201.

41. James D. McCabe, Jr., *New York by Gaslight* (New York: Greenwich House, 1882), 663.

42. Ibid., 664.

43. DeVoe, *The Market Book*, 355.

44. Ibid., 441–42.

45. Ibid., 443–44. In the mistreatment of farmers in the public markets, DeVoe is extremely cynical and angry about an incident in New York City's Washington Market. He writes: "This shed was put up accordingly, and gave accommodations only for a short period to the country people, as other individuals again wanted; and their having but the Superintendents of Markets [after this period] and a Clerk or two to 'convince' of their superior rights to take the countrymen's allotted space, they were usually successful, especially if their 'arguments' were weighty; and then one stand after another were 'given' away to these 'proper persons,' as the law directs, until at last the countrymen had again to fill the gangways, side-walks, and streets."

46. Charles Cist, *Cincinnati in 1851* (Cincinnati: W. H. Moore and Company, Publishers, 1851), 276–77.

47. McCabe, *New York by Gaslight*, 664–65; and Warren and Warren, *Baltimore*, 48. Not all cities had ladies shopping in public markets. In New Orleans of the 1840s, the markets were considered too rough for ladies. As a Creole tradition, gentlemen did the shopping or sent their slaves to buy goods in the market. See Cable, *Lost New Orleans*, 34.

48. DeVoe, *The Market Book*, 57, 565–66.

49. Spann, *The New Metropolis*, 50.

50. Vernon A. Mund, *Open Markets* (New York: Harper and Brothers, 1948), 44.

51. DeVoe, *The Market Book*, 210–11; Wade, *The Urban Frontier*, 280–81.

52. DeVoe, *The Market Book*, 425.

53. Wade, *The Urban Frontier*, 281–82. Cities such as Pittsburgh and St. Louis responded by enforcing trading hours and increasing fines for merchants who became forestallers at market houses; see also DeVoe, *The Market Book*, 426.

54. DeVoe, *The Market Book*, 494-95, 547.

55. William T. Childs, "The Municipal Markets in Baltimore," *Municipal Journal* 33 (23, 1912): 828.

56. DeVoe, *The Market Book*, 546.

57. Ibid., 448–50.

58. Ibid., 532; and Childs, "Municipal Markets of Baltimore," 828.

59. Arthur E. Goodwin, *Markets: Public and Private* (Seattle: Montgomery Printing Co., 1929), 38, 44–45, 152, 155, 206, 237.

60. Oscar E. Anderson, *Refrigeration in America* (Princeton: Princeton University Press, 1953), 8; DeVoe, *The Market Book*, 455–56.

61. Richard O. Cummings, *The American Ice Harvests* (Berkeley: University of California Press, 1949), 68–69.

62. Anderson, *Refrigeration in America*, 100.

63. Goodwin, *Markets*, 32.

64. Ibid., 109, 264.

65. Ibid., 85–87, 89; Frank Grad and George P. Hooper, "The New Centre Market, Newark, N.J.," *The American Architect*, 77 (March, 1925): 241–44. One of St. Louis' public markets also had an upper floor for parking, but it was significantly smaller than Newark's Center Market. See Goodwin, *Markets*, 68; and Sweet, "History of Municipal Markets," 239–41.

66. Goodwin, *Markets*, 70–74.

67. Alice Shorett and Murray Morgan, *The Pike Place Market: People, Politics, and Produce* (Seattle, Wash.: Pacific Search Press, 1982), 10–11, 23–39, 58–59.

68. W. P. Hunter, "New City Markets in Norfolk and Roanoke," *The American City* 28 (3, 1923): 261–63. Although not as large as the Newark Market, the Norfolk Public Market demonstrated how a medium-sized city could become concerned about design details that presented an image of efficiency and sanitation.

69. Goodwin, *Markets*, 148–54, 159–63, 170–71, 191–93.

70. U.S. Bureau of the Census, *Municipal Markets in Cities Having a Population of Over 30,000* (Washington, D.C.: U.S. Government Printing Office, 1918), 24. This report notes that a second story addition for an auditorium was added to the public market in Montgomery, Alabama, but this addition so darkened the building that the entire market fell into disuse; and Goodwin, *Markets*, 78, 97, 101.

71. Goodwin. *Markets*, 153.

72. McFall Kerbey, *Open Types of Public Markets*, United States Department of Agriculture Bulletin No. 1002 (Washington, D.C.: U.S. Government Printing Office, 1921), 10. Federal officials recommended that public markets be near main business zones and the most important subordinate business centers. Department stores were major retail magnets in such zones. For an explicit commentary about locating public markets near department stores, see Goodwin, *Markets*, 65.

73. U.S. Bureau of the Census, *Municipal Markets in Cities Having a Population of Over 30,000*, 24. Some cities, such as New Orleans, required less financing for public market improvements than other cities, because these cities still opted to have some of their markets built in the middle of public streets. As a result, there was no bonded indebtedness needed to retire property costs.

74. Goodwin, *Markets*, 271–74.

75. Ibid., 103.

76. Shorett and Morgan, *The Pike Place Market*, 62; and Goodwin, *Markets*, 246–50.

77. Goodwin, *Markets*, 217. Market managers who organized cooperative buying for stall merchants were acting in their own self-interest. By collectively lowering overhead costs for stall merchants, the market as a whole was seen as offering lower prices when compared to grocery store competitors. Because grocery stores offered conveniences, it was imperative for managers to make their markets as price competitive as possible.

78. Ibid., 235–36.

79. Ibid., 151. Such management techniques were characteristic of Taylorism. By standardizing equipment, processing procedures, and even worker movements, the only remaining variable was worker productivity. Even in public markets, some stall merchants were analyzed and managed as assembly-line workers, and they were judged on their ability to produce the highest rate of return in their stalls. This type of management control was probably greatest in those markets where the management had profit-sharing leases with stall merchants.

80. J. W. Sullivan, *Markets for the People: The Consumer's Part* (New York: MacMillan, 1913), 53–75.

81. J. F. Carter, "Public Markets in American Cities," in Cyrus C. Miller, John P. Mitchell, and George McAneny, eds., *Report of the Mayor's Market Commission of New York City* (New York: J. J. Little and Ives Company, 1913), 67.

82. Shorett and Morgan, *The Pike Place Market*, 67–75.

83. Robert A. Sauder, "Municipal Markets in New Orleans," *Journal of Cultural Geography* 2 (1, 1981): 82–87. New Orleans expanded its municipal markets into the suburbs, especially between 1881 and 1911. Because of laws restricting the operation of private markets, municipal markets dominated the food trade, even into the suburbs.

84. Mund, *Open Markets*, 127.

85. Jane Pyle, "Farmers' Markets in the United States: Functional Anachronisms," *Geographical Review* 61 (2, 1971): 179.

86. Miller, Mitchell, and McAneny, *Report of the Mayor's Market Commission of New York City*, 13.

87. Pyle, "Farmers' Markets in the United States," 179.

88. J. F. Carter, "Public Markets and Marketing Methods," *The American City* 8 (2, 1913): 121.

89. Alfred D. Chandler, Jr., *The Visible Hand: The Managerial Revolution in American Business* (Cambridge: Belknap Press, 1977), 391–402; and Anderson, *Refrigeration in America*, 142–78.

CHAPTER 2

1. Carl Bridenbaugh, *Cities in the Wilderness: The First Century of Urban Life in America, 1625–1742* (New York: Ronald Press, 1938), 40–41.

2. Ibid., 42.

3. Ibid., 341–43; Carl Bridenbaugh, *Cities in Revolt: Urban Life in America, 1743–1776* (New York: Alfred A. Knopf, 1955), 278.

4. Bridenbaugh, *Cities in the Wilderness*, 343–44.

5. Ibid., 344. The presence of retail trade in Charleston demonstrates the same capitalist forces that existed in the North. Large cities escaped the economics of agriculture, and as Charleston asserted itself as a trade center independent of agriculture, retail trade with a cash economy became more prevalent.

6. Gerald Carson, *The Old Country Store* (New York: Oxford University Press, 1954), 14.

7. Bridenbaugh, *Cities in Revolt*, 121–22.

8. Bridenbaugh, *Cities in the Wilderness*, 46, 340–42. As in traditional agricultural settings, children were seen by parents as a source of inexpensive labor.

9. Ibid., 11.

10. Bridenbaugh, *Cities in Revolt*, 14.

11. Samuel Bass Warner, Jr., *The Private City* (Philadelphia: University of Pennsylvania Press, 1968), 17–18.

12. Bridenbaugh, *Cities in Revolt*, 15; Robert F. Looney, *Old Philadelphia in Early Photographs, 1839–1914* (New York: Dover Publications, 1976), 38.

13. Warner, *The Private City*, 7.

14. Kenneth H. Dunshee, *As You Pass By* (New York: Hastings House, 1952), 95.

15. David R. Goldfield and Blaine A. Brownell, *Urban America: From Downtown to No Town* (Boston: Houghton Mifflin, 1979), 138.

16. Edward K. Spann, *The New Metropolis: New York City, 1840–1857* (New York: Columbia University Press, 1981), 127.

17. Paul E. Johnson, *A Shopkeeper's Millennium: Society and Revivals in Rochester, New York, 1815–1837* (New York: Hill and Wang, 1978), 78, 131.

18. Spann, *The New Metropolis*, 34, 73, 148.

19. Maury Klein and Harvey A. Kantor, *Prisoners of Progress: American Industrial Cities, 1850–1920* (New York: Macmillan, 1976), 123.

20. Warner, *The Private City*, 53.

21. Richard C. Wade, *The Urban Frontier* (Chicago: University of Chicago Press, 1959), 1–71.

22. Ibid., 119. Financial diversification enabled store owners to advance from being petty entrepreneurs to developing a merchant class. With multiple investments, merchants secured themselves better from financial failure when one of their business ventures failed. Moreover their investments in goods, loans, and real estate allowed them to diversify in regard to the types of capital they owned. If loans went bad, they still had their goods and real estate. If commodity prices went down, their loan and real estate investments could sustain them.

23. Ibid., 214.

24. Alfred D. Chandler, Jr., *The Visible Hand: The Managerial Revolution in American Business* (Cambridge, Mass.: Belknap Press, 1977), 17–18.

25. Lewis E. Atherton, *The Frontier Merchant in Mid-America* (Columbia: University of Missouri Press, 1971), 33.

26. Carson, *The Old Country Store*, 21. The movement of commodities was very dependent on local terrain and weather conditions. Roads were typically primitive in all rural areas.

27. Lewis E. Atherton, *The Southern Country Store, 1800–1860* (Baton Rouge: Louisiana State University, 1949), 65; Carson, *The Old Country Store*, 17.

28. Richard Lingeman, *Small Town America: A Narrative History 1620–The Pres-*

ent (Boston: Houghton Mifflin, 1980), 149; and Atherton, *The Southern Country Store*, 65.

29. Will Rose, "The Passing of the Country Store," *Scribner's Magazine* 80 (4, 1926): 362; and Atherton, *The Southern Country Store*, 63.

30. Atherton, *The Southern Country Store*, 65.

31. Ibid., 63.

32. Lawrence A. Johnson, *Over the Counter and On the Shelf: Country Storekeeping in America: 1620–1920* (New York: Bonanza Books, 1961), 31.

33. Ibid., 31.

34. James D. Norris, "One-Price Policy among Antebellum Country Stores," *Business History Review* 36 (4, 1962): 455–58. Although country storekeepers overwhelmingly used a multiple-pricing system before the Civil War, Norris has found that a small number of country storekeepers used a one-price system. He speculates that these particular stores served a very limited geographical area, and as a result, prices on basic commodities rapidly became common community knowledge.

35. Johnson, *Over the County and on the Shelf*, 31–32.

36. Chandler, *The Visible Hand*, 217; and Carson, *The Old Country Store*, 151. Wholesaling was concentrated on the eastern seaboard until the 1850s. Both factors in the South and storekeepers in the West normally had to make two buying trips per year.

37. Carson, *The Old Country Store*, 156.

38. Johnson, *Over the County and on the Shelf*, 26.

39. William E. Dodd, *The Cotton Kingdom: A Chronicle of the Old South* (New Haven: Yale University Press, 1919), 24.

40. Atherton, *The Southern Country Store*, 92.

41. Atherton, *The Frontier Merchant in Mid-America*, 80–82, 95.

42. Herbert M. Hart, *Tour Guide to Old Western Forts* (Ft. Collins, Colo.: The Old Army Press, 1980). This book documents all forts and camps in the West, and numerous maps of these installations show the presence of trading posts.

43. Hiram M. Chittenden, *The American Fur Trade of the Far West* (New York: Barnes and Noble, 1935), 1–8.

44. Don C. Rickey, Jr., *Forty Miles a Day on Beans and Hay* (Norman: University of Oklahoma Press, 1963), 116–22. Rickey's analysis of fort food trade describes post life after the Civil War, but these activities undoubtedly occurred before this conflict.

45. Carson, *The Old Country Store*, 116–34.

46. John R. Stilgoe, *Common Landscape of America, 1580 to 1845* (New Haven: Yale University Press, 1982), 73–74.

47. Johnson, *Over the County and on the Shelf*, 35–36. Storekeepers were resigned to the fact that they were unable to escape providing some food to the social circle about the stove. Sometimes the loungers were given whiskey, but the greatest invasion was upon the cracker barrel.

48. Atherton, *The Frontier Merchant in Mid-America*, 124.

49. Ibid., 117, 141; I. M. McFadden, "A Hoosier General Store in 1847," *Indiana Magazine of History* 35 (3, 1939): 299. Storekeepers also played the role of banker by helping customers to avoid cash shipments and to deal with cash shortages. When a local person wanted to transfer funds to a distant city, the storekeeper made a simple transfer of debits and credits with a firm in the far away city.

50. Atherton, *The Southern Country Store*, 117–29; Lingeman, *Small Town Amer-*

ica, 99–100. Before the Panic of 1837, speculators in the West increasingly bought property on credit, and with land speculation creating higher prices and little hard currency used for payment, land mortgages were being paid with bank notes that had insufficient deposits to support their face value. When President Andrew Jackson and the U.S. Congress approved the Distribution Act of 1836, the legislation allowed only gold or silver as acceptable payment at governmental land offices. As a result, many underfunded banks failed, and an economic depression followed.

51. Chandler, *The Visible Hand*, 84–85.

53. Atherton, *The Frontier Merchant in Mid-America*, 98; Chandler, *The Visible Hand*, 219.

54. Thomas D. Clark, *Pills, Petticoats and Plows: The Southern Country Store* (New York: Bobbs-Merrill, 1944), 21–22.

56. Johnson, *Over the Counter and on the Shelf*, 90; Chandler, *The Visible Hand*, 294–299. It was not until the 1880s that mass production of canned goods became a large business. Continuous processing machinery was a critical development to mass production. Those food companies that were able to sustain annual versus seasonal production of food goods were the most successful enterprises. Carnation Milk, Campbell Soup, H. J. Heinz, Pet Milk, and Libby were all companies that were able to match continuous processing machinery with a continuous supply of food for production.

57. Johnson, *Over the Counter and on the Shelf*, 95.

58. Clark, *Pills, Petticoats and Plows*, 50; Phyllis Fenner, "Grandfather's Country Store," *The American Mercury*, 61 (December, 1945): 672–77. Fenner's descriptions illustrate how the country store continued to be rather disorganized long after packaged goods had been made available.

59. Carson, *The Old Country Store*, 272.

62. Clark, *Pills, Petticoats and Plows*, 35, Carson, *The Old Country Store*, 191.

63. Daniel J. Boorstin. *The Americans: The National Experience* (New York: Random House, 1965), 115–23.

64. Lewis E. Atherton, *Main Street on the Middle Border* (Bloomington: Indiana University Press, 1954), 5–6; John W. Reps, *The Making of Urban America* (Princeton: Princeton University Press, 1965), 382–413.

65. Lingeman, *Small Town America*, 151; Atherton, *Main Street on the Middle Border*, 28, 97.

66. Atherton, *Main Street on the Middle Border*, 51; Chandler, *The Visible Hand*, 290. After 1870, mass food marketers no longer relied on local coordination of mass advertising. Advertising agencies were hired by these companies to orchestrate product promotion. Such agencies focused on writing copy and buying newspaper space in local communities, which included the promotion of grocery goods.

67. Atherton, *Main Street on the Middle Border*, 225; Susan Strasser, *Satisfaction Guaranteed* (New York: Pantheon Books, 1989), 90–94.

68. Atherton, *Main Street on the Middle Border*, 43–49.

69. Boris Emmet and John E. Jeuck, *Catalogues and Counters: A History of Sears, Roebuck and Company* (Chicago: University of Chicago Press, 1950), 101.

70. Atherton, *Main Street on the Middle Border*, 230; Charles M. Harger, "The Country Store," *Atlantic Monthly* 85 (1, 1905): 91–98. The country store was affected by food orders from mail-order catalogues just as much as the stores on Main Street. The Main Street shopkeeper, especially the grocer, could depend on customers who needed fresh food items and who did some impulse and emergency buying. Yet, the country storekeepers carried numerous goods without individual variety, and they had not relied on high turnover. The country storekeeper could not easily compete with a mail-order house's variety and rural free delivery. Harger's text also includes a dialogue from a farmer who points to what he sees as the hypocrisy of merchants. The farmer argues that storekeepers want the benefits of mass distribution as retailers while denying the same advantage to customers.

71. Samuel Bass Warner, Jr., *The Urban Wilderness* (New York: Harper and Row, 1972), 72–73.

72. Klein and Kantor, *Prisoners of Progress*, 124–29; Warner, *The Private City*, 53.

73. Maxwell F. Marcuse, *This Was New York* (New York: LIM Press, 1969), 20–21.

74. Ibid., 291.

75. W. H. Simmonds, *The Practical Grocer* (London: Gresham Publishing, 1904), 45–46.

76. Edwin G. Nourse, *The Chicago Produce Market* (Boston: Houghton Mifflin, 1918), 94–97. As late as 1918, five Chicago department stores maintained grocery departments, but with all their variety, these stores only captured an extremely small portion of the city's grocery trade.

77. Kenneth T. Jackson, *Crabgrass Frontier: The Suburbanization of the United States* (Oxford: Oxford University Press, 1985), 87–115. Jackson provides an excellent consolidated analysis relating the development of mass transportation and residential development in the American suburbs during the nineteenth and early twentieth centuries.

78. Frederic M. Miller, Morris J. Vogel, and Allen F. Davis, *Still Philadelphia: A Photographic History, 1890–1940* (Philadelphia: Temple University Press, 1983), 62.

CHAPTER 3

1. Alfred D. Chandler, Jr., *The Visible Hand: The Management Revolution in American Business* (Cambridge, Mass.: Belknap Press, 1977), 233–34.

2. Robert W. Mueller, *A&P: Past, Present and Future* (New York: Progressive Grocer, 1971), 3.

3. George Laycock, *The Kroger Story: A Century of Innovation* (Cincinnati: Kroger, 1983), 24.

4. Mueller, *A&P*, 3.

5. Ibid., 10.

6. Ibid., 4; Laycock, *The Kroger Story*, 27.

7. Mueller, *A&P*, 10.

8. Chester Liebs, *Main Street to Miracle Mile: American Roadside Architecture* (Boston: Little, Brown and Company, 1985), 11–12.

9. Godfred M. Lebhar, *Chain Stores in America, 1859–1959* (New York: Chain Store Publishing Co., 1963), 53.

10. Liebs, *Main Street to Miracle Mile*, 10–15.

11. William J. Baxter, *Chain Store Distribution and Management* (New York: Harper and Brothers, 1928), 10; Lebhar, *Chain Stores in America*, 53.

12. William I. Walsh, *The Rise and Decline of the Great Atlantic and Pacific Tea Company* (Secaucus, N.J.: L. Stuart, 1986), 27; Mueller, *A&P*, 18.

13. Mueller, *A&P*, 19.

14. Walsh, *The Rise and Decline of the Great A&P*, 29.

15. Richard Edwards, *Contested Terrain: The Transformation of the Workplace in the Twentieth Century* (New York: Basic Books, 1979), 97–104.

16. Walsh, *The Rise and Decline of the Great A&P*, 29–30.

17. Liebs, *Main Street to Miracle Mile*, 119–20.

18. William H. Marnell, *Once Upon a Store: A Biography of the World's First Supermarket* (New York: Herder and Herder, 1971), 150–1.

19. Ibid., 80–81.

20. Laycock, *The Kroger Story*, 27.

21. Charles M. Harger, "The Country Store," *Atlantic Monthly* 85 (1, 1905): 96–97.

22. John A. Jakle, *The American Small Town: Twentieth-Century Place Images* (Hamden, Conn.: Archon Books, 1982), 123.

23. Boris Emmet and John E. Jeuck, *Catalogues and Counters: A History of Sears Roebuck and Company* (Chicago: University of Chicago Press, 1950), 101, 228–29, 453. Groceries had never been expected to yield high profits, and in the 1920s the food chains such as A&P had severely limited Sears Roebuck's ability to effectively compete in the grocery trade. In 1929, the grocery department was discontinued.

24. William A. Gerbosi, "What About Wagon Route Selling?" in Paul Sayres, ed., *Foodmarketing* (New York: McGraw-Hill, 1950), 92–93.

25. Ibid., 88–94.

26. William J. Baxter, *Chain Store Distribution and Management* (New York: Harper and Brothers, 1928), 195–96.

27. Lebhar, *Chain Stores in America*, 29, 53.

28. Ibid., 68; and Theodore N. Beckman and Herman C. Nolen, *The Chain Store Problem: A Critical Analysis* (New York: McGraw-Hill, 1938), 34. The grocery chains were also the dominant type of chain among all other chain companies. Of the total chain store sales in 1929, grocery chains made 33% of these sales.

29. C. S. Duncan, *Marketing: Its Problems and Methods* (New York: D. Appleton and Company, 1920), 70–72.

30. Edwin G. Nourse, *The Chicago Produce Market* (Boston: Houghton Mifflin, 1918), 177; Cyrus C. Miller, John P. Mitchell, and George McAneny, *Report of the Mayor's Market Commission of New York City* (New York: J. J. Little and Ives Company, 1913), 13.

31. Beckman and Nolan, *The Chain Store Problem*, 43–44.

32. Ibid., 44–45.

33. Chandler, *The Visible Hand*, 294–95.

34. Walter S. Hayward and Percival White, *Chain Stores: Their Management and Operation* (New York: McGraw-Hill, 1922), 86–88.

35. Mueller, *A&P*, 20; Walsh, *The Rise and Decline of the Great A&P*, 32.

36. Walsh, *The Rise and Decline of the Great A&P*, 32.

37. Mueller, *A&P*, 26–27; Laycock, *The Kroger Story*, 67–68.

38. Walsh, *The Rise and Decline of the Great A&P*, 36–37.

39. Mueller, *A&P*, 24–25.

40. Charles W. Wood, *The Passing of Normalcy* (New York: B.C. Forbes, 1929), 185.

41. Ibid., 69–70.

42. Ibid., 215.

43. Godfrey M. Lebhar, *The Chain Store—Boon or Bane?* (New York: Harper and Brothers, 1932), 64–68. A ten-cent differential was also found to exist in large cities. In a Chicago study of price differentials between chain and independent grocers in 1930, an average chain store was found to charge ten cents less on the dollar for the same product than an independent grocery store. See Einer Bjorklund and James L. Palmer, *A Study of the Prices of Chain and Independent Grocers in Chicago* (Chicago: Chicago University Press, 1930), 54–55.

44. Wood, *The Passing of Normalcy*, 195.

45. *Congressional Record*, Seventy-First Congress, January 8, 1930, Vol. 72, Pt. 2, 1139–40.

46. Lebhar, *Chain Stores in America*, 112–16.

47. John P. Nichols, *The Chain Store Tells Its Story*, (New York: Institute of Distribution, 1940), 128–30; Lebhar, *Chain Stores in America*, 118, 134.

48. Nichols, *The Chain Store Tells Its Story*, 130–33; Lebhar, *Chain Stores in America*, 130–34.

49. Nichols, *The Chain Store Tells Its Story*, 130.

50. John P. Nichols, *Chain Store Manual* (New York: Institute of Distribution, 1936), 72–75; Nichols, *The Chain Store Tells Its Story*, 155–56.

51. Beckman and Nolen, *The Chain Store Problem*, 283–84; Lebhar, *Chain Stores in America*, 106–08.

52. Wright Patman, *The Robinson-Patman Act* (New York: Ronald Press, 1938), 7–48.

53. Ibid., 99–112; Beckman and Nolen, *The Chain Store Problem*, 277.

54. Wright Patman, *The Robinson-Patman Act*, 69–85; Lebhar, *Chain Stores in America*, 223.

55. Lebhar, *Chain Stores in America*, 213–22.

56. Beckman and Nolen, *The Chain Store Problem*, 275; Lebhar, *Chain Stores in America*, 182–98.

57. Lebhar, *Chain Stores in America*, 230–40.

58. Ibid., 247–85.

CHAPTER 4

1. Max M. Zimmerman, *The Super Market: A Revolution in Distribution* (New York: McGraw-Hill, 1955), 17–18.

2. Craig Davidson, *Voluntary Chain Stores* (New York: Harper and Brothers, 1930), 6–7; Editorial Research Staff, *The Voluntary Chains, No. 2* (New York: American Institute of Food Distribution, 1930), 14–25.

3. Zimmerman, *The Super Market*, 11–12; Davidson, *Voluntary Chain Stores*, 31–45; Editorial Research Staff, *The Voluntary Chains, No. 2*, 23.

4. Editorial Research Staff, *The Voluntary Chains—An Evolution in Distribution*,

No. 3 (New York: American Institute of Food Distribution, 1930), 10–16. By 1930, 49.6 percent of all affiliated independents were in wholesaler-sponsored groups. Moreover, of all retail grocery stores that belonged to an affiliated independent, 57.5 percent were members of this wholesaler group arrangement. In reality, there was a wide variety of retailer-wholesaler organizational arrangements, but these three types were considered to be the major general types.

    5. Ibid., 11. In a 1930 survey of 201 affiliated independents, only 14 of these affiliates were in existence before 1920. Also in 1930, there were estimated to be 551 affiliated independents. By calculating ratios (14/201 = X/551), a rough estimate of 38 affiliated independents existed before 1920. This calculation assumes that the 1930 study sample of 201 groups by the American Institute of Food Distribution was unbiased.

    6. Ibid., 8; and Godfrey M. Lebhar, *Chain Stores in America, 1859–1959* (New York: Chain Store Publishing, 1959), 68. In 1929, the U.S. Department of Commerce reported in its Retail Census that 53,466 grocery stores belonged to corporate chains. In 1930, it was estimated by the American Institute of Food Distribution that 59,640 grocery stores belonged to 551 affiliated independents. Although corporate chains, such as A&P, experienced some growth after 1919, the increases were marginal.

    7. Hector Lazo, *Retailer Cooperatives: How to Run Them* (New York: Harper and Brothers, 1937), 5.

    8. Carl W. Dipman, *Modern Food Stores* (New York: Progressive Grocer, 1935), 7–61, 70–74.

    9. Davidson, *Voluntary Chain Stores*, 84, 90–116.

    10. Ibid., 98.

    11. Ibid., 213–18.

    12. E. L. Rhodes, *Voluntary Chains as Distributors of Meats and Other Perishable Foods* (Chicago: University of Chicago, 1930), 3–4; Davidson, *Voluntary Chain Stores*, 205–6.

    13. Davidson, *Voluntary Chain Stores*, 69, 280–91.

    14. Ibid., 248–50.

    15. Ibid., 27–28; and Lazo, *Retailer Cooperatives*, 66.

    16. Editorial Research Staff, *The Voluntary Chains, No. 2*, 28–38; Davidson, *Voluntary Chain Stores*, 25–30.

    17. Davidson, *Voluntary Chain Stores*, 298–99.

    18. Rhodes, *Voluntary Chains as Distributors of Meats and Other Perishable Foods*, 19; Davidson, *Voluntary Chain Stores*, 175.

    19. John P. Nichols, *Chain Store Manual* (New York: Institute of Distribution, 1936), 79–80.

    20. Godfrey M. Lebhar, *The Chain Store—Boon or Bane?* (New York: Harper and Brothers, 1932), 121–30.

    21. John P. Nichols, *The Chain Store Tells Its Story* (New York: Institute of Distribution, 1940), 30–31.

    22. Davidson, *Voluntary Chain Stores*, 63.

    23. Lebhar, *Chain Stores in America*, 68.

    24. Alfred D. Chandler, Jr., *The Visible Hand: The Managerial Revolution in American Business* (Cambridge, Mass.: Belknap Press, 1977), 349, 398, 473.

    25. Ibid., 334–35. Quaker Oats, Pillsbury Flour, and Nabisco are examples of food companies that consolidated and centralized the administration of their manufacturing

facilities through mergers. The policy of centralizing was carried further by having a small number of large plants and eliminating small ones.

26. Ibid., 287–88; Glenn Porter and Harold C. Livesay, *Merchants and Manufacturers* (Baltimore: Johns Hopkins University Press, 1971), 166–79. Although food companies specializing in perishable goods moved forward into marketing, their efforts to control purchasing were often limited. For example, Swift and Company continued to work with independent cattle commission houses, but Swift set up their own buyers to work in the stockyards for more systematic buying. In contrast, the United Fruit Company owned its own banana plantations and operated its own fleet of steamships for transporting goods.

27. John B. Rae, *The American Automobile* (Chicago: University of Chicago Press, 1965), 92.

28. Frank J. Charvat, *Supermarketing* (New York: Macmillan, 1961), 38–39.

29. Chester H. Liebs, *From Main Street to Miracle Mile: American Roadside Architecture* (Boston: Little, Brown and Company, 1985), 122.

30. William J. Baxter, *Chain Store Distribution and Management* (New York: Harper and Brothers, 1928), 23–24; Liebs, *From Main Street to Miracle Mile*, 29–30.

31. Arieh Goldman, "Stages in the Development of the Supermarket," *Journal of Retailing* 51 (4, 1975): 57.

32. William H. Marnell, *Once Upon a Store* (New York: Herder and Herder, 1971), 32, 150–51.

33. Liebs, *From Main Street to Miracle Mile*, 121–23; William I. Walsh, *The Rise and Decline of the Great Atlantic & Pacific Tea Company* (Secaucus, N. J.: L. Stuart, 1986), 46–48. Although the combination store was an architectural means for independent grocers to compete, some affiliated independents and corporate chains, such as Red & White and A&P, did have stores that were either combined shops or freestanding buildings. Affiliated-independent members were certainly able to act on their own and to develop larger stores. In contrast, management in corporate chains dictated store design, and in the case of A&P, their stores essentially remained in small buildings of the same size until the 1930s.

34. Zimmerman, *The Super Market*, 24–29; Davidson, *Voluntary Chain Stores*, 60–62; Charvat, *Supermarketing*, 17.

35. H. M. Foster, "Threat of the Supermarket," *Sales Management* 32 (9, 20 April 1933): 436; and C. B. Larrabee, "Grocery Manufacturers Condemn Super-market Price Cutters," *Printers Ink*, 142 (2 March 1937): 41.

36. Zimmerman, *The Super Market*, 34–35.

37. Ibid., 40.

38. Ibid., 42; Charvat, *Supermarketing*, 154–55.

39. Max M. Zimmerman, *The Super Market Grows Up* (New York: Super Market Publishing, 1939), 4.

40. Walsh, *The Rise and Fall of the Great A&P*, 47.

41. William Greer, *America the Bountiful: How the Supermarket Came to Main Street* (Washington, D.C.: Food Marketing Institute, 1986), 86.

42. Charvat, *Supermarketing*, 161.

43. Larrabee, "Grocery Manufacturers Condemn Super-Market Price Cutters," 41–43; Zimmerman, *The Super Market*, 40–45.

44. Greer, *America the Bountiful*, 154–55.

45. Ibid., 154.

46. Charvat, *Supermarketing*, 162.

47. Ibid., 164; Walsh, *The Rise and Fall of the Great A&P*, 47–49; Edwin P. Hoyt, *That Wonderful A&P!* (New York: Hawthorn Books, 1969), 158–59. Hoyt is particularly critical of George Hartford's lack of understanding about the retail grocery business. He did not grasp the supermarket's ability to produce volume sales per square foot at a higher rate than an A&P economy store.

48. Charvat, *Supermarketing*, 162–67; Rom J. Markin, *The Supermarket: An Analysis of Growth, Development, and Change* (Pullman: Washington State University Press, 1968), 16–17; Zimmerman, *The Super Market*, 61, 110. Having made up his mind to convert to the supermarket approach, John Hartford contacted Michael Cullen who led him on tours through the King Kullen stores. Hartford was so impressed that he offered Cullen a position with A&P to take charge of supermarket operations, but being a successful entrepreneur, Cullen refused.

49. Robert W. Mueller et al., *A&P: Past, Present, and Future* (New York: Progressive Grocer, 1971), 38.

50. Liebs, *From Main Street to Miracle Mile*, 127.

51. Terry P. Wilson, *The Cart that Changed the World* (Norman: University of Oklahoma Press, 1978), 77–117.

52. Liebs, *From Main Street to Miracle Mile*, 129–30; Spiro Kostof, *America by Design* (New York: Oxford University Press, 1987), 108–12.

53. Greer, *America the Bountiful*, 154–55.

54. Pat Watters, *Fifty Years of Pleasure: The Illustrated History of Publix Supermarkets, Inc.* (Lakeland, Fl.: Publix Super Markets, Inc., 1980), 60–61.

55. Hoyt, *That Wonderful A&P*, 162–67.

56. Greer, *America the Bountiful*, 152–53.

57. Zimmerman, *The Super Market*, 69–76, 109–16.

58. Hoyt, *That Wonderful A&P*, 151–53; Greer, *America the Bountiful*, 27–44.

CHAPTER 5

1. Susan M. Hartmann, *The Home Front and Beyond: American Women in the 1940s* (Boston: Twayne Publishers, 1982), 15–29; Randolph McAusland, *Supermarkets: 50 Years of Progress* (Washington, D.C.: Food Marketing Research, 1980), 39, 47.

2. Max M. Zimmerman, *The Super Market: A Revolution in Distribution* (New York: McGraw-Hill, 1955), 132–33.

3. Ibid., 134.

4. Ibid., 28; Edward A. Brand, *Modern Supermarket Operations* (New York: Fairchild Publications, 1963), 32-34. The counter glass refrigerator with a sloped front was developed by Joe Weingarten, Inc., which was a grocery chain in Houston, Texas. Although it was an advancement over the refrigerator locker, this counter glass type did not lend itself to self-service. World War II heavily curtailed meat cabinet manufacturing, but factory production resumed immediately following the war.

5. Zimmerman, *The Super Market*, 222.

6. Edwin W. Williams, *Frozen Foods: Biography of an Industry* (Boston: Cahners Publishing, 1970), 21, 24.

7. McAusland, *Supermarkets*, 46.

8. Kenneth T. Jackson, *Crabgrass Frontier: The Suburbanization of the United States* (Oxford: Oxford University Press, 1985), 231–45; Rom J. Markin, *The Supermarket: An Analysis of Growth, Development, and Change* (Pullman: Washington State University Press, 1968), 45–48.

9. Zimmerman, *The Super Market*, 140.

10. Godfrey M. Lebhar, *Chain Stores in America, 1859–1962* (New York: Chain Store Publishing, 1959), 363–68. Lebhar's combined statistics for his list of chain stores (except for Winn-Dixie where data is incomplete) were used. American, Colonial, First National, Food Fair, Grand Union, A&P, Jewel Tea, Kroger, National Tea, and Safeway had a combined total of 15,194 stores in 1946. By 1954, this combined total had decreased to 11,580, down 31.2 percent. This decrease was even more dramatic for the largest chains—A&P, Kroger, and Safeway.

11. Julie A. Matthaei, *An Economic History of Women in America* (New York: Schocken Books, 1982), 238–39.

12. Markin, *The Supermarket*, 55, 66; Zimmerman, *The Super Market*, 141. Zimmerman notes that there was more room for supermarket expansion in 1953 than was actually exploited by grocery management.

13. Richard Longstreth, "The Neighborhood Shopping Center in Washington, D.C., 1930–1941," *Journal of the Society of Architectural Historians* 51 (1, 1992): 9–13, 20.

14. Chester H. Liebs, *Main Street to Miracle Mile: American Roadside Architecture* (Boston: Little, Brown and Company, 1985), 30; J. Ross McKeever, *Shopping Centers Re-Studied: Part Two—Practical Experiences, Technical Bulletin No. 30* (Washington, D.C.: Urban Land Institute, 1957), 9.

15. William I. Walsh, *The Rise and Decline of the Great Atlantic and Pacific Tea Company* (Secaucus, N.J.: L. Stuart, Inc., 1986), 82.

16. William Applebaum et al., *Guide to Store Location Research: With Emphasis on Super Markets* (Reading, Mass.: Addison-Wesley, 1968), 3–4.

17. George E. Kline, "There's Big Volume in Shopping Center Locations," *Progressive Grocer* 33 (3, 1954): 64–76; George J. Schulte, Jr., "Chicago Independent Finds Advantages in New Shopping Center," *Progressive Grocer* 32 (7, 1953): 56–59.

18. Geoffrey Baker and Bruno Funaro, *Shopping Centers: Design and Operation* (New York: Reinhold, 1950), 12; J. Ross McKeever, *Shopping Centers: Planning Principles and Tested Policies, Technical Bulletin No. 20* (Washington, D.C.: Urban Land Institute, 1953), 31.

19. J. Ross McKeever, *Shopping Centers Re-Studied: Part One—Emerging Patterns, Technical Bulletin No. 30* (Washington, D.C.: Urban Land Institute, 1957), 9–10, 30.

20. Ibid., 29–30.

21. Applebaum, *Guide to Store Location Research*, 54; Pat Watters, *Fifty Years of Pleasure: The Illustrated History of Publix Super Markets, Inc.* (Lakeland, Fla.: Publix Super Markets, 1980), 82–87.

22. Esther R. Cramer, *The Alpha Beta Story: An Illustrated History of a Leading Western Retailer* (LaHabra, Calif.: Alpha Beta Food Markets, Inc. 1973), 125.

23. Editorial Staff, "Wholesaler Sponsored Financing Strengthens Washington In-

dependents," *Progressive Grocer* 35 (12, 1956): 50–55; Robert W. Mueller, "Twenty-Fourth Annual Survey of Food Retailing," *Progressive Grocer* 36 (4, 1957): 54.

24. Carl W. Dipman, "Impressive Gains Reported by Independent Supermarkets and Superettes," *Progressive Grocer* 33 (4, 1954): 41; Robert W. Mueller, "Supermarkets Did 43.5% of Total Independent Sales in 1955," *Progressive Grocer* 35 (4, 1956): 45.

25. Editorial Staff, "What Kind of Super Markets Are They Building Today?" *Progressive Grocer* 35 (4, 1954): 80; Editorial Staff, "1955's Typical Super 18,000 Square Feet," *Progressive Grocer* 35 (3, 1956): 67.

26. Baker and Funaro, *Shopping Centers*, 172–73, 210–11, 242–45, 274–78.

27. Ibid., 104, 122.

28. B. Sumner Gruzen, "Automobile Shopping Centers," *Architectural Record* 76 (3, 1934): 43–48; B. Sumner Gruzen, "Big Bear Shopping Center—A Supermarket," *Architectural Record* 76 (1, 1934): 204–6.

29. Zimmerman, *The Super Market*, 182.

30. B. Sumner Gruzen, "Building a Distinctive Selling-Personality Through Store Layout and Design," *How to Build a Distinctive Selling Personality: Business Program of the 17th Annual Convention of the Super Market Institute* (Chicago: Super Market Institute, 1954), 30.

31. Joseph J. Trout, "Are These New Ideas in Store Design Here to Stay?" *Progressive Grocer* 32 (1, 1953): 44–49.

32. Editorial Staff, "How Leading Store Engineers Plan New Super Markets," *Progressive Grocer* 37 (5, 1958): 57.

33. John E. Lewis, "Winn-Dixie's Store Planning Concept: One Basic Plan—Four Different Sizes," *Progressive Grocer* 36 (10, 1957): 72.

34. National Association of Food Chains, *Progress in Food Distribution* (Washington, D.C.: National Association of Food Chains, 1962), 18; McAusland, *Supermarkets*, 58.

35. McAusland, *Supermarkets*, 42; Carl W. Dipman, *Modern Food Stores* (New York: Progressive Grocer, 1935), 49–55, 58.

36. Zimmerman, *The Super Market*, 185, 217.

37. McAusland, *Supermarkets*, 45.

38. Zimmerman, *The Super Market*, 145, 185.

39. McAusland, *Supermarkets*, 68.

40. Zimmerman, *The Super Market*, 143, 152–53.

41. William Greer, *America the Bountiful: How the Supermarket Came to Main Street* (Washington, D.C.: Food Marketing Institute, 1986), 157; McAusland, *Supermarkets*, 65. Training cashier clerks to operate cash registers without looking at the keys began as early as 1940, but the method became popular during and after World War II.

42. Brand, *Modern Supermarket Operations*, 56; Curt Kornblau, "Does the Super Market Industry Have a Solid Foundation for Growth?" *A Blueprint for Profits in an Inflationary Economy: Proceedings of the 1957 Mid-Year Conference* (Chicago: Super Market Institute, 1958), 14–15.

43. Henry J. Eavey, "Opportunities in Your Self-Service Meat Department," *How to Build a Distinctive Selling Personality: Business Program of the 17th Annual Convention of the Super Market Institute* (Chicago: Super Market Institute, 1954), 21–24; Zimmerman, *The Super Market*, 145–50.

44. McAusland, *Supermarkets*, 68, 74; Zimmerman, *The Super Market*, 266–79; Editorial Staff, "Public Wedding Provides Successful, Low-Cost Promotion," *Progressive Grocer* 33 (10, 1953): 152–56.

45. Brand, *Modern Supermarket Operations*, 86–88; Markin, *The Supermarket*, 101–2.

46. Tom Mahoney and Leonard Sloane, *Great Merchants* (New York: Harper and Row, 1966), 180; Robert W. Mueller et al., *A&P: Past, Present and Future* (New York: Progressive Grocer, 1971), 58; Walsh, *The Rise and Fall of the Great A&P*, 91–92.

47. Markin, *The Supermarket*, 66.

48. With the pioneering supermarkets in southern California (such as Ralphs) and in Texas (such as Henke and Pillot) store location was an important issue. The economic rise of King Kullen and Big Bear in the East was due partially to good site selection. Yet, supermarkets in the 1950s were typically larger in size and more expensive to operate due to air conditioning and mechanical equipment. As a result, grocery management had to be more careful in choosing a location than in the past.

49. Morris A. Adelman, *A&P: A Study in Price Cost Behavior and Public Policy* (Cambridge: Harvard University Press, 1959), 398.

50. Mueller et al., *A&P*, 46–51.

51. Frank J. Charvat, *Supermarketing* (New York: Macmillan, 1961), 82–83; Markin, *The Supermarket*, 28.

52. Ibid., 245.

53. U.S. Federal Trade Commission, *Economic Inquiry into Food Marketing, Part I* (Washington, D.C.: U.S. Government Printing Office, 1960), 128.

54. Ibid., 138.

55. Charvat, *Supermarketing*, 180–81; Lebhar, *Chain Stores in America*, 366.

56. Markin, *The Supermarket*, 29; Daniel I. Padberg, *Economics of Food Retailing* (Ithaca, N.Y.: Cornell University Press, 1968), 287–92. Padberg provides a summary account of the Von Grocery Company case.

57. Bruce W. Marion et al., *The Food Retailing Industry: Market Structure, Profits, and Prices* (New York: Praeger, 1979), 19–25.

58. O. W. Richard, "Special Session on Financing, Personnel, Etc.," *A Report of the Mid-Year Discussion Meeting, 1956* (Chicago: Super Market Institute, 1956), 34; Charvat, *Supermarketing*, 144.

59. Mueller et al., *A&P*, 56–57.

60. Zimmerman, *The Super Market*, 150–51. Many manufacturers found themselves in a no-win situation as they tried to maximize sales to both supermarkets and drug retailers while avoiding boycotts by the latter.

61. Michael Harrington, *The Retail Clerks* (New York: John Wiley and Sons, 1962), 6; Herbert R. Northrup and Gordon R. Storholm, *Restrictive Labor Practices in the Supermarket Industry* (Philadelphia: University of Pennsylvania Press, 1967), 36, 40.

62. Zimmerman, *The Super Market*, 285.

63. David Brody, *The Butcher Workmen: A Study of Unionization* (Cambridge: Harvard University Press, 1964), 131.

64. Marten S. Estey, "Patterns of Union Membership in the Retail Trades," *Industrial and Labor Relations Review* 8 (July 1955): 558–62.

65. Brody, *The Butcher Workmen*, 258.

66. Northrup and Storholm, *Restrictive Labor Practices in the Supermarket Industry*, 26, 32.

67. Ibid., 86–119.

68. Ibid., 42, 70–71; Harrington, *The Retail Clerks*, 70. The Meat Cutters were the instigators and primary users of wall-to-wall contracts with the RCIA using very few. Eventually, George Meany, president of the AFL-CIO, helped to mediate this dispute concerning union jurisdiction within the supermarket.

69. Harrington, *The Retail Clerks*, 77.

70. Northrup and Storholm, *Restrictive Labor Practices in the Supermarket Industry*, 38.

71. Harrington, *The Retail Clerks*, 40, 54.

72. Northrup and Storholm, *Restrictive Labor Practices in the Supermarket Industry*, 39.

73. Harrington, *The Retail Clerks*, 3.

74. Northrup and Storholm, *Restrictive Labor Practices in the Supermarket Industry*, 43–44, 60.

75. Padberg, *Economics of Food Retailing*, 12–13.

76. Editorial Staff, "The Dillon Study: Why the Study Was Made," *Progressive Grocer* 39 (12, 1960): D8.

CHAPTER 6

1. Rom J. Markin, *The Supermarket: An Analysis of Growth, Development, and Change* (Pullman, Wash.: Washington State University Press, 1968), 120.

2. Pat Watters, *Fifty Years of Pleasure: The Illustrated History of Publix Super Markets, Inc.* (Lakeland, Fla.: Publix Super Markets, 1980), 116.

3. William Appelbaum et al., *Guide to Store Location Research: With an Emphasis on Super Markets* (Reading, Mass.: Addison-Wesley, 1968), 13–42; Bernard J. Kane, Jr., *A Systematic Guide to Supermarket Location Analysis* (New York: Fairfield Publications, 1966), 26–86.

4. Markin, *The Supermarket*, 116.

5. Appelbaum et al., *Guide to Store Location Research*, 13–42.

6. Ibid., 36–40.

7. William I. Walsh, *The Rise and Decline of the Great Atlantic and Pacific Tea Company* (Secaucus, N.J.: L. Stuart, 1986), 129. Whereas corporate chains developed new stores in the suburbs during the 1960s, A&P's management lagged significantly behind their competitors in suburban expansion.

8. *SN Distribution of Grocery Store Sales, 1988* (New York: Fairfield Publications, 1988), 351.

9. Markin, *The Supermarket*, 29.

10. Thomas Calak, "The Big Change in Store Fronts," *Progressive Grocer* 39 (12, 1960): 75–79; Glenn Snyder, "From Roadside Stand to Store of the Month," *Progressive Grocer* 43 (7, 1964): 120–35.

11. Thomas Calak, "The Big Change in Store Fronts," 77, 82.

12. Leonard E. Daykin, *Outstanding New Supermarkets* (New York: Progressive Grocer, 1969), 7–9; Chester H. Liebs, *Main Street to Miracle Mile: American Roadside Architecture* (Boston: Little, Brown and Company, 1985), 133–34.

13. Daykin, *Outstanding New Supermarkets*, 6.

14. Editorial Staff, "How Safeway Turned Jeers into Cheers for New Market," *Progressive Grocer* 43 (9, 1964): 170–76. From October 1965 to March 1966, the *Progressive Grocer* presented a series of six articles on the topic of consumer dynamics. It was a major theme during an annual convention of the Super Market Institute.

15. Daykin, *Outstanding New Supermarkets*, 8; Leonard E. Daykin, "New Six-Sided Store Breaks 'Four-Wall Merchandising' Mold," *Progressive Grocer* 47 (5, 1968): 68–74; Glenn Snyder, "New Design Trends Stimulate Customers, Sales, Profits," *Progressive Grocer* 39 (12, 1960): 57–71; Editorial Staff, "Store of the Month: Radial Layout Draws the Long-Hour Shopper," *Progressive Grocer* 51 (1, 1972): 32–38; Editorial Staff, "Dimension Added to X-Layout Design," *Progressive Grocer* 44 (12, 1965): 74–77.

16. Robert E. O'Neill and Duane Shelton, "Top Designers' Biggest Successes," *Progressive Grocer* 51 (5, 1972): 39–55.

17. Robert W. Mueller, "Six Major Factors Contribute to Store Rebuilding Boom," *Progressive Grocer* 45 (5, 1966): 144–45.

18. Randolph McAusland, *Supermarkets: 50 Years of Progress* (Washington, D.C.: Food Marketing Institute, 1980), 88–90; Lew Milkovics, "In-Store Bake-Off Products Score for Genetti's," *Progressive Grocer* 43 (3, 1964): 163–74; Leonard E. Daykin, "Flowers Bloom as a New Profit Category," *Progressive Grocer* 51 (2, 1972): 36–50.

19. Lee W. Dyer, "Nautical Theme Attracts High-Income Customers," *Progressive Grocer* 45 (8, 1966): 147–61; Daykin, *Outstanding New Supermarkets*, 10–19.

20. Editorial Staff, "Showmanship: The Game That Moves the Merchandise," *Progressive Grocer* 51 (6, 1972): 98–119.

21. Editorial Staff, "Publix Shoppers Like Carpet Underfoot," *Progressive Grocer* 45 (10, 1966): 231–32.

22. Daykin, *Outstanding New Supermarkets*, 20–29.

23. Editorial Staff, "1955's Typical Super 18,000 Square Feet," *Progressive Grocer* 35 (3, 1956): 65–67; Markin, *The Supermarket*, 64, 66. The average 1955 supermarket had 18,000 square feet and sold 4,723 items for a ratio of 3.8 square feet per item. In 1965, the average supermarket had 28,000 square feet and sold 7,100 items for a ratio of 3.9 square feet per item.

24. Editorial Staff, "38th Annual Report of the Grocery Industry," *Progressive Grocer* 50 (4, 1971): 66.

25. Editorial Staff, "The Dillon Study, Part 3: How to Allocate Space to Groceries," *Progressive Grocer* 39 (7, 1960): D38–D39; Fred Powledge, *Fat of the Land* (New York: Simon and Schuster, 1984), 123–30.

26. Editorial Staff, "The Dillon Study, Part 3," D36.

27. Editorial Staff, "Centralized Meats—From Red Ink to Black Ink in 18 Months," *Progressive Grocer* 44 (1, 1965): 138–49.

28. McAusland, *Supermarkets*, 105.

29. Allen Liles, *Oh Thank Heaven! The Story of the Southland Corporation* (Dallas, Tex.: Southland Corporation, 1977), 19–20, 67.

30. Editorial Staff, "Convenience—The Right Idea at the Right Time," *Progressive Grocer* 50 (9, 1971): 201.

31. Alan R. Andreason, "Automated Grocery Shopping," *Journal of Marketing* 26

(4, 1962): 64–66; Editorial Staff, "Vending Machine Drive-In Forecasts New Food Retailing Technique," *Progressive Grocer* 40 (6, 1961): 58–61, 145.

32. Editorial Staff, "Convenience," 203.

33. Ibid., 201, 206; Lewis Milkovics, "A Report on Drive-In Food Markets," *Progressive Grocer* 39 (1, 1960): 73–77.

34. Jim Hightower, *Eat Your Heart Out: Food Profiteering in America* (New York: Crown Publishers, 1975), 74–111.

35. Jennifer Cross, *The Supermarket Trap: The Consumer and the Food Industry* (Bloomington: Indiana University Press, 1970), 27–61; William Robbins, *The American Food Scandal* (New York: William Morrow and Sons, 1974), 135–37.

36. Robbins, *The American Food Scandal*, 131–32.

37. Hightower, *Eat Your Heart Out*, 58; A. Q. Mowbray, *The Thumb on the Shelf: Or the Supermarket Shell Game* (Philadelphia: J. B. Lippincott Company, 1967), 1–22.

38. Co-op Handbook Collective, *The Food Co-op Handbook* (Boston: Houghton Mifflin, 1975), 29.

39. Powledge, *Fat of the Land*, 225–32.

40. Ronald C. Curhan and Edward G. Wertheim, "Consumer Food Buying Cooperatives Revisited: A Comparison from 1971 to 1974," *Journal of Retailing* 51 (4, 1975): 22–33, 86.

41. Robert Sommer, *Farmers Markets of America: A Renaissance* (Santa Barbara, Calif.: Capra Press, 1980), 26–27.

42. The cultural character of Boston's Haymarket was partially preserved through a photographic essay and a collection of oral histories from vendors. See Wendy Snyder, *Haymarket* (Cambridge: MIT Press, 1970).

43. Alice Shorett and Murray Morgan, *The Pike Place Market: People, Politics, and Produce* (Seattle, Wash.: Pacific Search Press, 1982), 120–51.

44. Ibid., 133.

45. Sommer, *Farmers Markets in America*, 44–45; Robert Sommer, John Herrick, and Ted R. Sommer, "The Behavioral Ecology of Supermarkets and Farmers' Markets," *Journal of Environmental Psychology* 1 (1, 1981): 15–17.

46. A. H. Kizilbash and E. T. Garman, "Grocery Retailing in Spanish Neighborhoods," *Journal of Retailing* 51 (4, 1975): 19.

47. Daniel J. McLaughlin, Jr., and Charles A. Mallowe, eds., *Food Marketing and Distribution* (New York: Chain Store Publishing, 1971), 63, 172. A lasting effect of the discount movement was the elimination of trading stamps and games. The postwar importance of trading stamps reached its zenith between 1963 and 1965, but their importance steadily declined after this period. Games were largely discarded after 1966.

48. Liebs, *From Main Street to Miracle Mile*, 134–35; McAusland, *Supermarkets*, 99–101.

49. McLaughlin and Mallow, *Food Marketing and Distribution*, 310.

50. Allen J. Mayer, "Supermarkets in a Crunch," *New York Times Magazine* (2 February 1976): 10–12, 46–54.

51. The author wishes to thank Kenneth Keefer of Dillon Stores for these historic insights.

52. McAusland, *Supermarkets*, 109.

53. Jon M. Hawes, *Retailing Strategies for Generic Grocery Products* (Ann Arbor, Mich.: U.M.I. Research Press, 1982), 14–15, 31–33.

54. Ibid., 19; Charlene C. Price and Doris J. Newton, *U.S. Supermarkets: Characteristics and Services* (Washington, D.C.: U.S. Department of Agriculture, 1986), 5; Debra J. Levin, *The Supermarket Industry—Review and Outlook for the 1990s* (New York: Salomon Brothers, 1990), 6.

55. J. A. Dawson, "Hypermarkets in France," *Geography* 61 (4, 1975): 259–62; Deborah Wise, "French Hypermarket Adjusts to U.S.," *New York Times*, 20 February 1989, C26; Willard Bishop Consulting, Ltd., "Update on Store Formats Trends," *Competitive Edge* 11 (9, 1990): 1–2; Priscilla Donegan, "Hypermarkets: Is America Ready?" *Progressive Grocer* 67 (7, 1988): 26; Thomas C. Hayes, "The Hypermarket: 5 Acres of Store," *New York Times*, 4 February 1988, C26.

56. Spiro Kostof, *America By Design* (New York: Oxford University Press, 1987), 110–12.

57. Hayes, "The Hypermarket: 5 Acres of Store," C26.

58. Levin, *The Supermarket Industry*, 8.

59. Michael Lev, "Hard Times? Not for These Stores," *New York Times*, 13 December 1990, C6; and United Food and Commercial Workers Union Research Office, *Membership Warehouse Clubs: A Special Report* (Washington, D.C.: UFCWU, 1991), 9.

60. UFCWU Research Office, *Membership Warehouse Clubs*, 6–8.

61. Ibid., 5–6.

62. Ibid., 11–13; Willard Bishop Consulting, Ltd., "Update on Store Formats," 1.

63. *Leadership for the 21st Century* (Washington, D.C.: United Food and Commercial Workers International Union, 1990), 5. Considering only the supermarket trade, the conventional supermarket fell from 85 percent in 1980 to 65 percent in 1984. In the same time period, superstores increased from 9 to 18 percent, and warehouse stores increased from 5 to 13 percent. See Charlene C. Price and Doris J. Newton, *U.S. Supermarkets: Characteristics and Services, Agricultural Bulletin No. 502* (Washington, D.C.: U.S. Department of Agriculture, 1986), 3.

64. Gordon F. Bloom, 1972, *Productivity in the Food Industry: Problems and Potential* (Cambridge: MIT Press, 1972), 220; James L. Brock, *A Forecast of the Grocery Retailing Industry in the 1980s* (Ann Arbor, Mich.: UMI Research Press, 1981), 17, 64.

65. *Leadership for the 21st Century*, 10.

66. R. McFall Lamm, "Unionism and Prices in the Food Industry," *Journal of Labor Research* 3 (1, 1982): 70.

67. Ibid., 70; Michael Goldfield, *The Decline of Organized Labor in the United States* (Chicago: University of Chicago Press, 1987), 146.

68. *Leadership in the 21st Century*, 7; Levin, *The Supermarket Industry*, 11.

69. Lamm, "Unionism and Prices in the Food Industry," 73.

70. Walsh, *The Rise and Decline of the Great A&P*, 82, 92, 148, 244.

71. Ibid., 155–56, 208, 212, 232.

72. Robert Stewart, "The Fall of Milgram," *Corporate Report Kansas City* 15 (8, 1989): 21.

73. Ibid., 26.

74. Susan C. Faludi, "The Reckoning: Safeway LBO Yields Vast Profits But Exacts

a Heavy Human Toll," *Wall Street Journal*, 16 May 1990, A1, A8–A9; Duane R. Norris, *The Supermarket Industry: Exploiting Trends in a Non Cyclical Sector* (New York: Salomon Brothers, 1990), 49.

75. Lydia Chavez, "Why Kroger Was Ripe for Attack," *New York Times*, 26 September 1988, C29, C31; Philip E. Ross, "Kroger Plans Asset Sale as Part of Restructuring," *New York Times*, 27 September 1988, C45.

76. Susan C. Faludi, "Facing Raiders, Kroger Took Another Path," *Wall Street Journal*, 16 May 1990, A8.

77. Ibid., A8.

78. Dennis Clark and Merry Guben, *Future Bread: How Retail Workers Ransomed their Jobs and Lives* (Philadelphia, Pa.: O&O Investment Fund, Inc., 1983), 4.

79. Ibid., 17.

80. Ibid., 20.

81. Ibid., 28–39.

CHAPTER 7

1. Lisa Gubernick, "Small Towns, Big Money," *Forbes* 138 (11, 1986): 50, 52.

2. Roberta Deering and Gregory Ptucha, "Super Marketing," *Planning* 53 (10, 1987): 27–29.

3. Isaac Asimov, "The Supermarket of 2077 A.D.," *Progressive Grocer* 56 (6, 1977): 52–53.

4. The ideas for the smart store were conceived by Glen Terbeck of Anderson Consulting, Dallas, Texas. The remarks noted in the text are extracted from the firm's promotional memorandums.

5. Christopher Alexander et al., *The Timeless Way of Building* (New York: Oxford University Press, 1979), 7.

6. Ibid., 441–43.

BIBLIOGRAPHY

Adelman, Morris A. 1959. *A&P: A Study in Price Cost Behavior and Public Policy.* Cambridge: Harvard University Press.

Alexander, Christopher, et al. 1977. *A Pattern Language.* New York: Oxford University Press.

———. 1979. *The Timeless Way of Building.* New York: Oxford University Press.

Anderson, Oscar E. 1953. *Refrigeration in America.* Princeton: Princeton University Press.

Andreasen, Alan R. 1962. "Automated Grocery Shopping." *Journal of Marketing* 26(4):64–66.

Applebaum, William, et al. 1968. *Guide to Store Location Research: With an Emphasis on Super Markets.* Reading, Mass.: Addison-Wesley.

Asimov, Isaac. 1977. "The Supermarket of 2077 A.D." *Progressive Grocer* 56(6):52–53.

Atherton, Lewis E. 1949. *The Southern Country Store, 1800–1860.* Baton Rouge: Louisiana State University Press.

———. 1954. *Main Street on the Middle Border.* Bloomington: Indiana University Press.

———. 1971. *The Frontier Merchant in Mid-America.* Columbia: University of Missouri Press.

Baker, Geoffrey, and Bruno Funaro. 1950. *Shopping Centers: Design and Operation.* New York: Reinhold.

Baxter, William J. 1928. *Chain Store Distribution and Management.* New York: Harper and Row.

Beckman, Theodore N., and Herman C. Nolen. 1938. *The Chainstore Problem: A Critical Analysis.* New York: McGraw-Hill.

Bjorklund, Einar, and James J. Palmer. 1930. *A Study in the Prices of Chain and Independent Grocers in Chicago.* Chicago: University of Chicago Press.

Bloom, Gordon F. 1972. *Productivity in the Food Industry: Problems and Potential.* Cambridge: MIT Press.

Boorstin, Daniel J. 1965. *The Americans: The National Experience.* New York: Random House.

Brand, Edward A. 1963. *Modern Supermarket Operation.* New York: Fairchild Publications.

Bridenbaugh, Carl. 1938. *Cities in the Wilderness: The First Century of Urban Life in America, 1625–1742.* New York: Ronald Press.

———. 1955. *Cities in Revolt: Urban Life in America, 1743–1776.* New York: Alfred A. Knopf.

Brock, James L. 1981. *A Forecast of the Grocery Retailing Industry in the 1980's.* Ann Arbor, Mich.: UMI Research Press.

Brody, David. 1964. *The Butcher Workmen: A Study of Unionization.* Cambridge: Harvard University Press.

Cable, Mary. 1972. *Lost New Orleans: The American Sector.* New York: American Legacy Press.

Calak, Thomas. 1960. "The Big Change in Store Fronts." *Progressive Grocer* 39(12):72–82.

Carson, Gerald. 1954. *The Old Country Store.* New York: Oxford University Press.

Carter, J. F. 1913. "Public Markets and Marketing Methods." *The American City* 8(2):121–38.

Chandler, Alfred D., Jr. 1977. *The Visible Hand: The Managerial Revolution in American Business.* Cambridge, Mass.: Belknap Press.

Charvat, Frank J. 1961. *Supermarketing.* New York: MacMillan.

Chavez, Lydia. 1988. "Why Kroger Was Ripe for Attack." *New York Times,* 26 September, C29, C31.

Childs, William Talbott. 1912. "The Municipal Markets in Baltimore." *Municipal Journal* 33(23):825–30.

Chittenden, Hiram M. 1935. *American Fur Trade of the Far West.* New York: Barnes and Noble.

Christovich, Mary L., et al. 1972. *New Orleans Architecture: The American Sector.* Gretna, La.: Pelican Publishing Company.

Cist, Charles. 1851. *Cincinnati in 1851.* Cincinnati: Wm. M. Moore and Company, Publishers.

Clark, Dennis, and Merry Guben. 1983. *Future Bread: How Retail Workers Ransomed Their Jobs and Lives.* Philadelphia, Pa.: O&O Investment Fund, Inc.

Clark, Thomas D. 1944. *Pills, Petticoats and Plows: The Southern Country Store.* New York: Bobbs-Merrill.

Congressional Record. Seventy-First Congress, 1930. Vol. 72, Pt. 2.

Co-op Handbook Collective. 1975. *The Food Co-op Handbook.* Boston: Houghton Mifflin.

Cross, Jennifer. 1970. *The Supermarket Trap: The Consumer and the Food Industry.* Bloomington: Indiana University Press.

Cramer, Esther R. 1973. *The Alpha Beta Story: An Illustrated History of a Leading Western Retailer.* LaHabra, Calif.: Alpha Beta Food Markets, Inc.

Cummings, Richard O. 1949. *The American Ice Harvests.* Berkeley: University of California Press.

Curhan, Ronald C., and Edward G. Wertheim. 1975. "Consumer Food Buying Cooperatives Revisited: A Comparison from 1971 to 1974." *Journal of Retailing* 51(4):22–33, 87.

Davidson, Craig. 1930. *Voluntary Chain Stores*. New York: Harper and Brothers.

Dawson, J. A. 1975. "Hypermarkets in France." *Geography* 61(4):259–62.

Daykin, Leonard E. 1968. "New Six-Sided Store Breaks 'Four-Wall Merchandising' Mold." *Progressive Grocer* 47(5):68–74.

———. 1969. *Outstanding New Markets*. New York: Progressive Grocer.

———. 1972. "Flowers Bloom a New Profit Category." *Progressive Grocer* 51(2):36–50.

Deering, Roberta, and Gregory Ptucha. 1987. "Super Marketing." *Planning* 53(10):27–29.

DeVoe, Thomas F. 1970. *The Market Book: A History of the Public Markets of New York City*. New York: Augustus M. Kelley Publishers.

Dipman, Carl W., ed. 1935. *Modern Food Stores*. New York: Progressive Grocer.

———. 1954. "Impressive Gains Reported by Independent Supermarkets and Superettes." *Progressive Grocer* 33(4):40–49.

Dodd, William E. 1919. *The Cotton Kingdom: A Chronicle of the Old South*. New Haven: Yale University Press.

Donegan, Priscilla. 1988. "Hypermarkets: Is America Ready?" *Progressive Grocer* 67(7):21–34.

Duncan, C. S. 1920. *Marketing: Its Problems and Methods*. New York: D. Appleton and Company.

Dunshee, Kenneth H. 1952. *As You Pass By*. New York: Hastings House.

Dyer, Lee W. 1966. "Nautical Theme Attracts High-Income Customers." *Progressive Grocer* 45(8):147–61.

Eavey, Henry J. 1954. "Opportunities in Your Self-Service Meat Department." *How to Build a Distinctive Selling Personality: Business Program of the 17th Annual Convention of the Super Market Institute*, 21–24. Chicago: Super Market Institute.

Editorial Staff. 1953. "Public Wedding Provides Successful, Low-Cost Promotion." *Progressive Grocer* 33(10):152–56.

———. 1954. "What Kind of Super Markets Are They Building Today?" *Progressive Grocer* 35(4):78–90.

———. 1956. "1955's Typical Super 18,000 Square Feet." *Progressive Grocer* 35(3):65–67.

———. 1956. "Wholesaler Sponsored Financing Strengthens Washington Independents." *Progressive Grocer* 35(12):50–55.

———. 1958. "How Leading Store Engineers Plan New Supermarkets." *Progressive Grocer* 37(5):54–61, 155.

———. 1960. "The Dillon Study: Why the Study Was Made." *Progressive Grocer* 39(5):D1–D16.

———. 1960. "The Dillon Story, Part 3: How to Allocate Space to Groceries." *Progressive Grocer* 39(7):D33–D48.

———. 1961. "Vending Machine Drive-In Forecasts New Food Retailing Technique." *Progressive Grocer* 40(6):58–61, 145.

———. 1964. "How Safeway Turned Jeers into Cheers for New Market." *Progressive Grocer* 43(9):170–76.

———. 1965. "Centralized Meats—From Red Ink to Black Ink in 18 Months." *Progressive Grocer* 44(1):138–49.

————. 1965. "Dimension Added to X-Layout Design." *Progressive Grocer* 44(12):74–77.

————. 1966. "Publix Shoppers Like Carpet Underfoot." *Progressive Grocer* 45(10):231–35.

————. 1971. "38th Annual Report of the Grocery Industry." *Progressive Grocer* 50(4):59–106.

————. 1971. "Convenience—The Right Idea at the Right Time." *Progressive Grocer* 50(9):200–218.

————. 1972. "Store of the Month: Radial Layout Draws the Long-Hour Shopper." *Progressive Grocer* 51(1):32–38.

————. 1972. "Showmanship: The Game That Moves the Merchandise." *Progressive Grocer* 51(6):98–119.

Editorial Research Staff. 1930. *The Voluntary Chains, No. 2.* New York: American Institute for Food Distribution.

————. 1930. *The Voluntary Chains—An Evolution in Distribution, No. 3.* New York: American Institute for Food Distribution.

Edwards, Richard. 1979. *Contested Terrain: The Transformation of the Workplace in the Twentieth Century.* New York: Basic Books.

Emmet, Boris, and John E. Jenck. 1950. *Catalogues and Counters: A History of Sears Roebuck and Company.* Chicago: University of Chicago Press.

Estey, Marten S. 1955. "Patterns of Union Membership in the Retail Trades." *Industrial and Labor Relations Review* 8(July):558–62.

Faludi, Susan C. 1990. "Facing Raiders, Kroger Took Another Path." *Wall Street Journal*, 16 May, A8.

————. 1990. "The Reckoning: Safeway LBO Yields Vast Profits but Exacts a Heavy Human Toll." *Wall Street Journal*, 16 May, A1, A8–A9.

Fenner, Phyllis. 1945. "Grandfather's Country Store." *The American Mercury* 61(December):672–77.

Foster, H. M. 1933. "Threat of the Supermarket." *Sales Management* 32(9, April 20):436, 450.

Gerbosi, William A. 1950. "What About Wagon Route Selling?" In *Foodmarketing*, edited by Paul Sayres. New York: McGraw-Hill.

Goethe, Wilhelm. 1885. *Italian Journeys.* London: George Bell and Sons.

Goldfield, David R., and Blaine A. Brownell. 1979. *Urban America: From Downtown to No Town.* Boston: Houghton Mifflin.

Goldfield, Michael. 1987. *The Decline of Organized Labor in the United States.* Chicago: University of Chicago Press.

Goldman, Arieh. 1975. "Stages in the Development of the Supermarket." *Journal of Retailing* 51(4):49–64.

Goode, James M. 1979. *Capital Losses: A Cultural History of Washington's Destroyed Buildings.* Washington, D.C.: Smithsonian Institution Press.

Goodwin, Arthur E. 1929. *Markets: Public and Private.* Seattle: Montgomery Printing Co.

Grad, Frank, and George B. Hooper. 1925. "The New Centre Market, Newark, N.J." *The American Architect* 77(March):241–44.

Greer, William. 1986. *America the Bountiful: How the Supermarket Came to Main Street.* Washington, D.C.: Food Marketing Institute.

Gruzen, B. Sumner. 1934. "Automobile Shopping Center." *Architectural Record* 76(3):43–48.

———. 1934. "Big Bear Shopping Center—A Supermarket." *Architectural Record* 76(1):204–6.

———. 1954. "Building a Distinctive Selling-Personality Through Store Layout and Design." *How to Build a Distinctive Selling Personality: Business Program of the 17th Annual Convention of the Super Market Institute*, 30–34. Chicago: Super Market Institute.

Gubernick, Lisa. 1986. "Small Towns, Big Money." *Forbes* 138(11):50, 52.

Harger, Charles M. 1905. "The Country Store." *The Atlantic Monthly* 85(1):91–98.

Harrington, Michael. 1962. *The Retail Clerks*. New York: John Wiley and Sons.

Hart, Herbert M. 1980. *Tour Guide to Old Western Forts*. Ft. Collins, Colo.: The Old Army Press.

Hartmann, Susan M. 1982. *The Home Front and Beyond: American Women in the 1940s*. Boston: Twayne Publishers.

Hawes, Jon M. 1982. *Retailing Strategies for Generic Grocery Products*. Ann Arbor, Mich.: U.M.I. Research Press.

Hayes, Thomas C. 1988. "The Hypermarket: 5 Acres of Store." *New York Times*, 4 February, C25–C26.

Hayward, Walter S., and Percival White. 1928. *Chain Stores: Their Management and Operation*. New York: McGraw-Hill.

Hightower, Jim. 1975. *Eat Your Heart Out: Food Profiteering in America*. New York: Crown Publishers.

Hoyt, Edwin P. 1969. *That Wonderful A&P!* New York: Hawthorn Books.

Hunter, W. P. 1923. "New City Markets in Norfolk and Roanoke." *The American City* 28(3):261–63.

Jackson, Kenneth T. 1985. *Crabgrass Frontier: The Suburbanization of the United States*. Oxford: Oxford University Press.

Jakle, John A. 1982. *The American Small Town: Twentieth-Century Place Images*. Hamden, Conn.: Archon Books.

Johnson, Laurence A. 1961. *Over the Counter and On the Shelf: Country Store-keeping in America: 1620–1920*. New York: Bonanza Books.

Johnson, Paul E. 1978. *A Shopkeeper's Millennium: Society and Revivals in Rochester, New York, 1815–1837*. New York: Hill and Wang.

Kane, Bernard J., Jr. 1966. *A Systematic Guide to Supermarket Location Analysis*. New York: Fairfield Publications.

Kerbey, McFall. 1921. *Open Types of Public Markets*. U.S. Department of Agriculture Bulletin No. 1002. Washington, D.C.: U.S. Government Printing Office.

Kizilbash, A. H., and E. T. Garman. 1975. "Grocery Retailing in Spanish Neighborhoods." *Journal of Retailing* 51(4):15–21, 86.

Klein, Maury, and Harvey A. Kantor. 1976. *Prisoners of Progress: American Industrial Cities, 1850–1920*. New York: Macmillan.

Kline, George E. 1954. "There's Big Volume in Shopping Center Locations." *Progressive Grocer* 33(3):64–76.

Kornblau, Curt. 1958. "Does the Super Market Have a Solid Foundation for Growth?" *A Blueprint for Profits in an Inflationary Economy: Proceedings of the 1957 Mid-Year Conference*, 11–17. Chicago: Super Market Institute.

Kostof, Spiro. 1987. *America by Design*. New York: Oxford University Press.

Lamm, R. McFall. 1982. "Unionism and Prices in the Food Retailing Industry." *Journal of Labor Research* 3(1):69–79.

Larrabee, C. B. 1933. "Grocery Manufacturers Condemn Super-Market Price Cutters." *Printers Ink* 142(March 2):41–44.

Laycock, George. 1983. *The Kroger Story: A Century of Innovation*. Cincinnati, Ohio: Kroger Co.

Lazo, Hector. 1937. *Retailer Cooperatives: How to Run Them*. New York: Harper and Brothers.

Leadership for the 21st Century. 1990. Washington, D.C.: United Food and Commercial Workers Union.

Lebhar, Godfrey M. 1932. *The Chain Store—Boon or Bane?* New York: Harper and Brothers.

————. 1959. *Chainstores in America, 1859–1962*. New York: Chain Store Publishing Co.

Lev, Michael. 1990. "Hard Times? Not For These Stores." *New York Times*, 13 December, C1, C6.

Levin, Debra J. 1990. *The Supermarket Industry—Review and Outlook for the 1990s*. New York: Salomon Brothers.

Lewis, John E. 1957. "Winn-Dixie's Store Planning Concept: One Basic Plan—Four Different Sizes." *Progressive Grocer* 36(10):72–77.

Liebs, Chester H. 1985. *Main Street to Miracle Mile: American Roadside Architecture*. Boston: Little, Brown and Company.

Lightfoot, Frederick S. 1981. *Nineteenth-Century New York: In Rare Photographic Views*. New York: Dover.

Liles, Allen. 1977. *Oh Thank Heaven! The Story of the Southland Corporation*. Dallas, Tex.: Southland Corporation.

Lingeman, Richard. 1980. *Small Town America: A Narrative History 1620–The Present*. Boston: Houghton Mifflin.

Longstreth, Richard. 1992. "The Neighborhood Shopping Center in Washington, D.C., 1930–1941." *Journal of the Society of Architectural Historians* 51(1):5–34.

Looney, Robert F. 1976. *Old Philadelphia in Early Photographs, 1839–1914*. New York: Dover Publications.

Mahoney, Tom, and Leonard Sloane. 1966. *Great Merchants*. New York: Harper and Row.

Marcuse, Maxwell F. 1969. *This Was New York*. New York: LIM Press.

Marion, Bruce W., et al. 1979. *The Food Retailing Industry: Market Structure, Profits, and Prices*. New York: Praeger Publishers.

Markin, Rom J. 1968. *The Supermarket: An Analysis of Growth, Development, and Change*. Pullman: Washington State University Press.

Marnell, William H. 1971. *Once Upon a Store: A Biography of the World's First Supermarket*. New York: Herder and Herder.

Matthaei, Julie A. 1982. *An Economic History of Women in America*. New York: Schocken Books.

Mayer, Allen J. 1976. "Supermarkets in a Crunch." *New York Times Magazine* (2 February):10–12, 46–54.

Mayer, Harold M., and Richard C. Wade. 1969. *Chicago: Growth of a Metropolis*. Chicago: University of Chicago Press.

McAndrew, John. 1965. *The Open-Air Churches of Sixteenth-Century Mexico.* Cambridge: Harvard University Press.

McAusland, Randolph. 1980. *Supermarkets: 50 Years of Progress.* Washington, D.C.: Food Marketing Research.

McCabe, James D., Jr. 1882. *New York by Gaslight.* New York: Greenwich House.

McFadden, I. M. 1939. "A Hoosier General Store in 1847." *Indiana Magazine of History* 35(3):299–302.

McKeever, J. Ross. 1953. *Shopping Centers: Planning Principles and Tested Policies, Technical Bulletin No. 20.* Washington, D.C.: Urban Land Institute.

———. 1957. *Shopping Centers Re-Studied: Part One—Emerging Patterson, Technical Bulletin No. 30.* Washington, D.C.: Urban Land Institute.

———. 1957. *Shopping Centers Re-Studied: Part Two—Practical Experiences, Technical Bulletin No. 30.* Washington, D.C.: Urban Land Institute.

McLaughlin, Daniel J., Jr., and Charles A. Mallowe, eds. 1971. *Food Marketing and Distribution.* New York: Chain Store Publishing.

Milkovics, Lewis. 1960. "A Report on Drive-In Markets." *Progressive Grocer* 39(1):73–77.

———. 1964. "In-Store Bake-Off Products Score for Genetti's." *Progressive Grocer* 43(3):163–74.

Miller, Carol P. 1987. "Markets and Market Houses." In *The Encyclopedia of Cleveland History,* edited by David D. Van Tassel and John J. Grabowski. Bloomington: Indiana University Press.

Miller, Cyrus C., John P. Mitchell, and George McAneny. 1913. *Report of the Mayor's Market Commission of New York City.* New York: J. J. Little and Ives Company.

Miller, Frederick M., Morris J. Vogel, and Allen F. Davis. 1983. *Still Philadelphia: A Photographic History, 1890–1940.* Philadelphia: Temple University Press.

Mowbray, A. Q. 1967. *The Thumb on the Scale: Or the Supermarket Shell Game.* Philadelphia: J. P. Lippincott Company.

Mueller, Robert W. 1956. "Super Markets Did 43.5% of Total Independent Sales in 1955." *Progressive Grocer* 35(4):44–51.

———. 1957. "Twenty-Fourth Annual Survey of Food Retailing." *Progressive Grocer* 36(4):54–70.

———. 1966. "Six Major Factors Contribute to Store Rebuilding Boom." *Progressive Grocer* 45(5):144–45.

Mueller, Robert W., et al. 1971. *A&P: Past, Present and Future.* New York: Progressive Grocer.

Mund, Vernon A. 1948. *Open Markets: An Essential of Free Enterprise.* New York: Harper and Brothers.

National Association of Food Chains. 1962. *Progress in Food Distribution.* Washington, D.C.: National Association of Food Chains.

Nichols, John P. 1936. *Chain Store Manual.* New York: Institute of Distribution.

———. 1940. *The Chain Store Tells Its Story.* New York: Institute of Distribution.

Norris, Duane R. 1990. *The Supermarket Industry: Exploiting Trends in a Noncyclical Sector.* New York: Salomon Brothers.

Norris, James D. 1962. "One-Price Policy Among Antebellum Country Stores." *Business History Review* 36(4):455–58.

Northrup, Herbert R., and Gordon R. Storholm. 1967. *Restrictive Labor Practices in the Supermarket Industry.* Philadelphia: University of Pennsylvania Press.

Nourse, Edwin G. 1918. *The Chicago Produce Market.* Boston: Houghton Mifflin.

O'Neill, Robert E., and Duane Shelton. 1972. "Top Designers' Biggest Successes." *Progressive Grocer* 51(5):39–55.

Padberg, Daniel I. 1968. *Economics of Food Retailing.* Ithaca, N.Y.: Cornell University Press.

Patman, Wright. 1938. *The Robinson-Patman Act.* New York: Ronald Press.

Peterson, Arthur E., and George W. Williams. 1967. *New York City as an Eighteenth Century Municipality.* Port Washington, N.Y.: Ira J. Friedman, Inc.

Porter, Glenn, and Harold C. Livesay. 1971. *Merchants and Manufacturers.* Baltimore: Johns Hopkins University Press.

Powledge, Fred. 1984. *Fat of the Land.* New York: Simon and Schuster.

Price, Charlene C., and Doris J. Newton. 1986. *U.S. Supermarkets: Characteristics and Services, Agricultural Bulletin No. 502.* Washington, D.C.: U.S. Department of Agriculture.

Primm, James N. 1981. *The Lion of the Valley: St. Louis, Missouri.* Boulder, Colo.: Pruett Publishing Company.

Pyle, Jane. 1971. "Farmers' Markets in the United States: Functional Anachronisms." *Geographical Review* 61(2):167–97.

Rae, John B. 1965. *The American Automobile.* Chicago: University of Chicago Press.

Reps, John W. 1965. *The Making of Urban America.* Princeton: Princeton University Press.

———. 1979. *Cities of the American West.* Princeton: Princeton University Press.

Rhodes, E. L. 1930. *Voluntary Chains as Distributors of Meats and Other Perishable Foods.* Chicago: University of Chicago Press.

Richard, O. W. 1956. "Special Session on Financing, Personnel, Etc." *A Report of the Mid-Year Discussion Meeting, 1956,* 30–36. Chicago: Super Market Institute.

Rickey, Donald C., Jr. 1963. *Forty Miles a Day on Beans and Hay.* Norman: University of Oklahoma Press.

Robbins, William. 1974. *The American Food Scandal.* New York: William Morrow and Sons.

Rose, Will. 1926. "The Passing of the Country Store." *Scribner's Magazine* 80(4):362–67.

Ross, Philip E. 1988. "Kroger Plans Asset Sale as Part of Restructuring." *New York Times,* 27 September, C45.

Sauder, Robert A. 1981. "Municipal Markets in New Orleans." *Journal of Cultural Geography* 2(1):82–95.

Scharf, John Thomas. 1881. *History of Baltimore City and County, Vol. I.* Philadelphia: L. H. Everts.

———. 1883. *History of Saint Louis City and County Vol. I.* Philadelphia: L. H. Everts.

Schulte, George J., Jr. 1953. "Chicago Independent Finds Advantages in New Shopping Center." *Progressive Grocer* 32(7):56–59.

Shorett, Alice, and Murray Morgan. 1982. *The Pike Place Market: People, Politics, and Produce.* Seattle, Wash.: Pacific Search Press.

Silver, Nathan. 1967. *Lost New York.* New York: Houghton Mifflin.

Simmonds, W. H. 1904. *The Practical Grocer*. London: Gresham Publishing.

SN Distribution Study of Grocery Store Sales, 1988. 1988. New York: Fairfield Publications.

Snyder, Glenn. 1960. "New Design Trends Stimulate Customers, Sales, Profits." *Progressive Grocer* 39(12):57–71.

———. 1964. "From Roadside Stand to Store of the Month." *Progressive Grocer* 43(7):120–35.

Snyder, Wendy. 1970. *Haymarket*. Cambridge: MIT Press.

Sommer, Robert. 1980. *Farmers Markets of America: A Renaissance*. Santa Barbara, Calif.: Capra Press.

Sommer, Robert, John Herrick, and Ted R. Sommer. 1981. "The Behavioral Ecology of Supermarkets and Farmers' Markets." *Journal of Environmental Psychology* 1(1):13–19.

Spann, Edward K. 1981. *The New Metropolis: New York City, 1840–1857*. New York: Columbia University Press.

Stewart, Robert. 1989. "The Fall of Milgram." *Corporate Report Kansas City* 15(8):19–26.

Stilgoe, John R. 1982. *Common Landscape of America, 1580 to 1845*. New Haven: Yale University Press.

Strasser, Susan. 1989. *Satisfaction Guaranteed*. New York: Pantheon Books.

Sullivan, J. W. 1913. *Markets for the People: The Consumer's Part*. New York: MacMillan.

Sweet, Morris L. 1961. "History of Municipal Markets." *Journal of Housing* 18(6):237–47.

Tatum, George B. 1961. *Penn's Great Town*. Philadelphia: University of Pennsylvania Press.

Trout, Joseph J. 1953. "Are These New Ideas in Store Design Here to Stay?" *Progressive Grocer* 32(1):44–49.

United Food and Commercial Workers Union Research Office. 1991. *Membership in Warehouse Clubs*. Washington, D.C.: UFCWU.

U.S. Bureau of the Census. 1918. *Municipal Markets in Cities Having a Population of Over 30,000*. Washington, D.C.: U.S. Government Printing Office.

U.S. Federal Trade Commission. 1960. *Economic Inquiry into Food Marketing, Part I*. Washington, D.C.: U.S. Government Printing Office.

Van Trump, James D. 1983. *Life and Architecture in Pittsburgh*. Pittsburgh: Pittsburgh History and Landmarks Foundation.

Wade, Richard C. 1959. *The Urban Frontier*. Chicago: University of Chicago Press.

Walsh, William I. 1986. *The Rise and Decline of the Great Atlantic and Pacific Tea Company*. Secaucus, N.J.: L. Stuart.

Wann, John L., and Edwin W. Cake. 1948. *Farmers' Produce Markets in the United States*. Washington, D.C.: U.S. Department of Agriculture.

Warner, Samuel Bass, Jr. 1968. *The Private City*. Philadelphia: University of Pennsylvania Press.

———. 1972. *The Urban Wilderness*. New York: Harper and Row.

Warren, Marion E., and Mame Warren. 1983. *Baltimore: When She Was What She Used to Be, 1850–1930*. Baltimore: Johns Hopkins University Press.

Watters, Pat. 1980. *Fifty Years of Pleasure: The Illustrated History of Publix Super Markets, Inc.* Lakeland, Fla.: Publix Super Markets, Inc.

Whitehill, Walter M. 1968. *Boston: A Topographical History*. Cambridge: Harvard University Press.

Willard Bishop Consulting, Ltd. 1990. "Update on Store Format Trends." *Competitive Edge* 11(9):1–4.

Williams, Edwin W. 1970. *Frozen Foods: Biography of an Industry*. Boston: Cahners Publishing.

Wilson, Terry P. 1978. *The Cart that Changed the World: The Career of Sylvan Nathan Goldman*. Norman: University of Oklahoma Press.

Wise, Deborah. 1989. "French Hypermarket Adjusts to U.S." *New York Times*, 20 February, C26.

Wood, Charles W. 1929. *The Passing of Normalcy*. New York: B.C. Forbes.

Zimmerman, Max M. 1939. *The Super Market Grows Up*. New York: Supermarket Publishing.

———. 1955. *The Super Market: A Revolution in Distribution*. New York: McGraw Hill.

INDEX

A&P. *See* Atlantic and Pacific Tea Company

advertising: affiliated independents, 119–20, 124; allowances, 110–12; chain stores, 78–79; grocery stores, 68; loss leaders, 208; public markets, 34; supermarkets, 141, 144–45; warehouse clubs, 221

Advertising Retail Grocers' Association, 119

affiliated independents: adaptation to supermarkets, 144–47, 168; chain store competition, 118, 120, 193; eating-out challenge, 217; education programs, 123; equipment exchange, 124; financing, 167; food additives, 208; loss leaders, 123–24; management, 123–24, 126–27, 132; market share, 138, 168, 189–90; racial discrimination, 129; shopping centers, 166–67; store design, 121–23, 138; takeovers, 227; tax legislation, 126–27; types of, 119–20; unions, 187, 225; warehousing, 121, 140

Albers, William H., 153

Albers Super Markets, 85, 117, 147

Alexander, Christopher, 244

Allegheny Market, Pittsburgh, 14, 16

Alpha Beta Food Markets, Inc., 85, 138, 167

Amalgamated Meat Cutters and Butcher Workmen of North America, 184–85, 224. *See also* unions

American Federation of Labor, 145

American Retail Federation, 112

American Stores, 84–85, 94, 99

American Wholesale Grocers' Association, 146

anti-chain movement, 107–15. *See also* corporate chains

architectural styles: Art Deco, 150, 152, 168–69; blending technique, 196, 198, 242; colonial, 194, 199; Modern, 194; modernism, 194; Streamline Moderne, 150–51, 168

Arkansas Wholesale Grocers' Association, 107

Armour and Company, 40, 77, 130

Art Deco, 150, 152, 168–69

Ashton Supermarkets, 182

Asimov, Isaac, 243

Associated Grocers of Chicago, 119

Association Grocery Manufacturing Association, 145–46

Atlantic and Pacific Tea Company: anti-chain movement, 115; Atlantic Com-

About the Author

JAMES M. MAYO is a professor in the School of Architecture and Urban Design at the University of Kansas. He is the author of *War Memorials as Political Landscape: The American Experience and Beyond* (Praeger, 1988). He has published articles in the *Journal of Architectural Education, Environment and Behavior, Journal of the American Planning Association, Journal of Architectural and Planning Research*, and numerous other journals. He is the Associate Editor for the *Journal of Architectural Education* and for the *Journal of Architectural and Planning Research*. His research is particularly known for relating political ideology to the built environment and design practice.

02.06.97, Hennessy, 07.50, 65843